D0152184

NASCAR Nation

NASCAR NATION

*A History of Stock Car Racing
in the United States*

Scott Beekman

 PRAEGER

AN IMPRINT OF ABC-CLIO, LLC
Santa Barbara, California • Denver, Colorado • Oxford, England

Copyright 2010 by Scott Beekman

All rights reserved. No part of this publication may be reproduced, stored in a retrieval system, or transmitted, in any form or by any means, electronic, mechanical, photocopying, recording, or otherwise, except for the inclusion of brief quotations in a review, without prior permission in writing from the publisher.

Library of Congress Cataloging-in-Publication Data
Beekman, Scott.
    NASCAR nation : a history of stock car racing in the United States / Scott Beekman.
        p. cm.
    Includes bibliographical references and index.
    ISBN 978-0-275-99424-2 (hard copy : alk. paper) — ISBN 978-1-56720-661-6 (ebook) 1. Stock car racing—Social aspects—United States—History. 2. NASCAR (Association)—History. I. Title.
    GV1029.9.S74.B46 2010
    796.720973—dc22   2009051144

ISBN: 978-0-275-99424-2
EISBN: 978-1-56720-661-6

14 13 12 11 10   1 2 3 4 5

This book is also available on the World Wide Web as an eBook.
Visit www.abc-clio.com for details.

Praeger
An Imprint of ABC-CLIO, LLC

ABC-CLIO, LLC
130 Cremona Drive, P.O. Box 1911
Santa Barbara, California 93116-1911

This book is printed on acid-free paper ∞

Manufactured in the United States of America

Dedicated to the memories of Bill and John Hoeckh,
both of whom loved NASCAR

CONTENTS

ACKNOWLEDGMENTS

As with any book, the name on the cover tells only part of the story behind the work. In the process of delving into the history of stock car racing, I gained invaluable assistance from Suzanne Wise, Eddie Samples, Neal Thompson, and Gordon White. All, including myself, who study the history of this sport owe a debt of gratitude to Greg Fielden and his pioneering works on motor sports history. Dan Harmon at Praeger has once again shown himself to be a remarkably patient and supportive editor. The idea to write a book on NASCAR originated with Dan, so I can truthfully say this book would not exist without him. Thanks Dan. The process of completing this monograph proved to be far longer than anyone involved hoped, and my family assisted in many ways during the entire (extended) journey. My parents, Blaine and Frances Beekman, encouraged me all along the way. Kimberly Little acted as both a kind and supportive wife and as a hard-nosed proofreader. This is a much stronger work thanks to her efforts. I would love to say helping me with this volume turned Kim into a NASCAR fan, but that is probably a stretch. She will at least now acknowledge, however, that stock car racing is not just a bunch of cars going around in circles for five hours. And, as always, this is for Miller.

INTRODUCTION

*History is a funny thing. If you got ten people and they all
see the same thing, you'll get ten different stories from them.*
                                                        —Richard Petty

The previous accounts detailing stock car racing's past validate "King"
Richard Petty's assertion that history is a subjective art. Earlier volumes
on stock car racing feature disparate claims over the sport's very origins.
Efforts to understand the early years of the sport derail immediately
thanks to various chroniclers both placing the birth of the sport in different locales across the United States and offering alternative versions
of what actually constitutes a "stock car." Along with these geographical
and technical disputes come arguments over who actually "invented" this
form of motor sport. Unlike battles over creation myths in other sports,
which typically pit one alleged founder against another, stock car racing's fight revolves around different socioeconomic groups. Indicative of
the high level of confusion surrounding stock's origins, diametrically opposed views on creators have emerged, with claims that the elite invented
the sport countered by assertions that credit should belong to lower-class
criminals involved in illegal liquor operations. To further muddy the wa-
ters, NASCAR (the de facto governing body for all American stock car
racing) vehemently defends its "official" version of the sport's history,
which shifts over time depending on the organization's current economic
and promotional imperatives.

From the maze of differing accounts, a consensus story of stock car racing's origins has gained strength in recent years. According to the popular
myth of stock's birth, southern bootleggers invented stock car racing as a
means of determining who owned the fastest customized vehicle. Unable
to compete against each other on open roads thanks to law enforcement,
these moonshine haulers began challenging each other on crudely laid

out dirt ovals across the rural South. News of these spirited races then spread to the wider populace, who began attending the events as spectators. Once these spectators started paying admission to watch the races, prize money could be offered to the competitors and thus a sport was born. The widespread acceptance of this account of stock car racing's development can be primarily attributed to NASCAR, who, in recent years, has repeatedly asserted the veracity of a bootlegger genesis. As the controlling body of stock car racing, NASCAR holds a status in the sport that lends great credence to their claims. Alas, the "official" version of stock car racing's development contains more myth than truth. Like Major League Baseball's false claim that Abner Doubleday invented baseball, NASCAR's story does not hold up to close scrutiny.

In this study I attempt to put forth a counter to this popular trope that bootleggers invented stock car racing by offering a more nuanced and verifiable perspective on the sport's history. It is my contention that the wide disparity in previous creation accounts stems from the inherent difficulty in ascribing inventor status to any one individual, group, or location. Put simply, both the elite and the working class share responsibility for the creation of stock car racing. Wealthy motor racing supporters helped build tracks, establish auto meets, and organize sanctioning bodies, but working class Americans (including bootleggers) filled grandstands and supplied drivers to compete in stock car races. While the gentry dominated early motor sports, the middle and working classes embraced auto racing and—especially in the case of stock—helped it flourish. By the mid-20th century, stock car racing had developed into a sport supported almost exclusively by the middle and working classes. Although they can be counted among the working class supporters of stock car racing, moonshine haulers served as an important part of the sport only for a brief period—roughly the late 1930s to early 1950s. Bootleggers clearly played a significant role in stock car racing's history, but the sport did not begin with them.

Technically, stock car racing began in 1895 (40 years before the period of bootlegger prominence) with a race in Chicago. Although credited as the first recorded motor race in American history, this 1895 event poses problems in its own right. Not only did earlier races involving stock vehicles occur in other countries, but unrecorded impromptu contests between early car owners surely predate the Chicago race. The northern location of this 1895 event also illustrates the pitfalls in viewing stock car racing as a purely southern endeavor. As I will detail, all parts of the United States can take credit for hosting early stock car races. Thanks to a host of cultural and economic factors, however, this form of motor sports became most popular in the American South. By the mid-20th century, despite races in other regions, the bulk of stock car fans, events, and governing bodies were found in the Southeast. The common assertion that stock car racing is a southern sport, although correct, tells only part of the story. It is far more accurate to describe stock car racing as a sport with national roots that became a regional (southern) sport. Much of the focus of this work, therefore, revolves around the importance of stock car racing in the American South.

A decade ago Edward Ayers, among others, warned that a focus on "southern culture" created a fiction that arbitrarily and obfuscatingly created a rigid distinction between the states of the former Confederacy and the rest of the United States. Although his point is well taken, it is also important to note David Potter's defense of attention to regional differences (at the expense of examining the similarities) in order to gain a fuller understanding of the nation's southeastern quadrant. If we accept the proposition that the South is somehow, someway, distinct from the rest of the nation, it becomes incumbent upon us to seek out those cultural artifacts that illustrate the area's unique attributes. It is my contention that stock car racing represents a sport that became an important part of the southern cultural landscape in the mid-20th century, and that even in its current nationalized condition, it retains vestiges of this southern heritage. Further, NASCAR and the sport's corporate sponsors actively seek to reinforce this lineage as part of a campaign to position stock car racing as a traditional, patriotic, family-friendly, and politically conservative sports form. As I will discuss later, modern stock car racing's blending of national and regional locales positions the sport as "transcultural," thanks to its ties to a sense of regionalism not found in any other major professional sport.[1]

Studies of the "South" often use that term as a replacement for "white," thereby unwittingly eliminating half the southern population from the discussion. In the case of this examination of stock car racing, however, I use "South" and southerners with the explicit understanding that these references apply purely to white residents of the country's southeastern corner. Stock car racing in the states of the former Confederacy developed as a cultural endeavor for whites and, to a significant extent, remains a preserve for them. Unlike all other major sports in the United States, minority athletes play little role in stock car racing. The absence of color in stock car racing initially developed out of the white dominance of all forms of early 20th century motor sports, but became even more pronounced as stock racing established itself as a cultural form embraced by mid-20th century middle and working class southern whites. When coupled with the racially conservative leadership of NASCAR, efforts by southern stock car fans to position races as havens from the pressures of the civil rights movement succeeded in creating a segregated sport.

Along with being openly right-wing, the NASCAR leadership is unique among major American sports organizations in that it is a family-owned business. The France family, in the person of "Big" Bill France, helped create NASCAR and then moved during the 1950s to wrest control of the sanctioning body from all other stakeholders. Subsequently, two additional generations of the family have shaped the direction of NASCAR. As majority stockholders in what is now the undisputed ruler of stock car racing in the United States, the France family effectively owns the sport. With this unfettered control of NASCAR, the Frances have possessed the freedom to imbricate stock car racing with their personal views. NASCAR's reputation as a socially and politically conservative organization can be traced to the family's efforts to shape the sanctioning body in their image. This ability to direct NASCAR gave the France family a position of enormous influence throughout the last 60 years of stock car history. As such, "Big" Bill and his descendants are key to my narrative throughout this work.

The France family built NASCAR with the assistance of corporate America and the automobile industry. Without Detroit products, there simply would have been no cars on the track. American auto makers began their direct relationship with NASCAR in the early 1950s and, despite occasional periods of retreat, continue to work with stock car racing today. And without deep-pocketed sponsors, drivers could not have afforded to compete in the expensive world of motor racing. Although corporate sponsorship plays a growing role in all American sports, the level of involvement in stock car racing supersedes that found in any other athletic endeavor. The modern stock car has effectively been converted into a rolling billboard plastered with the names of sponsors. Given the importance of American corporations and auto makers in the evolution and success of stock car racing, their roles are frequently foregrounded in this volume.

Although the Frances and NASCAR loom large in the story of stock car racing, it is important to note the contributions of other leaders and organizations. Much like the bootlegger myth, a version of stock car racing's history that excludes all other sanctioning bodies has recently gained momentum thanks to the pronouncements of NASCAR. Also, like Vince McMahon in professional wrestling, NASCAR's last man standing status in stock car racing naturally invites accounts of its inevitable supremacy. While I spotlight NASCAR in this account, discussions of other organizations (and the travails of NASCAR) are also included in an effort to avoid a whiggish history of NASCAR's rise. NASCAR's role in the development of American stock car racing, however, towers over all other sanctioning bodies to a degree that warrants placing that organization at the center of the story. To most motor sports fans in this country, NASCAR *is* stock car racing. This merging of the sport and its sanctioning body can be seen in the name millions of stock car racing fans have adopted for themselves—NASCAR nation.

I

BIRTH OF A SPORT

In December 1947, Bill France Sr. and a group of fellow stock car racing promoters and enthusiasts gathered in the Ebony Lounge atop Daytona Beach's Streamline Hotel for three days of discussions. They drank, fraternized, and vied for the attentions of the local swimsuit models France had hired to entertain them. Amidst the revelry they also transacted important business. France arranged the meeting in the hope that this group could coalesce into a unified organization to control stock car racing in the United States. After some debate they settled on the rather repetitious name National Association for Stock Car Automobile Racing (NASCAR), which was suggested by World War II hero and ace racing mechanic Red Vogt. Initially, NASCAR represented just another entry into the welter of alphabet soup organizations struggling to rule stock car racing—France himself previously organized the National Championship Stock Car Circuit (NCSCC) in 1946—but this new group would eventually succeed in dominating American stock car racing. France's dictatorial leadership, a host of popular folk-hero drivers, millions of sponsorship dollars, and stock car racing's ability to connect with the psyche of American racing fans eventually made the initially humble NASCAR into one of the country's most popular sports organizations.

Stock car racing dates back to the dawn of motor racing. Expensive, high-tech racing involving purpose-built vehicles, however, quickly established itself as the most popular and highly regarded form of motor sports—a circumstance that continued for almost the entire 20th century. Often viewed as the primitive stepchild of open-wheel auto racing, stock cars spent much of the century ignored by the national media, periodically disdained by the very manufacturers whose products were being raced, and ghettoized in the Southeast. Pre-NASCAR sanctioning bodies promoted occasional open-wheel races in the South, but these groups focused more attention on other parts of the country. Although pockets of stock car racing enthusiasts operated throughout the United States, the Southeast emerged as the area of the most sustained stock activity. Although factors in the South weighed heavily in the popularity of stock car racing in the region, inattention to the area by national racing organizations helped this form of racing take root by offering little competition from open-wheelers. Although NASCAR made sporadic mid-century efforts to extend the organization's territory, stock car racing remained wedded to its southern base, with a few annual forays into the Far West and New England. Only in the last two decades of the 20th century was stock car racing able to exert itself in a truly national fashion. NASCAR now rules American auto racing thanks to a host of national, social, economic, and cultural changes; it survived long enough to flourish thanks to particular conditions in the American South.[1]

Southern sports of the 19th century featured time-tested diversions such as horse racing and cock fighting, coupled with emerging forms promoted by the burgeoning national sporting press. In many instances—baseball, for example—the sports landscape of the southeastern quadrant mirrored that of the rest of the United States. Thanks to the cross-country reach of pioneering sporting journals such as *Sign of the Times* and the *National Police Gazette*, sports-minded southerners stayed abreast of professional athletics occurring throughout the United States. Southerners could therefore watch the evolution of professional baseball and the legal struggles faced by boxing, and follow the blossoming of new popular sports such as wrestling, rowing, and pedestrianism. In many cases, however, watching was all they could do. The low population density, relative paucity of newspapers, poverty, and lack of significant urban centers meant that the South did not emerge as a center of major sporting activities similar to the Northeast and Midwest. The South did occasionally play host to significant prizefights, but these bouts typically occurred thanks to promoters from other areas finding the region easier to maneuver than more tightly regulated eastern states. Viewed as the periphery both politically and economically, the states of the former Confederacy suffered a similar fate culturally.

Although baseball and other sports penetrated the southern markets, the Southeast's lack of involvement at the highest levels of these sports helped keep traditional and uniquely southern sporting endeavors alive at a time when regionalism in sports was being slowly eliminated by the spread of a national sporting culture. For example, Major League Baseball positioned itself as the nation's leading sport during the late 19th century, but until the 1960s its "southern" teams were located in Baltimore and St. Louis. States in the temperate South supported a great deal of barnstorming and spring training games, proving the presence of hungry sports fans in the area, but major professional sports organizations hesitated in locating franchises there. Minor league and semipro baseball reached fans in the South, but the second-class nature of baseball in the area allowed for the continued demand for other sports. Much of the early growth of auto racing hinged on the survival of horse racing, a sport that remained popular in the South thanks to southern sportsmen's ability to compete at its highest levels. Although the types of sports embraced by southerners changed over time, the uniqueness of southern sports culture continued into the 20th century.

Prosperity in many parts of the country helped support growing associations between sports fandom, leisure, and masculinity, which allowed increasing numbers of professional sports to develop national reaches, but rural and southern fans bereft of local professional teams of the highest order turned college football and stock car racing into regionally significant sports. Even after the National Football League boosted the reputation of professional football in most parts of the country, college football retained its preeminence in the South. Neither of the two major professional football leagues bothered locating teams in any southern states save Texas until the late 1960s, which gave college football room to flourish. A regional affinity for college football helped the amateur form of the sport retain its significance in the South even after professional football franchises arrived. The largest American sanctioning body for auto racing similarly ignored the South, helping the growth of stock car racing. As with college football, stock car racing's place in the southern sports culture remained intact even when later confronted with challenges from other forms of motor sports.

The cultures surrounding both southern football and stock car racing are often linked to regional notions of honor. Southern honor (and its concomitant effects on masculinity) played a critical role in the development of a distinct regional sporting culture, a culture that, in turn, would color the behavior of stock car drivers of the 20th century. The violation of southern honor (among all white socioeconomic classes) required immediate and direct responses. Honor effectively coded acceptable actions outside of written laws. Although courts served as a mechanism for redressing material losses, the erosion of reputation and respect caused by an attack on one's honor could be addressed only through personal initiative. The fragility of honor created the need for constant, vigilant protection. Honor blended with class often constituted more of the public's perceptions of an individual than any material possessions. Bertram Wyatt-Brown noted that the importance of defending honor contributed greatly to the levels of violence in southeastern states, as a full display of southern masculinity mandated spirited defenses of one's honor. Even among southern adolescents, violent behavior could be condoned (if not promoted) by parents if these confrontational actions represented responses to threats to a boy's honor. Notions of honor existed in northern states during the 19th century, but for still disputed reasons, more muted responses to personal slights prevailed.[2]

For 20th-century southern stock car drivers, the related issues of honor and masculinity often dictated actions on the track. To be bumped out of the way by a competitor demanded some sort of response. NASCAR's officials might penalize a confrontational driver (thereby serving the role of a court), but a driver with a sense of honor felt compelled to personally respond. Retaliating either in kind on the track or through a verbal or physical altercation in the pits after the race represented an essential defense of one's honor. By not doing so, a driver ran the risk of being viewed as soft, which opened one up to both frequent, similar bumping and questions about the driver's manhood. As Bobby Allison, leader of NASCAR's Alabama Gang, explained after an on-the-track altercation with Curtis Turner, "I decided that if I was ever gonna race and be respected, then I was gonna have to give him what he had already given to me." Abiding by traditional notions of southern honor established drivers such as Allison as popular and highly regarded racers among southeastern stock car fans.[3]

Notions of honor, coupled with race and masculinity, undergirded one of the uniquely southern sporting endeavors of the 19th century—ring-and-lance tournaments. Based on fanciful notions of medieval chivalry, the tournaments provided the southern gentry opportunities to reinforce gender roles, honorable behavior, and the superior horsemanship of the well-heeled. Members of the gentry (men as armored knights with lances on horseback, women as fair maidens) reenacted medieval tilting contests to determine a champion knight, who then selected one of the female spectators as his queen. As part of what Wilbur J. Cash called the South's "cardboard medievalism," the tournaments attempted to create a linkage between medieval knights, southern cavaliers, and 19th-century gentry in an effort to reinforce social hierarchy.[4]

Vestiges of these events can be discerned in the more democratic world of modern stock car racing. The crowning of a "queen" as the trophy for the victor in both the tournaments and motor racing may be the most immediately visible linkage, but other connections exist as well. An 1898 account of one tournament describes the beginning of the event in the following manner: "there is a blast from the trumpet, the flag in the hands of another herald drops to the ground, and the rider is flying down the course at break-neck speed." Such a description bears a striking resemblance to the beginning of a NASCAR event with the roar of the engines followed by the drop of a flag and the subsequent blast of speed. Surrounded by (as opposed to clothed in) steel, guiding a vehicle whose strength is measured in horsepower, and competing for a trophy and kiss from a race queen, stock car drivers afford ample opportunities for knight-related metaphors. Examples of the conflation of stock car racing and ring-and-lance tournament traditions can be seen in reporter Chris Economaki's 1970 description of drivers as knights jousting on the road and in racing historian Sylvia Wilkinson's comparison of the steel-bodied, overweight American cars run in NASCAR to suits of armor.[5]

The remarkable horsemanship displayed in the ring-and-lance tournaments reflected the enormous cultural significance of horses in the South. Owning a saddle horse demonstrated one's status; meeting someone on a horse while walking made visibly clear that the pedestrian was beneath the rider. The southern gentry also strove to establish hierarchy within their own ranks through owning the fastest of horses, which gave rise to the most popular sport in the South—horse racing. Two different types of races emerged in the South, and both of them involved honor and status. Regularly scheduled racing events on well-known tracks offered opportunities for formal challenges among members of the gentry. Informal challenges between gentlemen who had congregated to drink and socialize were settled on the nearest piece of available flat land. Both types of races provided opportunities for gentlemen to engage in gambling, an abiding pursuit of many members of the southern gentry. Although the high-stakes gambling and expense of the best-bred horses eliminated the middle and lower classes from participation for financial reasons, the gentry outright banned those below them from competing as a matter of honor and hierarchy. By allowing nonelite whites to attend only as spectators, horse racing helped reinforce hierarchical standards. This intersection of horse ownership and its attendant status was replicated with automobile ownership in the first half of the 20th century. As NASCAR champion Ned Jarrett noted, "in the South an automobile is a matter of pride." Such attitudes also help explain why one form of motor sports—the demolition derby—did not succeed in the South. To destroy an automobile in such a willful fashion simply could not be justified.[6]

The connections between horse racing and southern motor sports cannot be overstated. In the South the love of speed, gambling, and bragging rights contributed directly to the development of stock car racing. As with horse racing, formal motor racing events were coupled with impromptu challenges settled on dusty back roads. In addition, road racing's popularity in early motor racing quickly became superseded by track racing, which offered both more safety (although unbanked turns created their own dangers) and better vantage points for paying spectators. The ubiquitous dirt oval tracks constructed for horse racing provided a convenient environment for motor racing as well, with much of stock car racing's early history occurring on horse tracks. Enterprising track owners sometimes even added a short motor race into the middle of a regular horse meet to generate excitement. The spread of motor racing in general would have suffered mightily without the presence of these dirt ovals. NASCAR no longer races on dirt tracks, but the legacy of this lineage is that races are conducted in a counterclockwise fashion, a practice initially adopted to placate the sensibilities of horse racing fans accustomed to watching races proceed in this fashion.[7]

The emergence of motor racing in the late 19th century occurred during a period of transition in America's sporting culture. In many parts of the country, a number of the sports associate with the post-Civil War birth of professional athletics (such as wrestling, rowing, and pedestrianism) skittered toward irrelevance as baseball, football, and boxing came to dominate the sporting landscape. In the South a similar transformation created an environment conducive to the rise of new pastimes. For example, this period witnessed widespread efforts to clean up traditional southern sports viewed as "rough amusements." New restrictions on hunting and drinking emerged in many places, and during the last quarter of the 19th century, every southern state passed laws against the long-lived sport of cockfighting. With older amusement forms circumscribed, southerners found themselves forced to embrace new entertainment forms, including motor racing. One by-product of this shifting cultural landscape was the wild popularity of county fairs in the early 20th century. As part of their growth, many southern fairgrounds expanded to include new, elaborate horse racing tracks. Motor racing, then, did not merely rise as a result of the South's changing sporting culture; it also benefited from the new infrastructure constructed for other purposes. In the wake of significant cultural alterations, especially after horse racing faced its own series of difficulties, motor racing grew in stature.

The roots of the stock car racing that came to prominence in the transformed southern sports culture can be traced to the November 1895 event sponsored by the *Chicago Times-Herald*. This first significant automobile race in the United States, a road course event from Chicago to Evanston and back, was won by auto manufacturer Frank Duryea. The next year a race occurred at the Rhode Island State Fair, thereby initiating the era of oval track racing that would eventually give rise to open-wheel and stock car racing. These earliest races frequently served as promotional devices for the hundreds of manufacturers that dotted the American landscape. Desperate to distinguish themselves from their competitors, manufacturers participated in races that served primarily as tests of durability and reliability. Participation in one such event meant that, technically, Henry Ford was a stock car driver. He won the only race he ever competed in, at Grosse Pointe, Michigan, in 1901, while piloting his own car. Although the NASCAR axiom "what wins on Sunday sells on Monday" lay decades in the future, early motor racing served a similar function for the fledgling automakers.[8]

By 1902, the United States possessed its first legitimate racing sanctioning body, the then-Chicago-based American Automobile Association (AAA). The AAA served as an all-purpose organization for those interested in automobiles, transportation improvements, and motor racing. Sanctioning from the organization, which eventually removed itself from the world of automobile racing in 1956, immediately granted an event status and respectability. Furthermore, only events with AAA representation could make legitimate claims to setting new American speed or endurance records. The initial American races certified by the AAA used road courses in emulation of European Grand Prix events. Most famous of these early American efforts was the Vanderbilt Cup, initially run on Long Island, which began in 1904. Although the initial Cup event featured only slightly modified street vehicles, by the second year purpose-built racing machines dominated the event. As the entrants became increasingly exotic, an effort was made to return to the initial spirit of the event in 1909 by requiring all cars to have stock chassis. Because of the horrible attrition rate of these machines, the 1910 race once again allowed for modifications. The AAA continued to operate a stock chassis series for the next few years, but a combination of manufacturer apathy and greater fan excitement over purpose-built racers led to its abandonment. Forty years later NASCAR would learn a similar lesson after attempting to run completely stock vehicles; without modification, a Detroit product straight from the assembly line simply could not withstand the stresses of racing. And in response, NASCAR, too, would begin to allow alterations that turned "stock" cars into something very different.

Public road course racing of the Vanderbilt Cup variety proved to be challenging to organize, tough on the fragile vehicles, and extremely dangerous. Promoters also found it difficult to make these events profitable because of the lack of crowd control. An example of how racing promoters might survive, however, emerged in August 1909 with the opening of the macadam-surfaced Indianapolis Motor Speedway, the nation's first track built specifically for motor racing. Despite initial problems, Carl Fisher's track proved that motor racing fans would willingly pay for grandstand seats in a state-of-the-art facility. The viability of similar purpose-built race tracks increased when efforts to continue public road course racing collapsed in 1916 after a series of fatalities involving both drivers and spectators. Fearful of future calamities, the AAA responded with a declaration that the organization would no longer sanction road racing events. This ban eventually proved to be less than a total abandonment of road courses, but the AAA primarily focused on speedways. Economic realities, public safety concerns, and the continued need for official sanctioning created an environment ripe for this new style of racing. Most involved in motor racing, however, could not afford to follow the lead of Indianapolis's Fisher and build their own track; they needed to use existing facilities. Horse racing ovals, already a popular venue for motor racing events, provided both safe environments and crowd control. The drive to shift the nation's motor racing to dirt tracks received an additional boost when several state legislatures enacted laws restricting wagering on horse races. Track owners now facing their own economic ruin turned to the struggling motor racing promoters for assistance. Out of these dire financial circumstances the uniquely American motor sport of oval track racing emerged.

Although blessed with many dirt track ovals, the South's levels of automobile ownership (and racing) initially lagged behind the Northeast's for several reasons. With most of the manufacturers based in the Northeast and Midwest, automobile acquisition was more difficult in the South than in other parts of the country. In addition, the area's lower income level translated into fewer potential buyers in the region. Because of the large rural population in need of connections to urban centers and county seats, the South did not suffer from a dearth of roads, but the bulk of these roads were unimproved and difficult for motor vehicles to use. Rural residents across the country, therefore, embraced the automobile more cautiously. In the agricultural South this caution translated into a more gradual increase in automobile ownership than in other parts of the country. As a result of significant purchase and repair costs, automobile ownership remained overwhelmingly limited to the economic elite. In the deeply socially stratified South, this disparity of ownership served to further reinforce class status in a manner similar to gentry control of the best horse blood lines. Later in the 20th century, when private ownership among the middle and working classes rose to levels that corresponded to their numbers in the population, the ability to use automobiles to compete against the gentry in stock car races became a challenge, however limited, to the existing social structure.

To those southern boosters who promoted the economic expansion, modernization, and increased national integration embedded in the "New South" creed at the turn of the 20th century, involvement in the new automobile industry offered an important opportunity to improve national perceptions of the region. The region's poor public image and transportation conditions, however, represented significant obstacles to merging with the burgeoning car culture of other regions. The South's promoters, with tourist dollars in mind, therefore began the process of linking urban centers in the South and Northeast via new railroads and highways. To demonstrate the improved transportation network of the South, reliability runs, automobile shows, and actual motor races became heavily promoted events. By the second decade of the 20th century, tentacles of the national Good Roads Movement reached the South, which began the process of improving both national highways and local connector roads. These developments also served to undercut the traditional provinciality of the region, an alteration initially viewed by rural residents with some measure of suspicion, but hailed by "New South" advocates as enormous progress.[9]

Urban proponents of the automobile found car shows and organized races a valuable tool in their efforts to promote the "New South." Atlanta, the seat of the "New South" creed, actively sought to become part of the modernization associated with the arrival of the automobile, with the city hosting the National Association of Automobile Manufacturers national show in November 1909. During the first few years of the 20th century, motor races also occurred in several southern cities including Louisville, San Antonio, Nashville, and Daytona-Ormond Beach. As part of the effort to use these events as a means of connecting the "New South" with the rest of the country, hastily organized automobile clubs in southern cities often applied for AAA sanctioning for these races. For southern boosters, AAA approval was essential if they hoped to receive national attention for their efforts.[10]

As demonstrating the modernity of the "New South" lay at the core of these often municipal government-promoted races, it naturally followed that most of the early southern automobile events involved vehicles either designed for racing or modified heavily, with professional drivers at the wheel. Most of these Progressive-era races offered several days of festivities with multiple races, parades, and banquets. Parades frequently included local automobile owners who, given the expense of early cars, represented the socioeconomic elite of their communities. This gentry dominance of private automobile ownership also meant that even when these events included stock car races, the working class residents of the area could not compete. Like southern horse racing before it, early automobile racing reflected the rigidly hierarchical social structure of the South. With the expansion of private automobile ownership into the lower socioeconomic classes, however, elite dominance waned. Part of the appeal of motor racing for the middle and working classes became this ability to compete with their social betters. Not surprisingly, elite attention to stock car racing declined as lower classes became more prominent in this form of motor racing.[11]

Although the early motor age races and gentry-dominated parades helped southern boosters showcase their own cities, those looking to promote regional progress needed to create an event of truly national importance. The effort to create an automobile-related event to promote the entire South resulted in the creation of a southern version of the Vanderbilt Cup—the Savannah Grand Prize of 1908. A road course event intended to attract international competitors, the Grand Prize meet included several lesser events, some of which involved stock vehicles driven by wealthy local residents. The paucity of owners willing to compete, however, made the stock races a secondary part of the meet. Moreover, an event dominated by stock cars, even if driven by the local elite, not only would do nothing to establish Savannah as a progressive city on the cutting edge of technology, but also would reinforce notions of southern backwardness. The Savannah boosters involved in organizing the Grand Prize viewed this event as a promotional tool for both the city and the "modern" South, which necessitated the participation of prominent and international drivers in purpose-built racing machines. As supposed demonstrations of modernity, events such as the Savannah Grand Prize marginalized the participation of the simple passenger cars off the streets, even if operated by the local elite. The perception of stock car racing as a second-tier form of motor sports, then, can be seen as early as the first decades of the 20th century.[12]

The events of the Savannah Grand Prize also demonstrated that the sites for southern motor racing generally followed the pattern for early motor races seen in other parts of the country, with initial events on road courses, followed by the rise of oval track racing. One enormous divergence of great import for racing in the South in general and NASCAR in particular, however, developed during the early 20th century. Unlike racing in the North, southern events began using beaches. By the early 20th century, Florida boosters had already established the state as a haven from bitter northern winters, and improving transportation networks made excursions to Florida increasingly viable. Representatives from *Automobile Magazine* visited coastal Florida during the winter of 1902 as part of one of these motor trips and became enamored with the Daytona-Ormond Beach area. They began promoting it as a destination for northern motorists thanks to the miles of smooth and firm sand that made the beach a fantastic location for automobiling. These conditions also created an almost perfect natural racetrack, prompting *Automobile Magazine* to send promoter William J. Morgan to Daytona-Ormond with instructions to organize a March 1903 auto meet.

The beach events at Daytona-Ormond inaugurated in 1903 would continue for the rest of the decade. By 1905, the bulk of the event occurred at Daytona Beach, and that location became known as a Mecca for automobile enthusiasts. The annual event grew to include several races and AAA-sanctioned attempts to set land speed records. In 1906, meet organizers, the Florida East Coast Automobile Association (FECAA), enlarged the speed-related activities to include a contest to find the "prettiest girl in Florida." Officials anointed the victor, 14-year-old Mary Simrall of Ormond, as the event's queen, and she then crowned feature race winner Victor Demogeot as the "Speed King of the World." From this point forward, like the ring-and-lance tournaments before them, the resolution of motor races frequently involved a "race queen" as part of the concluding ceremonies. Serving as a living trophy, with rare exceptions, represented the only role women would be allowed in motor racing for decades to come.

Although more successful than the abortive efforts to establish Savannah as a motor racing hub, the Daytona Beach meets suffered a series of setbacks that made the event increasingly difficult to maintain. By 1907, the actual races had taken a backseat to the accompanying attempts to set land speed records, and that year purpose-built steam-powered vehicles dominated a meet fraught with wrecks. In subsequent years FECAA established new qualifying rules that mandated vehicles attempting to set new speed records must first participate in a 100-mile race, persuaded racing star Barney Oldfield to appear as a special attraction, and encouraged the attendance of high-speed motorcycles. Not only did these endeavors fail to reignite the excitement of Daytona's earliest meets, but they drove away international competitors. Those seeking to set new speed records then began using the wide and flat Bonneville Salt Flats of Utah for their attempts. In 1911, Daytona leaders responded to the declining importance of the annual automobile meet by hosting a flying exhibition on the beach instead. Occasional efforts to set speed records continued at Daytona for the next few decades, but full-fledged meets did not accompany these attempts. Only in 1936 did organized beach racing return to Daytona and then in the very different form of a stock car race. The Depression-era renewal of racing at Daytona cemented the importance of the city in southern motor racing, a prominence it retains to this day.[13]

The oval tracks dominated the interregnum between periods of Daytona's importance. As early as 1903, Louisville's Churchill Downs oval hosted a motor race, and purpose-built racers sped around dusty Virginia fairgrounds tracks by the middle of the decade. The horse tracks of the South served as the primary location of motor racing in the pre–World War I era, but sporadic attempts to create automobile-specific racing facilities also occurred. Soft drink magnate Asa Candler arranged for the 1909 auto showcase in Atlanta to correspond with the opening of his new two-mile, mixed-surface speedway in that city. Designed to compete with the new track at Indianapolis, Atlanta Speedway's opening proved successful, and one reporter noted that "motor racing has taken a hold on the fancy of Southerners." Despite the initial burst of excitement, however, the track proved costly to maintain and was eventually converted into an airport.[14]

High-banked wooden tracks built specifically for motor racing also briefly supplemented the dirt ovals of fairgrounds. Although safer for spectators than public road courses, the dirt ovals posed their own problems. Unbanked turns were not conducive to poorly handling high-speed automobiles, and potholes (Daytona Beach's equivalent were sand ripples) caused deadly crashes. Board tracks, capable of handling both high speeds and banking, seemed to offer a viable alternative. Beginning in 1910, high-banked (some with 50-degree turns) wooden race tracks started appearing across the country. Construction of most of the board tracks occurred in the racing hubs of the Midwest and West Coast, but the South sported short-lived tracks in Charlotte, near Miami, and in the border city of Baltimore. Although fast and relatively safe, the board tracks did not offer especially exciting racing. Their speedy surfaces tended to offset any advantages a particular car or driver might have, which led to single-file racing and little passing. Even worse, their wooden surfaces, in an era before satisfactory preservatives, suffered damage from weather, termites, and fire. Although most tracks simply rotted away thanks to rain, a more spectacular weather-related fate befell the board track in Miami. The track hosted only one race meet before its destruction in the hurricane of 1926. Cheaper and easier to maintain, dirt tracks continued to host races during the board track fad and regained their status as the dominant racing venue during the late 1920s. By one estimate, 90 percent of all motor races in the 1920s and 1930s occurred on dirt tracks designed for horse racing.[15]

The South sported so few purpose-built motor racing tracks because of the combined effects of poverty and low population density. Local farm board-supported dirt ovals provided the only viable means of hosting motor races under these dire circumstances. Drawing crowds to motor racing events in the South also meant bringing in spectators from a much larger radius than in the Northeast or Midwest. With a poorer, albeit improving, transportation network than other regions, the South had inherent difficulties attracting large crowds. Even in areas with good roads, the low percentage of automobile ownership in the South meant the range of travel for most southerners was rather limited. Given these circumstances, it is not surprising that Lakewood Speedway of Atlanta, the South's urban hub, established itself as the preeminent purpose-built southern track. Few other locales provided populations large enough to support a dedicated motor racing track. Further, low income levels among this predominantly rural population resulted in less disposable income available for entertainment purposes. Professional entertainment, common in northern cities by the late 19th century, took longer to reach the South for these reasons, and motor racing of the early 20th century followed a similar pattern.[16]

For the automobile (and motor racing) to become an important aspect of southern life, the conditions arrayed against motor vehicles needed to change. In the years just before and after World War I, a significant transformation did occur. Local and federal funding contributed to an increasingly modern transportation network throughout the southeastern United States. Southern income levels also rose, while the price of automobiles declined. Also, the new urban areas in the South, bereft of the congested cores built for horse-and-buggy travel common in the North, aided the development of a car culture by using planning techniques conducive to automobile travel. Boosters for southern cities perceived expansion arranged around motorized transportation as a reflection of the region's increasing modernity. These automobile-age cities of the South fostered a sense of the automobile's centrality to life and therefore encouraged increased private ownership of cars. And, most important, rural residents across the country came to embrace all sorts of motorized vehicles. For the South, these alterations exacted fundamental changes in the region. Automobility affected all parts of the country, but the South felt the car's impact most deeply.[17]

Like other rural Americans, southerners initially balked at the rise of automobiles. The early cars' loud motors disrupted the tranquility of outlying areas and frightened livestock, and the unreliable vehicles often blocked roads as a result of mechanical failures or by sinking into the muddy quagmires that passed for rural roads. The dearth of available improved highways, coupled with the traditional lack of disposable income among small farmers, meant that rural Americans did not initially embrace the automobile in the fashion of urban residents. Although they were slower to accept motor vehicles, rural Americans quickly came to be firm proponents of the automobile. This acceptance stemmed partly from endorsements of motor vehicles by groups such as the National Grange, who, in 1908, declared that automobiles promised to make life easier for those involved in the agricultural sector. American auto manufacturers, struggling to establish their brand among the 500 different makes available, recognized that rural Americans represented a relatively untapped market and therefore launched campaigns geared specifically toward the group. Rural residents also began to see the car as a general source of power, both in terms of the automobile's ability to make agricultural tasks easier and the mobility it granted them. This shift in rural attitudes can be seen in the 1920 U.S. Census, which found that a higher percentage of farm households owned an automobile than did nonfarm households. Many of the early stock car racers grew up in these car-loving farm households.[18]

Accustomed to working on farm machinery, rural residents discovered they could not only repair their own automobiles, but they could also earn extra money working on those belonging to both stranded motor tourists and their less mechanically inclined neighbors. For impoverished rural residents, employment as an auto mechanic became a new means of escaping the family farm. The new southern cities, built during the automobile age, expanded through the development of car-friendly suburbs and wide urban streets. With so many cars in operation, these cities needed enormous numbers of mechanics. Not all of the mechanics operating in southern cities during the first few decades of the 20th century migrated from rural areas, but a large number did, and these men, such as the legendary Raymond Parks, would eventually contribute to the development of southern stock car racing. Despite the notoriety associated with early NASCAR drivers involved in the illegal liquor business, an essential aspect of the sport's development lies with those who worked in more respectable fields such as auto mechanics.

Whether or not they migrated to the cities, rural southerners embraced the automobile, as one contemporary account noted, as "the mechanical means for a greater degree of self-direction and self-expression." Rural residents found this life-changing machine easier to acquire by the early 1920s thanks to falling car prices and the widespread availability of installment buying. The transition from horse to car wrought a fundamental change in the equality of southern transportation. Where the gentry previously dominated through their ability to purchase the best saddle horses and the fastest thoroughbreds, in an era of experimentation and simple car design, the democratic automobile allowed for the rural and working class to tune their cars to make them equal to those of the socioeconomic elite. Further, this leveling could not be easily escaped. The elite could still afford to purchase better quality automobiles than the lower classes, just as they had with 19th-century horses, but they needed working class mechanics to perform the required maintenance on those vehicles. Also, the number of working class youth trained as mechanics grew in wake of the 1917 Smith-Hughes National Vocational Education Act. Smith-Hughes helped the perennially cash-strapped southern educational system provide vocational training to adolescents, thereby markedly increasing the number of young men who could thoroughly work on others' automobiles or tune their own for ad hoc competitions.[19]

As in the rest of the country, the car most beloved by working class southerners was the Ford Model T. First introduced in 1908, the Model T proved to be both reliable and fast and, as the century wore on, increasingly inexpensive to purchase and repair. In its stock condition, the Model T was not an especially good race car, although it won several competitions before Henry Ford ended his factory racing program in 1913, but the "car for the great multitude" could be cut, chopped, and customized in remarkable ways. Equipped with Rajo or Frontenac ("Fronty") racing heads, the "hotted-up Model T did more to create a racing element in the United States than did anything else." A customized Model T could not compete with expensive purpose-built open-wheel racers on paved or long tracks, but on short dirt ovals and country pastures, it dominated; 30-year-old Fronty Fords were still winning races in the 1950s. For southern men replicating the time-tested tradition of impromptu racing challenges, the Model T served as a chariot capable of earning them status among their peers.[20]

The drop in Model T prices occurred concurrently with the growing strength of the American temperance movement. Temperance advocates scored a series of victories in the second decade of the 20th century that banned alcohol in many southern states. To keep these states truly dry, Congress passed the Webb-Kenyon Act in 1913, which banned the shipment of alcohol from a wet to a dry state. The growing momentum of the temperance campaign eventually resulted in the ratification of a national Prohibition amendment in January 1919. With legal distilleries idled, obtaining alcohol became a difficult proposition. The Prohibition decade of the 1920s is typically associated with the rise of organized crime, but it also witnessed a phenomenal growth in rural whiskey production, especially in the Southeastern and Appalachian regions. Distilling whiskey and selling it without paying federal taxes date back to the 18th century in these areas, but statewide and then national Prohibition increased the demand for this product. Even after national Prohibition's repeal in 1933, many southern states and counties remained dry, thereby continuing the demand for moonshine. With few economic opportunities available to rural southerners, distilling whiskey (moonshining) or transporting that product from producers to consumers (bootlegging or tripping) offered them a means to make a comfortable living in areas such as the Carolina Piedmont or North Georgia. NASCAR driver and convicted moonshiner Junior Johnson, a native of Wilkes County, North Carolina, later suggested "it was either make moonshine or starve."[21]

Despite current mythology, not all early NASCAR drivers previously hauled illegal whiskey; however, many of the most successful—and colorful—did trip. Along with Junior Johnson, admitted trippers included Buddy Shuman, the Flock brothers, Wendell Scott, Gwyn Staley, and Curtis Turner. Prominent pre-NASCAR stock car drivers Lloyd Seay, Roy Hall, and Ed Samples (later one of the founders of NASCAR) also ran moonshine. The effect of such participation is that it is possible to link all early NASCAR figures to the moonshine business. For example, Red Vogt, who invented the name NASCAR, worked as a mechanic on the race cars owned by Atlanta mechanic and moonshine kingpin Raymond Parks, and one of his cars was driven in the late 1930s by Bill France Sr., the acknowledged "father" of NASCAR. Such ties have given rise to the notion, now frequently promoted by NASCAR itself, that trippers invented stock car racing. Given the enormous significance of bootleggers in the sport, it is perhaps unsurprising that such an idea has taken root. It is therefore important to keep in mind that the rise of stock car racing involved men who were not part of the illegal liquor underworld and that the promotion and sponsorship of even the races that did include trippers required the funds and skills available only to municipalities and local elites. Moreover, "stock" car racing, in its purest form, began with the 1895 Chicago to Evanston race won by automobile manufacturer Frank Duryea.[22]

The significance of the trippers lay not in their invention of the sport of stock car racing, but for two other important reasons. First, their need for fast and reliable transportation fostered performance enhancement, which can be viewed as a continuation of the traditional southern love of horsepower. Developments first undertaken by trippers would have eventually occurred without their presence, but the imperatives of the moonshine business sped up the nonfactory evolution of passenger cars. Their actions, then, accelerated the process of converting truly "stock" vehicles into machines capable of the speed and durability needed for racing purposes. The second area in which trippers proved important to the sports development rested on their "gatekeeping" status of providing participants for southern stock car racing during the lean period between the early 20th century death of the first stock car racing era and the post-World War II rise of a more tightly regulated form of stock. By virtue of their mechanical aptitude, temperament, and driving experience, trippers proved to be a vast pool of willing and able stock car racers between the wars. Without their presence it is difficult to imagine full race fields for southern stock car races during the wildcat pre-NASCAR era.

To the undoubted chagrin of teetotaler Henry Ford, his products became an integral part of the moonshine business. After the discontinuation of the Model T, motors for that car became so inexpensive they were commonly used to drive cooling pumps on stills. During the 1920s, trippers increasingly embraced Fords, which also became the dominant vehicle of pre-NASCAR stock racing. Southern speed merchants of all types used the trusty Model T and its late 1920s replacement, the Model A, but found the most to love in the V8 introduced by Ford in the early 1930s. One of the great racing motors of all time, the Ford coupe equipped with a "flathead" V8 could be tuned and customized into an awesome machine, capable of speeds and handling beyond anything else on the road. Although law-abiding, mechanically inclined southerners deserve some credit for advancing the capabilities of these Fords, it was the men who prepared cars for tripping that discovered the ways to make these cars as fast as possible.[23]

Trippers not only found ways to increase the top speed of the Fords, but they also perfected techniques for strengthening a car's suspension. Hauling a full load of moonshine added an enormous amount of weight to a car that needed to have the capability to outrun law enforcement, which necessitated suspension improvements. The advances developed by trippers to deal with this problem on back country roads proved equally effective at assisting a stock car to speed through the unbanked corners of dirt oval tracks. These home efforts to improve the performance of the Ford V8 were also assisted by the Ford Motor Company, which made several adjustments to the motor during the decade. The "flathead" emerged in its perfected factory form by the end of the 1930s. As such, the 1940 Ford became the vehicle of choice for both trippers and stock car racers, a status it maintained for more than a decade.

As the experienced pilots of customized V8s, trippers also made excellent stock car drivers. Lonely country roads provided a possible setting for any car owner to test his ability to operate an automobile at full throttle, but only trippers felt compelled to do so on a regular basis. They learned not only how to handle a fast-moving V8, but also how to navigate unbanked dirt turns at high rates of speed, as well as how to set up a car to make that task as easy as possible. For moonshine haulers addicted to the adrenaline rush of a high speed chase with Internal Revenue Service agents, racing offered the only comparable thrill. These often unregulated early races were both deadly and poorly paying, with bragging rights standing as the primary reward. The high risks and low rewards served as deterrents to most southerners. Young and fatalistic trippers, however, relished the opportunities to compete with their peers. Therefore, with a few performance-minded mechanics and hobbyists added to the mix, the trippers constituted the majority of drivers in early southern stock races.

Fast Fords became increasingly important for southern race fans because they were so poorly served by national racing sanctioning bodies. From the very beginning of the Championship Trail circuit, the AAA focused most of its attentions on the Midwest and Northeast. Efforts to establish the modernity of the South, such as the Savannah Grand Prize, may have boosted general perceptions of the area, but they did little to establish the region as a hub of motor sports. When the championship circuit officially began in 1911, it included meets in 22 cities, with only two stops in former Confederate states. Neither of the two southern events proved sustainable, with one race at the ill-fated Candler track in Atlanta and the other the Savannah Grand Prize. The AAA made future sustained southern touring unlikely later in 1911 when it established new sanctioning rules that forced one-mile dirt oval operators to adopt stricter safety standards and outright banned racing on dirt ovals of lesser distances. Even the one-mile dirt ovals survived only because the AAA could not yet assemble a complete racing season on the much preferred paved surfaces. These rules effectively ended any chances of a significant AAA presence in the South. Overwhelmingly of the short and dirt variety, southern oval tracks simply did not meet the requirements for AAA sanctioning. Champ cars subsequently made occasional forays into the South, but the AAA evinced a marked reluctance to sanction events for these vehicles in the region.

The other national sanctioning body, the International Motor Contest Association (IMCA), made more regular stops in the South, but also found the region less supportive than the Midwest and Northeast. IMCA typically featured "big cars," so it also brought open-wheel racing to southerners. Far more lenient in its sanctioning standards than the staid AAA, IMCA governed more than 80 percent of the country's races by the late 1920s and promoted itself as the sanctioning body for dirt track racing. Like the AAA, however, IMCA focused its attentions on other regions of the country. Most of the actual races sanctioned by the group could be viewed as IMCA events in name only, with the organization simply lending its name to as many races as possible in an effort to defeat the rival AAA in a battle of quantity over quality.[24]

IMCA's premier open-wheel series actually acted more like a barnstorming troupe than a legitimate racing championship. J. Alex Sloan, head promoter of IMCA, staged daredevil stunts and match races, changed drivers' names to make them sound more exotic, and engaged in other promotional gimmicks disdained by the more respectable AAA. Their big car circuit also developed a reputation for hippodroming. Sloan put the top drivers on weekly salaries, so they were not actually running for the advertised purses, and, by the late 1930s, IMCA directly owned all the cars competing on the circuit. Although IMCA visited the South more often than did the AAA, the group's appearances were still rather infrequent and often served as part of the entertainment at state or county fairs, rather than as an ongoing championship to be followed over the course of a racing season. When coupled with their shady reputation, IMCA's scheduling strategy did little to improve the cause of open-wheel racing in the region.[25]

Already marginalized by the major sanctioning organizations, stock car racing was further regionalized by the onset of the Great Depression. Open-wheel racing continued to dominate, but in a new form. Forced to survive under extreme financial constraints, the nation's auto racing promoters latched on to midget cars as their economic salvation. Small, fast, and inexpensive to maintain, the midgets became the most common form of motor racing in the United States. One benefit to their small size was that they could be raced in a variety of locations. The midgets, therefore, competed not just on formal race tracks, but also on football and baseball fields and indoor arenas. Indoor racing allowed for midget competition year round, even in the dead of winter, which helped racing promoters continue to operate. Like other types of open-wheel racing, the midgets appeared in the South. The midgets also followed the earlier open-wheel pattern of both limited southern exposure and popularity. By the time of its arrival, low-budget stock car racing already ruled the motor racing world of middle and working class southerners.

2

BACK TO THE BEACH

After the shift toward the faster purpose-built race cars developed in the first decade of the 20th century, stock car racing languished as a lesser form of racing located beneath open-wheelers in the sport's pecking order. Despite the overwhelming dominance of open-wheel racing, stock car racing did manage to survive. Most of the stock car racing of the 1920s occurred well beyond the purview of the national sanctioning bodies. Challenges on country roads that blurred the line between motor racing and drag racing and localized dirt oval events constituted the bulk of these races. They could be considered "stock," however, only by using NASCAR's current notion of the term—a heavily altered car that looks like a showroom model. Pure stock car racing (what Bill France Sr. would call "strictly stock") did actually experience a brief recrudescence in the late 1920s, but revival proved short-lived. Stocks emerged as an increasingly popular form of racing again at the end of the 1930s, only to see their momentum cut short by World War II. Even the federally mandated end of motor racing precipitated by American involvement in the greatest conflagration in human history, however, could not stop stock's progress among racing fans, and the immediate postwar years witnessed both the birth of NASCAR and the beginning of stock's rise to national prominence.

Automobile racing began in the United States as a means of determining superiority among the confusing multitude of manufacturers, and a similar concern gave rise to a return of organized stock car racing in the 1920s. The field of companies had been reduced from hundreds to dozens by that point, but competition among the survivors proved just as fierce. In 1926, a few manufacturers attempted 24-hour endurance runs, independently of each other, to improve their market shares. These efforts spurred the promotion of pure stock car races sanctioned by the American Automobile Association (AAA) the next year. The AAA then began offering the Stevens Challenge Trophy to any strictly stock vehicle that could maintain a speed of 60 miles per hour for 24 consecutive hours at the Indianapolis Motor Speedway. This return of stock cars emerged out of an internal debate within the AAA over the expense and future course of motor sports. Rapid technological advances during the 1920s led to ever-increasing specialization within open-wheel racing, which forced drivers to possess a wildly expensive Deusenberg, Miller, or Offenhauser vehicle if they hoped to compete successfully. The rift within the AAA stemmed from these developments. A spirited debate arose over whether the organization should continue to promote cutting-edge technology to present spectators with the finest machines possible or whether they should adjust their rules so that less expensive machines closer to stock vehicles could also compete in sanctioned events. Underlying this fight was a recognition that motor sports were slipping in popularity and that this might be a result of having a limited number of drivers in possession of truly competitive equipment. The AAA attempted to resolve this problem by changing regulations to encourage open-wheel vehicles at least partly constructed by a manufacturer (semistock) to compete on the Championship Trail. It also developed rules to govern a new series of truly stock races.[1]

As part of its cautious return to stock car racing, the AAA held races for these production vehicles as preliminary events at Championship Trail meets during 1927, including one southern event in Charlotte, North Carolina. Cognizant of the limitations of true stock cars as racers, these events ran shorter distances than the Champ cars. Although 100 miles became the preferred distance, some stock races for smaller cars went only 25 miles. Reflecting the organizational split over high- and low-cost racing, the AAA promoted some stock races as events for semiprofessional drivers to enable those with limited funds to be involved in motor sports. Yet top Champ car drivers, backed by manufacturers desperate for victories, also competed in stock races. AAA stars such as Ralph Hepburn, Tom Rooney, and the ill-fated Frank Lockhart undoubtedly added excitement to stock events, but their presence must have also deterred many semiprofessionals from even attempting to compete.[2]

After these 1927 efforts, the AAA did not become deeply involved in stock racing again until after World War II. They sanctioned speed tests and a stock race at Daytona in 1928, but during the Great Depression decade, the organization only occasionally approved stock events. Typically, these 1930s meets featured races of more than 100 miles and ran on road racing courses. Most prominently, the AAA sanctioned a race in Elgin, Illinois in 1933, the Targo Florio event of 1934, on a road course that included part of Los Angeles's Legion Ascot Speedway, and a few mid-decade races at Mines Field in California. During the late 1930s, the AAA authorized annual events at Oakland Speedway, and Ralph Hankinson promoted AAA-sanctioned races at the legendary round track at Langhorne, Pennsylvania. Although the Oakland Speedway event represented the longest, best-publicized recurring stock car race in the nation, it also reflected the localized nature of stock. A newspaper article promoting the 1937 event, for example, singled out driver Edgar Lewis simply because he traveled all the way from Texas to compete. The infrequency of AAA events partly reflected that organization's continued dedication to open-wheel racing, but also indicated a waning interest on the part of manufacturers to participate in multiple races each year. For example, Stutz Motors was one of the leaders in returning to endurance tests in the mid-1920s, and their cars dominated the AAA stock events of 1927, but by the early 1930s, they no longer wanted to compete. Stutz executive E. S. Gorrell believed that the success of their cars in stock races actually hurt sales because it created an overly "sporty" image of the vehicles that drove away well-to-do consumers, women, and the safety conscious. In 1930, he told a reporter that "racing success no longer helps sell cars in the United States."[3]

With little pressure or support from manufacturers to continue to heavily promote stock car racing, the AAA continued to focus most of its energies on the open-wheel series. From the inception of the organization's Contest Board in 1909, the AAA viewed itself as the sanctioning body for the most advanced and professional forms of racing. For the AAA this meant the Champ series and other races involving open-wheel cars. It also meant sanctioning races on the most modern (preferably paved) and longest tracks, the bulk of which existed outside the South. The South possessed few of these types of tracks for two basic reasons. First, as a hotbed of horse racing, southern racing entrepreneurs focused on dirt tracks and typically viewed half-mile tracks as the standard. Also, the low population density and high poverty rates made the large initial investment required to build a long, paved oval track a risky proposition. With the AAA infrequently venturing into the southeastern quadrant, these expensive modern tracks possessed few opportunities to recoup the initial investment. And the AAA would not increase its southern operations without these types of tracks. For southern race fans, a low volume of AAA events resulted from these circumstances. Although short track stock car racing in other parts of the country faced stiff competition from the open-wheel racing available to local fans, it prospered in the South thanks to limited competition from open-wheel. Southern affinity for stock developed for several local reasons, but it also benefited greatly from the AAA's neglect of the South.

With the AAA sanctioning only a few stock car races and scrupulously avoiding short ovals, the bulk of 1930s stock racing occurred thanks to local promotional efforts. Most of these races, as a result, involved only local drivers, possessed no connections to any sort of national (or, in most cases, even regional) points championship, and were viewed at the time as "amateur races." Occasionally a more substantial regional event developed, such as Joe Littlejohn's 1938 "Southern Championship" race in Spartanburg, South Carolina, but even these races held no direct ties to real sanctioning bodies. Given the ephemeral nature of the Depression-era races, many more undoubtedly occurred than those preserved with written records. For newspaper editors with limited space to devote to motor racing, covering the more professional open-wheel version of the sport seemed the more logical choice. Whether or not covered by local news outlets, these sorts of one-off, purely local stock events developed out of the increasing speed and durability of passenger cars. As one editorialist noted, the new cars could go so fast that their owners could no longer completely open them up on the highway, so those curious about their vehicle's top performance felt compelled to take them to a track. Southern dirt track operators looking to supplement their income during the Great Depression therefore catered to local speed enthusiasts by offering them the occasional opportunity to venture onto a track.[4]

At a slightly more professional level stood the regularly scheduled events on horse track ovals and a few purpose-built speedways. Still overwhelmingly local in nature, these tracks often featured points standings and season champions. These series were often limited to local or "amateur" drivers, like the one-off races. Although there were strictly stock meets of this nature, "modified" stock cars, often shorn of their fenders and glass, ran more regularly. The adoption of some form of stock cars reflected a simple fact of racing—most locales could not muster a full field of open-wheel vehicles to compete on a regular basis. By featuring stocks, modifieds, or "jalopies" (old, low-value passenger cars)—vehicles much more readily available than open-wheelers—a track would be assured of full fields of local competitors. These connections to local, low-budget racing also reinforced the notion that stock racing stood well below the various forms of open-wheel in the hierarchy of racing.[5]

Stock emerged as the dominant form of racing in the South partly because it was the sole region of the country that offered little racing by the "professional" open-wheel types. The International Motor Contest Association (IMCA) and the AAA visited southern states throughout the 1930s, but only in a limited fashion. Hankinson promoted an annual southern "big car" swing in the fall for most of the decade, and Bill Breitenstein periodically worked with the AAA in Georgia and Florida, but the bulk of the races sanctioned by the national groups occurred in other parts of the country. They did not view the South as a primary market and responded accordingly. As racing journalist Russ Catalin noted in the 1950s, "it has long been accepted that auto racing south of the Mason-Dixon line has always been a losing proposition." IMCA appeared more often than the AAA, but even its appearances remained limited to events connected with fairs. This association with state and county agricultural fairs was not accidental. IMCA recognized the difficulty of attracting a large audience to a southern open-wheel event and, therefore, scheduled its races to correspond with those times when a large population of potential spectators would already be present in the vicinity of the dirt ovals. The AAA's focus on long and, preferably, paved tracks meant the South, which boasted a limited number of modern speedways, offered only a few sites that the organization would even consider sanctioning. Rural areas did not factor into the AAA's plans and, therefore, had little hope of landing a sanctioned race. The AAA did not sanction a race in the sparsely populated state of West Virginia, for example, until 1935. Facing the combined problems of few long tracks and low population density, southern racing fans found themselves forced to create their own races.[6]

The emergence of local racing was not unique to the South; however, because of the region's isolation, in terms of its relationship to national sanctioning bodies, local racing in the South developed its own unique, bottom-up culture that, in many ways, contrasted sharply with the areas of the country governed from the top by the AAA. Southern drivers began their racing careers (or, in most cases, hobby) with some form of stock and then typically ended their driving days in stock. Even if southern drivers were especially successful at the local level, moving up to national racing proved difficult for them. For most of the Depression decade not a single driver from south of the Mason-Dixon Line appeared in the end of the season Champ car points top 30 issued by the AAA. Bereft of the frequent big car and midget races found in other parts of the country, southern racers simply lacked chances to move up through the open-wheel ranks. The one exception in the region was Texas, which produced a significant number of lower level open-wheel drivers. The other former Confederate states operated almost independently of national racing trends. Closed out from moving up nationally in open-wheel, stock racing gained importance for southern drivers and fans. As Bill France Sr., who drove stocks during the 1930s, laconically noted, "the North and South were somewhat different in their racing likes and dislikes."[7]

Southerners embraced stock partly out of their marginalization by the national sanctioning bodies, but also because of specific cultural factors. Actions by the AAA reinforced notions of northern elitism for many racing-inclined southerners. The "northern" Contest Board of the AAA could declare that open-wheel racing was superior and that the southern states were peripheral, but this served only to stiffen the resolve of southern racers to maintain their more egalitarian and regional style of racing. For southerners imbued with the region's traditional love of speed, modified versions of passenger cars represented the most readily available and economical means of satisfying their passion. Heavily armored stock cars allowed for considerably more contact that the fragile open-wheel vehicles, so immediate responses to personal slights—in the form of purposeful car-to-car contact—proved much easier. This high impact nature of stocks resonated with honor-bound southerners. That Yankees declared southerners' preferred style of racing substandard freighted a racing form born from economic necessity with great cultural weight. From this initial wellspring of regional pride, a spirited defense of stock car racing as a "southern" sport developed

Southern stock car racing of the 1930s (and beyond) also represented an intersection of race and class with the issue of regionalism. Previously closed out of horse racing by the mandates of the southern elite, middle and working class whites could actively participate in motor racing. Unfortunately for them, the AAA operated in a haughty manner similar to the local gentry. West Coast AAA official Art Pillsbury later acknowledged that the organization represented a "fraternity . . . full of men of substantial wealth and culture" promoting racing with "aristocratic associations." With the expensive (and northern) world of open-wheel racing as exclusionary as thoroughbred competitions, stock cars offered nonelite southerners an entree into motor racing. The best thoroughbred bloodlines and high-tech Champ cars could never be matched by a working class southerner, but passenger cars converted into racing vehicles through the hard work of their owners could compete with stock cars owned by even the wealthiest patrons of racing. Neal Thompson pointed out that "in contrast to AAA events and their traveling bands of professionals, stock car races were often filled with amateur local drivers in local cars, which often erased the elitist taint from auto racing and, in the South, multiplied the thrills."[8]

Stock car racing finally gave working class white southern men the chance to demonstrate their honor and masculinity in a democratic public cultural endeavor. Working class stock drivers competed not just among themselves, as they had previously in horse racing, but with the entire community. Success against their peers, and potentially social betters as well, on the track gave these men both status and a public voice. Like Willie Stark's chauffeur Sugar-Boy in *All the King's Men*, a working class stock driver "couldn't talk, but he could express himself when he got his foot on the accelerator." Given the social implications of stock car racing, the disavowal of it by many within the southern elite as a "poor white trash" pursuit was not surprising, especially since that attitude could be buttressed by the pronouncements of the AAA. The New South promoters of the Savannah Grand Prize never envisioned their refined gathering would spawn contests between sweaty machinists banging fenders in a cow pasture, but the uncontrollable democratization of personal automobile ownership did just that.[9]

These middle and working class southern stock car drivers raced primarily on the dirt oval horse tracks. Stock cars typically did not frequent the few purpose-built southern tracks until the late 1930s. At the close of the decade, however, construction began on a spate of purpose-built speedways in the South that would host stock as well as open-wheel competitions. Those involved in the creation of speedways through central Virginia and North Carolina and the northern parts of South Carolina and Georgia discovered that those areas boasted the perfect soil for a dirt track. The tough red clay of those regions made farming difficult, but it could be converted into an exceptional smooth, slick, and fast race track. Southern speedways built with red clay and banked turns became some of the fastest dirt tracks in the country. With high speeds easily attainable, southern stock car racing became even more exciting for local supporters. Stock car executive H. A. "Humpy" Wheeler posited that stock emerged so successfully in the South both because it gave the "small town southerner [a place] to go and achieve something" and because that spirited racing on the area's red clay racing kept spectators coming back.[10]

Southerners with customized passenger cars also engaged in impromptu races on public roads, just as antebellum horsemen had before them, or on makeshift ovals cut into fields. It is these "field ovals" that sparked the myth that bootleggers invented stock car racing. Early NASCAR great Tim Flock often recalled that he watched his brothers racing against fellow bootleggers in fields in North Georgia during the mid-1930s; similar stories emerged from other sources and for other locations. Those who connect the birth of stock car racing with moonshine frequently cite these events as evidence of their claim. Further, as previously mentioned, many of the most prominent drivers during NASCAR's formative period worked as trippers, which seemingly adds credence to this notion. Even contemporary accounts sometimes linked trippers with racing. Newspaper accounts sometimes referenced chases between trippers and the law as "a motor car race." Although trippers' challenges did occur during the Great Depression, formally organized stock car races predated them by 40 years. Moreover, these more formal events continued, in all regions, during the 1930s; however, not all involved in impromptu street or field challenges were directly linked to illegal liquor operations. Car-loving nontrippers undoubtedly participated in these events, and documentation corroborates their competition in these more formal stock car races. Flashy and fatalistic trippers provide ready symbols for early stock racing, but even in the South they did not represent the entire sport.[11]

Stocks' rising tide of popularity in the South crested in the years immediately before World War II, with a host of new locations becoming available in the region. In a few instances older speedways also began hosting their first stock events. The round track at Langhorne, Pennsylvania, hosted the All-American Championship, a 200-mile strictly stock event, as well as a July 4th race for amateur stock drivers. Atlanta's Lakewood Speedway, in some years the only southern track to host a AAA event, organized its first stock race in 1939; Lakewood would eventually become one of the premier southern tracks for stock racing. Racing there had an added danger in that the track surrounded a lake that took up most of the infield. The growing attraction of stock can be easily deduced from the opening up in the late decade of the most prominent tracks in the South and in the area just to the north.[12]

Older horse tracks, which had previously hosted the occasional stock race, also became increasingly important centers for racing. For example, the Rowan County Fairgrounds track, near Salisbury, North Carolina, hosted infrequent stock races early in the 1930s, but by the end of the decade this horse track offered several races per year. Reflecting the growing importance of stock there, these events spanned two days, with qualifying on Saturday and the feature race on Sunday. A local reporter noted that these late 1930s meets attracted a "wide range of interest throughout several southern states," which led to entrants from six states. Fairgrounds tracks in important southern cities such as Charlotte, Raleigh, Winston-Salem, Greensboro, Spartanburg, and Columbia also began offering increasing numbers of stock races during these years. These prominent events soon began drawing drivers from multiple states as well. Although they were not technically professional drivers (in that they continued to hold down other, regular, employment during the week), growing numbers of southern stock drivers began to gain regional reputations thanks to their frequent appearances throughout the area. Stock drivers of the 1930s such as Harley Taylor, Bill Lewallen, Mark Light, T. T. Brown, and E. C. Stockman appeared as competitors at tracks far beyond their home bases.[13]

In addition to older tracks either beginning to run stocks or increasing the number of their events, new speedways emerged to attract the growing population of stock fans. Although some of these tracks constituted little more than barely improved fields, others offered exciting red clay racing, even if the facilities themselves proved rather crude. One of the finest new tracks was the High Point Speedway in North Carolina. A one-mile red clay track capable of speeds of more than 100 miles per hour, High Point attracted the South's best drivers to the handful of races held at the facility. Reflecting the modernity of the track, the AAA even sanctioned an open-wheel event here in 1940. The High Point facility did not reopen after World War II, but the prewar events at this location clearly reflected both the growing southern fascination with stock racing and the style's potential for future growth.[14]

Along with giving southern stock racing its first regionally recognized drivers, these pre-World War II events also witnessed the birth of the first stock car racing team. Open-wheel racing had long featured groups of cars linked via a common owner or factory sponsorship, but only during this late 1930s expansion did stock car racing witness a similar phenomenon. The man credited with introducing the team concept to stock was Atlanta bootlegger Raymond Parks. After working as a teenage tripper in his hometown of Dawsonville, Georgia, Parks moved to the city in 1930 and quickly built a financial empire based on moonshine and a numbers racket that he subsequently parlayed into more respectable public ventures. Parks used a cadre of young trippers to bring moonshine from North Georgia to Atlanta, including his cousins Lloyd Seay and Roy Hall. The cars these men drove represented the pinnacle of tripper customization of Ford V-8s thanks to the work of mechanic Jerome "Red" Vogt, a transplanted Washingtonian who grew up with Bill France Sr. During the late 1930s upswing in stock car racing popularity, Parks began outfitting new Fords for his cousins to race, which constituted the first stock racing team. In addition, Parks occasionally had moonshiners Bob and Fonty Flock and mechanic Bill France drive his race cars. Parks continued to field cars into the NASCAR era and served as an important bridge between the 1930s wildcat era of southern stock and the more tightly regulated postwar version of the sport.[15]

Equipped with the fantastically fast Ford V-8s tuned by Vogt, Seay and Hall became dominating forces in southern stock car racing. The two cousins competed against each other frequently, with Hall winning the majority of their duels. Although related, the two exhibited remarkably different personalities, which were also reflected in their disparate driving styles. The taciturn Seay typically held back early in races, saving his car for a late charge to the front. Hall, whose rakish lifestyle inspired musicians to immortalize him in songs, drove hard from the very beginning of races and liked to be the front-runner. In his study of early stock racing, Neal Thompson categorized the two as oozing "a fearlessness and insouciant cool that gave people something to dream of." Along with fellow moonshiner Harley Taylor, the Parks team helped make Atlanta a center of 1930s stock car racing activity.[16]

Stock's increasing visibility also led to a return of racing at Daytona Beach. During the 1920s, a few open-wheel beach races occurred there, but most of the motor sports activities at Daytona revolved around attempts to set land-speed records. Even this rather limited connection to racing dried up during the Great Depression, as those seeking high speeds completed the shift to the salt flats of Utah and away from the sands of Florida. In an effort to attract tourists, Daytona's leadership made a desperate bid to regain its status in the racing community by hosting a stock race in 1936, with retired open-wheel racer Sig Haugdahl as organizer of the event. Just as they had more than 30 years previously, Daytona's race promoters obtained AAA sanction to add legitimacy to the event. Won by Milt Marion, the 1936 race used a novel course that combined the paved Highway A1A as one straightaway and the beach as the other. With multiple cars mired in sand ruts, confusion at the scorer's table, and most of the crowd watching the race without purchasing tickets, the race proved disastrous for its sponsors. The spectators enjoyed the racing, but the city of Daytona lost thousands of dollars. For racing to continue in Daytona, private investment would have to be secured. In 1937, a local Elks Club chapter stepped in to promote the race, and Georgia tripper Smokey Purser emerged victorious. As with the previous year's race, fans loved the show, but the sponsors met with equally bad financial results. At that point an unlikely savior emerged, the man who finished fifth in the 1936 race—"Big" Bill France.[17]

William Henry Getty "Big Bill" France grew up in Washington, D.C. He dropped out of high school to become an auto mechanic, and this love of cars also led him to become involved in motor racing. During the late 1920s, France ran in open-wheel races, including on the board track at Laurel, Maryland. In 1935, France and his family moved to Daytona, where he established a garage and became more actively involved in motor racing. France began running stock cars and also devoted a great deal of attention to observing how race promoters operated. He assisted Haugdahl in lining up Elks Club sponsorship for the 1937 Daytona race and then became the primary promoter of the event the next year. The 1938 race offered a portent of the dictatorial style that France would use as head of NASCAR for its first 20 years. For the second year in a row, Smokey Purser finished first at Daytona, but in 1938 he immediately left the track and, therefore, his car was not available for postrace inspection. France, believing illegal parts to be the cause of Purser's hasty exit, promptly disqualified the Georgian and awarded the win to the second-place finisher (himself). Despite protest from Purser, France refused to change his decision. In the future, France's determination to demonstrate that he and not the drivers ruled NASCAR would lead him to make countless similar disqualifications. This steely resolve allowed France to guide NASCAR through its perilous early years, but earned him the enmity of numerous drivers.

In the late 1930s, however, France was just one of dozens of stock car promoters in the South and was actually better known as a driver. France proved to be a solid prewar racer, even winning the mythical 1940 national championship, but Hall and Seay remained the top drivers in the South. Through 1939 and early 1940, they traded wins at Daytona, Lakewood, and High Point. Hall won the initial Daytona race of 1940 (two more followed later in the season), but then went to the penitentiary in Chillicothe, Ohio on bootlegging charges. Recently freed, Hall won the Daytona Labor Day race in 1941, but it was Seay who had the more consistent season. In one remarkable stretch Seay won three consecutive races (Daytona, High Point, Lakewood) in August, but was then shot and killed by a relative in a moonshine-related incident. Hall, who ran several races under assumed names to avoid law enforcement, gained recognition as the unofficial national champion. On November 2, Lakewood Speedway paid tribute to Seay with the running of the Lloyd Seay Memorial Race, which attracted the South's leading drivers. Even with Seay dead and Hall's career in legal jeopardy, 1942 promised to continue the growing importance of stock car racing to the southern sporting scene. American involvement in World War II, however, brought the plans for 1942 to a screeching halt. Early that year the Office of Defense Transportation, as part the federal government's larger plan to curtail entertainment forms that siphoned off needed war materials, decreed that auto racing must stop for the duration of the war.

The federal government lifted the ban on motor racing in August 1945 and stock racing quickly resumed in the South. A Labor Day race at Lakewood represented the first significant postwar stock event. In a race dominated by prewar Fords, Roy Hall won, with Bill France finishing in second place. This Lakewood event also underlines both the reasons for the mythology of bootleggers inventing stock and why that view is inadequate in addressing the rise of this form of racing. In the buildup to the race, Atlanta's political leaders attempted to ban all contestants with criminal records, an effort geared specifically toward keeping trippers (particularly the notorious Roy Hall) from competing. The outcry by spectators on the day of the event threatened to fuel a riot, which led to a decision to allow Hall and others to race. From one perspective, then, the Lakewood race can be read as suggesting that a true stock race could not be held without trippers competing, and that stock fans of the time, through the protests over driver exclusions, held the belief that, in effect, trippers equaled stock car racing. The complaints, however, stemmed not from the banning of felons, but from the banning of popular drivers who also happened to be convicted felons. Fans at Lakewood objected because a few of their favorite drivers were not allowed to race, not because they perceived a race without trippers as a thoroughly delegitimized exercise. Equally important is that a full field of drivers could have still raced even without trippers. Clearly, then, not all stock car drivers emerged from the moonshine business.

For those who sought to reignite the prewar popularity of stock car racing, the postwar South appeared to offer an especially inviting environment. Unlike much of the rest of the country, the South experienced little by way of a postwar recession. The region continued to develop in terms of industry and urbanization and moved toward closing the economic gap between it and the rest of the country. The economic prosperity of the South led to more cars being sold in the South than in any other region of the country. Southern men not only continued to embrace automobiles for the speed and status they brought them, but they now possessed the financial ability to obtain increased numbers of these vehicles. And the Lakewood race demonstrated that there was an enormous, entertainment-starved southern audience for stock car racing. Despite this, the AAA continued its prewar policy of focusing on other regions of the country, which opened the door for other organizations.[18]

Under these circumstances, Bill France and others began exploring the idea of bringing stock car racing under some sort of centralized control. For France, this meant bringing stock car racing under his control. To do so, he first needed to establish himself as the most prominent stock car racing promoter. Although stock racing appeared to have lost none of its prewar momentum, France's career as a promoter suffered a serious postwar setback. The Daytona course he controlled before World War II, suffering from years of neglect, lay in ruins by the time France concluded his military service. To begin to rebuild his promotional work, France needed to operate from another track. France chose to promote his first prewar race at the Southern State Fairgrounds (also known as the Charlotte Agricultural Fairgrounds) in the stock hotbed of North Carolina. With a dubious claim to the title, he promoted the event as the southern stock car championship. Although the race proved a success, France also realized that promoting scattershot races throughout the Southeast would not allow him to rise in status above the other southern stock promoters who operated in a similar fashion. The situation in southern stock was so chaotic that during the next season three men—Roy Hall, France, and Glenn Dunnaway—would be promoted as having won the 1945 national championship.

France realized he needed to link his efforts in a way that would legitimize claims of his "championship" events and, therefore, separate him from the other regional promoters. Well aware of the respectability afforded the Championship Trail series through AAA sanctioning—and the group's occasional prewar approval of stock races—France approached that organization in early 1946. Unimpressed by France, the AAA decided both to continue its prewar focus on open-wheel racing and to sanction only a limited number of stock events. France's proposal to develop a national stock championship did not correspond with the organization's goals. The AAA would sanction occasional stock races in the next few years, typically as preliminary events before a Champ car race, before making a more determined effort to create its own national stock series in 1950. This decision to establish a more visible stock racing presence reflected the growing popularity of stock, which the AAA had neither expected nor could any longer ignore. Their rebuke of France would prove costly, as his own sanctioning organization became the greatest threat to AAA hegemony since the Contest Board's creation in 1909.[19]

France spent the early part of 1946 continuing to run his one-off shows while occasionally racing himself. In addition to Charlotte and a revived Daytona, France added tracks in Greensboro, Orlando, and Greenville, South Carolina, to his orbit. Unable to ingratiate himself into the AAA power structure, France then decided to create his own organization. During the summer of 1946, he created the National Championship Stock Car Circuit (NCSCC), which was neither truly national nor really extensive enough to be called a circuit. France also proposed creating a uniform set of rules for all stock races, regardless of promoter, which met with limited success. At the end of the year, France organized a meeting in Daytona with a few other promoters who also had their own sanctioning bodies, and they decided to crown Ed Samples stock car racing's national champion. That he had to work with other organizations to name a national champion reflected the fact that France operated at this point simply as one of the multitude of southern stock promoters.[20]

Raymond Parks, whom newspapers now cagily referred to as a "sportsman," found himself forced to reorganize his team for the 1946 season. Roy Hall ran well, but then mid-way through the season, he received a six-year prison sentence (he ended up serving three years), which led Parks to try out two other trippers—Glenn "Legs" Law and Billy Watson. Neither proved especially adept on a race track, but Parks struck gold with a former open-wheel driver named Robert "Red" Byron. Originally from Colorado, Byron moved to Alabama in the late 1930s to work as a mechanic. He first ran stock cars in 1938, but met with little success. During World War II, Byron suffered a serious leg injury that left him with a limp and limited use of his left leg. At Vogt's urging, Parks gave Byron a ride in early 1946. He proved an immediate success, made all the more remarkable because his left leg had to be physically pinned to the clutch in order for him to drive. Before his injuries finally forced him to end his career, Byron would become the first NASCAR strictly stock series champion.[21]

Over the next two seasons Parks also gave rides to members of the first great family of racers in NASCAR history—the Flocks. Born in Fort Payne, Alabama, into a family of thrill seekers, the Flock brothers seemed destined to become race car drivers. Their bicycle-racing father loved speed so much that he named his daughters Reo (in honor of the REO Speedwagon car) and Ethel (after high-test gasoline). Ethel followed her brothers Bob, Fonty, and Tim into stock car racing, and Reo became a wingwalker before her early death. A fourth brother, Carl, raced hydroplanes. All four brothers eventually moved to Georgia, where they worked as trippers for their cousin's moonshine operation. Bob and Fonty both became stock car drivers in the late 1930s, with Fonty suffering a horrific crash at the 1941 Daytona race. Stern-countenanced Bob began running for Parks in late 1945 and proved himself a worthy successor to the Seay-Hall lineage. The far less serious Fonty, who often raced wearing Bermuda shorts, also raced a bit for Parks, but found greater success in a car prepared by Atlanta mechanic Bob Osiecki. All three brothers would finish in the top 10 in points during NASCAR's inaugural strictly stock season of 1949, but Tim, the best driver of the three, did not reach his racing peak until the 1950s.[22]

The growing popularity of stock racing in the postwar South propelled an additional batch of sanctioning bodies to organize at the beginning of the 1947 season. One newspaper reporter noted that "stock car auto racing is rapidly becoming an institution in the Carolinas sports niche." To distinguish his NCSCC from the herd, France doggedly worked to increase the number of races he sanctioned. His efforts to build the organization especially paid dividends with the new North Wilkesboro track, which Enoch Staley partially built with moonshine money. After overseeing the track's first stock race on May 18, France and NCSCC made frequent visits to the five-eighths–mile oval. In September, France sanctioned the first races at the new track in Martinsville, which, as with North Wilkesboro, began a decades-long connection with the promoter in 1947. With more than two dozen races to its credit, NCSCC established itself as one of the premier stock associations in the nation, but it still faced competition from a number of similar sanctioning bodies. And as an added difficulty, France now found himself competing against the AAA. Promoter Sam Nunis convinced that organization to authorize a few southern stock car races, primarily at Atlanta's Lakewood, during the summer of 1947. Still stinging from the AAA's rebuff of his proposal to run stock races for them, France countered the organization's efforts to challenge him in the realm of stock car with an attempt to undercut their status in open-wheel racing. During the summer of 1947, France promoted midget and Champ-style races under the auspices of the Central States Racing Association (CSRA). France managed to separate his NCSCC from its competitors and lessen the impact of the AAA's entrance in stock by taking the revolutionary step of offering additional prize money to the driver with most NCSCC points at the end of the season. This novel move ensured that drivers would compete in as many NCSCC events as possible, which helped keep the best drivers from appearing in non-France races. After the season-ending early December race in Jacksonville, Florida, Fonty Flock became NCSCC's "national" champion and pocketed a $1,000 bonus.[23]

The 1947 arrival of the AAA into stock, however hesitant, proved to be a catalyst for action among the independent promoters. These promoters recognized that, with the national sanctioning body now increasing its involvement in stock racing, continuing to operate in competition with each other made all of them vulnerable. Bill France, who demonstrated his considerable promotional skills to all with the successful NCSCC season, then issued a public call to his fellow stock promoters, inviting them to Daytona (his base of operations) for another mid-December meeting. During this second annual gathering, France and eastern promoter Bill Tuthill steered a discussion of how each promoter could prosper into a compelling argument for banding together under the umbrella of a single organization. France and Tuthill noted that unscrupulous promoters both hurt the sport's image and caused drivers to move from one organization to another looking for fair treatment. If a sanctioning body with several promoters as members could establish itself as an honest broker, it would instill loyalty in drivers and help bring more fans to the track. Further, by creating a unified body of rules, especially those related to car modifications, such an organization could expand the geographical range of drivers, who often ran only on tracks they were familiar with out of fear of having their cars ruled ineligible at new ones. With the best drivers willing to travel to additional tracks, promoters could assure fans they would see the finest stock car racing possible. Such a system would also lend validity to claims of crowning a "national" champion.

France and Tuthill's efforts reflected broader attempts to modernize various professional sports during the 20th century. According to Allen Guttmann, the characteristics of modern sport are "secularism, equality of opportunity to compete and in the conditions of competition, specialization of roles, rationalization, bureaucratic organization, quantification, and the quest for records." France and Tuthill's plans involved all these characteristics. Although some present remained skeptical of the viability of a unified organization, the assembled group voted to create a new sanctioning body for the 1948 season. After some debate, they adopted Red Vogt's suggestion of National Association for Stock Car Auto Racing as the new organization's name. On December 14, 1947, in a Daytona hotel bar, NASCAR was born.[24]

The initial organizational structure of NASCAR reflected the tenuous condition of the new sanctioning body. Their "1948 Rules and Specifications" consisted of just one sheet of paper. A Technical Committee, chaired by driver Ed Samples, established the specifications for vehicles competing in the new circuit. Reflecting the desire of the promoters to have the series look as professional as possible, only vehicles manufactured in 1937 or later would be allowed to compete. France especially believed that fan support for the series rested on the ability of spectators to identify with the vehicles racing, so, along with mandating "late models," NASCAR banned foreign vehicles. The Technical Committee's regulations allowed for vehicle alterations that placed NASCAR's stocks within the rather nebulous realm of "modifieds"—completely factory-stock cars only appeared in races in 1949. Under the leadership of Fred Dagavar, the Competition Committee created rules for determining the series champion and how NASCAR-sanctioned events should be run. Above these two committees sat a board of governors, which consisted of representative drivers, mechanics, car owners, and promoters. Bill France served as president of the board. In a move intended to make NASCAR appear as tightly controlled as other professional sports leagues, an allegedly top-level position of commissioner oversaw the board and the two committees. To bolster legitimacy, legendary endurance racer E. G. "Cannonball" Baker, not present at the inaugural meeting, was asked to assume this position. France told reporters "Baker will be to us what [Major League Baseball Commissioner] Happy Chandler is to baseball."[25]

Baker did issue both public pronouncements and private suggestions, but his authority fell far short of that possessed by the baseball czar Chandler. All real power within NASCAR rested with France and Tuthill. The December organizational meeting served to create a sanctioning body informally supported by promoters, but France and Tuthill wanted to establish an entity of real legal standing. Therefore, they approached Daytona attorney Louis Ossinsky, who completed the necessary paperwork to have NASCAR incorporated with the state of Florida in February 1948. Unable to pay Ossinsky, they made him a partner in the company. France and Tuthill each received 40 percent of NASCAR's stock, with Ossinsky retaining 20 percent in return for continued legal services. Legal control of the NASCAR brand gave France and Tuthill the ability to shape the new organization in ways not initially apparent to the other attendees of the December meeting. The genius of France, who quickly superseded Tuthill as the dominant force in the organization, was that his promotional talents helped the new group succeed, which kept the other promoters (whom he desperately needed) affiliated until NASCAR established itself as the most prominent name in stock car racing. And once their brand name became associated with the nation's finest stock racing, all promoters would have to deal with NASCAR. By that point, as the majority owner of NASCAR (Tuthill gave up a portion of his stock), France controlled American stock car racing. France would later pass ownership of NASCAR to his descendants, and a third generation continues to control the organization. Unlike any other American sport, the highest level of stock car racing continues to operate as a family-owned business.

The newly created NASCAR sanctioned its first race in February 1948 at Daytona, with Red Byron emerging victorious. Over the course of the season the organization sanctioned more than 50 races, all of them featuring the same sort of modified stock cars that ran in NCSCC. Most of the races also occurred on the same tracks France worked with in previous years. The NASCAR circuit, as a result, included familiar stops in North Wilkesboro, Greensboro, Jacksonville, and Charlotte. The coalition of promoters, however, also booked dates at Langhorne, Atlanta, and Dover, New Jersey. By the end of the season, the NASCAR stocks blazed across tracks in seven different states. France's ploys to attract attention included running races on three different tracks in one day and creating the Southeastern Championship based on 10 mid-season contests (in effect, a championship within the season championship). The inaugural season received an enormous boost from a remarkably tight championship race, with Red Byron and Fonty Flock battling until the last event. Those two drivers won half the season's races, and Byron ended the 1948 campaign leading Flock by less than 35 points. As with Flock in NCSCC the previous year, Byron won an additional cash bonus ($1,250) as the season champion.[26]

Stock car racing's increased organization, welter of new tracks, and packed grandstands began to gain the sport national attention during the inaugural NASCAR season. In August, the venerable *Saturday Evening Post* ran a full-length story that introduced the Flocks, Red Byron, Ed Samples, and Buddy Shuman to those outside the South. And while the article hinted that stock cars might not seem like real (i.e., open-wheel) race cars, author Frank Harvey noted the action on the track offered a great deal of contact and excitement. Harvey also recognized that stock car racing now involved large amounts of money. The potential for financial windfalls not only kept the drivers on the track, but also spurred other sanctioning groups to compete with NASCAR. Along with the AAA, NASCAR faced challenges from the Mid-Atlantic-based American Stock Car Racing Association (ASCRA), Atlanta's National Stock Car Racing Association (NSCRA), and the CSRA. More regional operations such as the American Racing Association, Western Racing Association, and the Empire State Stock Car Racing Association provided lesser threats, but still complicated France's plans for NASCAR. Even IMCA began sanctioning increasing numbers of Midwest stock races. Early in the 1948 season, a reporter related that events would be "sanctioned by the powerful NASCAR governing body," but the organization's power was certainly not absolute.[27]

Although NASCAR ran only modified stock cars in 1948, the organization's long-term goals involved creating roadster and strictly stock divisions as well. In early 1949, it sanctioned its first roadster event. The roadsters (cut-down stocks that resembled street hot rods) proved unsuccessful at attracting large numbers of spectators, and plans for that series fell by the wayside. Unfortunately for NASCAR, the failure of the roadster series proved to be only the first difficulty of the 1949 season. A drivers' revolt proved to be a more serious threat to the long-term survival of the sanctioning body. The threat posed by other organizations, especially NSCRA, created additional challenges. NASCAR's response to these adversities fatefully altered the course of stock car racing history. Although the sanctioning body ran a full slate of races in 1948, it would be 1949 that became viewed as NASCAR's first season.

The unrest among drivers stemmed from NASCAR's payment system. Since the formation of NCSCC, France had offered guaranteed purses to the drivers instead of the standard 40 percent of the gate provided by the AAA, NSCRA, and others. This decision initially derived from the need to guarantee drivers they would receive a decent payday for competing in a NASCAR event, irrespective of the crowd size. With wildly fluctuating numbers of spectators attending races, these guarantees both calmed driver fears and worked to their advantage. Stock's increasing popularity, however, meant ever-increasing crowds, but NASCAR's guaranteed payouts did not keep pace. Drivers witnessed NASCAR making large amounts of money and believed they should be entitled to increased revenue as well. Angered over NASCAR's refusal to increase purses, some of the sport's biggest names, such as Bob Flock, Marshall Teague, and Buddy Shuman, defected to NSCRA. France responded by banning these drivers from future NASCAR events and then publicly attacked these men as malcontents who sabotaged his organization's races. Despite this public saber rattling, NASCAR, fearful of the loss of more drivers, did eventually raise the guarantees, although not enough to seriously affect the organization's profits.[28]

NASCAR's concerns over losing drivers stemmed from the growing success of NSCRA. In 1949, racing entrepreneur O. Bruton Smith became that group's leader, and he helped raise NSCRA's visibility by teaming with the ubiquitous Sam Nunis (who also promoted races for the AAA and ASCRA). Smith's abilities as a promoter rivaled those of France and, when coupled with a cadre of popular drivers, NSCRA posed a serious challenge to NASCAR in its southeastern home base. In 1948, NASCAR declared that non-NASCAR events would not count toward the season championship, hoping that move would dissuade drivers from missing their sanctioned races. Many of NASCAR's biggest names, while still competing for that organization's title, continued to run races for other groups (including NSCRA). France decided that NSCRA needed to be dealt with more harshly in 1949. NASCAR issued an edict that season declaring that competing in non-NASCAR events would no longer be tolerated. Drivers who chose to race for other sanctioning bodies faced disciplinary action from NASCAR, which included losing all the points those drivers had previously accumulated during the season. NSCRA responded by announcing they would begin holding races with recent vintage, strictly stock vehicles. Unlike the modified stocks previously run, these cars represented, if the rules were actually followed, unaltered Detroit products of the sort spectators drove to the track. A change of this nature augured enormous alterations to the nature of stock car racing.

France responded, in his typical fashion, swiftly and decisively. The founders of NASCAR listed strictly stock as one of the three divisions they hoped to race, but that series lay somewhere in the future. Challenged by Smith and NSCRA, they felt compelled to respond by inaugurating strictly stock events during the 1949 season. Although the threat posed by Smith propelled this action, the shift toward strictly stock vehicles actually corresponded to France's ultimate plan for stock racing. He remained convinced that part of stock's allure was that the vehicles on the track looked like the cars the spectators drove, which created immediate fan connections. A shift to strictly stock meant that the cars the fans drove were the vehicles on the track. Fan affiliation with specific makes of car became an integral part of the flavor of NASCAR. With the possible exception of Ferrari in Formula 1, no other racing series possesses a car brand affiliation among fans of the magnitude seen in NASCAR. The move to strictly stock also had the additional bonus of creating thousands of potential new NASCAR competitors. France noted that a strictly stock event gave "the hot chauffeurs a chance to work off their steam on a track instead of on the highway." A fan could come to the races, make a few safety adjustments to the family car, and then speed out onto the track and attempt to qualify. Before they could do so, however, these drivers would help fill NASCAR's coffers by paying for their required NASCAR membership and entry fees.[29]

In June 1949, Charlotte Speedway, initially built with moonshine money, hosted the first NASCAR strictly stock race. A motley crew of 33 drivers (in emulation of the Indianapolis 500) qualified for what became the first race of NASCAR's flagship series. Greg Fielden would later describe this band of NASCAR pioneers as a "collection of odd-balls." The excitement over witnessing the equivalent of the family car hurtling around a dirt track aroused the fans, but for the drivers the experience proved less pleasurable. Their efforts demonstrated the same simple fact seen in the AAA's stock races of 1927—a passenger car straight from an assembly line was not a race car. Scheduled for 150 miles, the race exposed the vehicles' weaknesses and much of the field did not finish the race. Veteran Gastonia, North Carolina driver Glenn Dunnaway crossed the finish line a full three laps ahead of the second place car of Jim Roper, earning $2,000 for his efforts. France estimated 13,000 paying spectators attended the event, which made the race an economic success, as well as a blow to NSCRA.[30]

Reporters and spectators alike left the track under the assumption that Dunnaway won NASCAR's first strictly stock race. Later that night, like Smokey Purser's 1938 win at Daytona, the Tar Heel's victory evaporated. NASCAR technical officials discovered a wedge inserted into the rear springs on Dunnaway's 1947 Ford to stiffen the suspension. The use of wedges was an old bootlegger's trick, and car owner Hubert Westmoreland had, in fact, used the car to haul moonshine earlier in the week. France immediately disqualified Dunnaway and awarded the victory to Roper. Any doubts that NASCAR viewed the notion of strictly "stock" seriously ended with that decision. Mechanics looking to give their cars an advantage would have to find ways to surreptitiously circumvent NASCAR regulations. These efforts quickly became codified in the racing mechanic's adage "it ain't cheatin' if you don't get caught."[31]

Although caught cheating, Hubert Westmoreland attempted to use the courts to overturn NASCAR's disqualification of his car. Westmoreland's suit in the U.S. District Court for the Middle District of North Carolina asked for $10,000 in damages. Westmoreland argued that by passing a prerace inspection, his car could not be ruled illegal after the race. In a decision of momentous import for NASCAR, Judge Johnson J. Hayes, who later sent driver Junior Johnson to prison on moonshine-related charges, ruled that the sanctioning body possessed the power to both establish the rules for their races and stand as the final arbiter of rules violations. The decision meant that NASCAR now had legal authority to operate as it saw fit. Drivers who agreed to compete in a NASCAR event effectively surrendered their right to object to NASCAR decisions. For France, this authority gave him dictatorial power over all NASCAR races. As drivers would discover in later years, France and NASCAR could (and would) adjust the rules whenever they believed it was in the organization's best interest, without consulting the drivers. The 1949 decision established an authoritarian power dynamic in NASCAR that continues to the present. As historian Dan Pierce later noted, "NASCAR's style of management is more typical of a cotton mill than a modern, billion-dollar, professional sporting enterprise."[32]

The success of the Charlotte race prompted NASCAR to organize an additional seven strictly stock races. With eight races of this type now on the schedule, NASCAR determined that strictly stock races could be deemed an actual championship series. NASCAR also decided to drop the unwieldy name "strictly stock" and dubbed the new series, after the elite British horse racing circuit, Grand National. With such a limited schedule, NASCAR tried to locate the Grand National events on premier tracks. Grand National races, therefore, occurred at the tracks in Daytona, North Wilkesboro, Martinsville, and Occoneechee Speedway (Hillsboro, North Carolina). The round track at Langhorne hosted an early September race as part of a northern swing that included races in Pittsburgh and Hamburg, New York. Many of the premier southern drivers declined to attend these new northern tracks, so no drivers actually competed in all eight events. Several future stock car racing stars, however, did see action in the limited Grand National season. Drivers such as Curtis Turner, Herb Thomas, Buck Baker, and Lee Petty—all destined to have great NASCAR careers—appeared in a few of the new strictly stock events. Even Roy Hall, fresh out of prison, competed in the season-ending race at North Wilkesboro. With two wins in his six starts, Red Byron easily won the title. The disabled veteran's back-to-back championships in NASCAR's premier divisions garnered him acclaim as the nation's finest stock car driver. These titles, however, marked the pinnacle of his racing career, as Byron never again won a Grand National event.

The inauguration of the Grand National series represented a pivotal moment in the young history of NASCAR. With the limiting "strictly stock" title discarded, the organization could now use the Grand National name as cover for putting slightly modified cars on the track that performed admirably, but still looked just like passenger cars. From this point on, the "stockness" of vehicles in NASCAR's top series slowly lessened as performance and safety enhancements became increasingly important. Along with the cars on the track, NASCAR itself would undergo significant changes over the next decade. Although not completely unchallenged by other sanctioning bodies, by the end of the 1950s, NASCAR emerged as the group most associated with stock car racing in the United States. This growth, however, did not come easily. The successes of 1949 quickly faded as a host of new threats to Bill France's burgeoning empire developed in 1950.

3

NASCAR RISING

For NASCAR, the 1950 season proved to be both a pivotal year and a continuing struggle against old and new competition alike. The sport of stock car racing underwent significant alterations during the 1950s, and great changes in NASCAR developed at the dawn of the decade. Like any nascent sports league, NASCAR essayed initially simply to survive. Unlike most sports organizations, however, NASCAR's survival was predicated on immediate and rapid expansion. NASCAR endured its early decade hardship to emerge as a viable, albeit overwhelmingly regional, sanctioning body. By the end of the decade, NASCAR, along with the successor to the AAA, positioned itself as one of the two significant national organizations for stock car racing at its highest level. NASCAR eventually gained the advantage over their rivals, but the final significant challenger to its dominance would not completely fade away until 1984. The NASCAR organization would also undergo dramatic changes over the course of the decade, with new tracks, an abortive effort to establish a significant northern presence, new series for different types of cars, and the arrival of a host of successful young drivers. Perhaps most important, Bill France tightened his control over NASCAR during the 1950s. Before he could rule NASCAR, however, France had to battle with other organizations to guarantee the continued viability of his sanctioning body.

The success of the limited 1949 strictly stock series resulted in a determination by NASCAR to promote the Grand National series as the organization's premier level of racing. NASCAR continued to sanction hundreds of modified and lower level series events, but it focused increasingly on building Grand National. For 1950, the top series expanded to 19 races, with many of them occurring outside the Southeast as part of an effort to both expand NASCAR's reach and eliminate competition. NASCAR's regional expansion proved unsatisfactory and, after several seasons, the organization effectively retreated to its southeastern base,

with only occasional forays in to other parts of the country. Its efforts to
drive out competing sanctioning bodies, however, did manage to establish
NASCAR as the preeminent southern series and one of the two primary
stock car racing organizations in the country.

At the dawn of the 1950s, NASCAR continued to face competition
from Bruton Smith's National Stock Car Racing Association (NSCRA),
International Motor Contest Association (IMCA), American Stock
Car Racing Association, and a handful of smaller, regional organizations. Its gravest threat, however, came from the American Automobile
Association (AAA). After half-hearted efforts to become involved
with stock car racing during the immediate postwar years, the AAA announced it would become more deeply involved with stock in 1950. Its
decision to do so stemmed from the growing importance of stock cars in
American racing. Low-level, local stock events now occurred with regu-
larity throughout most parts of the United States. Although only certain
regions drew especially large crowds for stock events, the organization
recognized that stock represented a permanent aspect of American motor
racing. Convinced that its mid-1940s view, that stock was only a passing
fad, had been ill-founded, the AAA decided to become more directly
involved. Its association with stock racing did not represent any sort of
significant shift in the perspective regarding the hierarchy of racing—the
Champ cars and other open-wheelers continued to hold a place of importance for them—but, as the body that oversaw all automobile racing
in this country, the AAA leadership felt it could no longer ignore stock.
As part of the continued notion of sanctioning only the highest level of
competition, the AAA declared it would not sanction stock car races on
tracks of less than one mile.

The AAA's limited 1950 effort consisted of less than 10 events, but
over the next few years, spurred by promoters Sam Nunis and J. C. "Aggie"
Agajanian, the organization increased its stock involvement into a full-
fledged championship series. With the addition of the AAA, the raft of
groups involved in southern stock car racing, including NASCAR, found
themselves confronted with a significant challenge to their survival. To
the benefit of these regional organizations, the popularity of stock car racing in the South gave them a substantial body of support with which
to counter the AAA's actions. Sportswriter Richard Minor posited that
"the popularity of stock car racing in North Carolina has taken much of
the spotlight away from conventional racing-type automobiles in the last
three or four years," and that support proved vital to organizations such
as NASCAR and NSCRA, which hoped to maintain their status in the
face of challenges from the nationally strong AAA. Implicit in Minor's
editorial was that stock represented a style of racing more appealing to Tar

Heels because it was local and immediate, rather than second-hand and distant like open-wheel. Greg Fielden more explicitly noted that "one of the major factors in the immediate success of NASCAR's Grand National division was the fact that the Southeast finally had a sport which it could call its own." The "southern" nature of NASCAR and NSCRA gave them significant leverage against the "northern" AAA in the battle for control of stock car racing.[1]

The AAA ventured into the South only once in 1950, at Lakewood in September, and IMCA limited its stock car efforts to sanctioning races affiliated with fairs in the Midwest and Great Plains. Therefore, those two organizations presented, at this juncture, limited threats to NASCAR in the Southeast. Bruton Smith's NSCRA, however, posed a greater challenge by operating in the same region as NASCAR. Despite being undercut by NASCAR's strictly stock efforts in 1949, his organization continued to battle with France's group for the next two seasons. Smith's efforts to supersede NASCAR included recruiting drivers unhappy with France's rules. During the 1950 season, disgruntled racers such as Buck Baker, Jack Smith, Ed Samples, and Buddy Shuman competed under the NSCRA banner. Smith went head-to-head with the Florida group by scheduling races on several tracks on which NASCAR also raced. In addition, Smith opened his new showcase track in July—a one-mile dirt oval outside Charlotte that, in an obvious provocation, he threatened to name Lakewood Speedway. NSCRA efforts in the South would rankle the NASCAR leadership until 1952, when the U.S. military's drafting of Smith finally ended the threat posed by the organization. Smith's rivalry with France never actually ended, but in later years the North Carolinian's provocations resurfaced while he worked as a track owner within the NASCAR structure.[2]

NASCAR responded to the increased efforts of other sanctioning bodies by making clear that it would not tolerate its affiliated drivers competing in events scheduled by other groups. Drivers who ran for other organizations witnessed their hard-earned NASCAR championship points wiped off the books in an effort to keep them loyal. Red Byron, 1949's strictly stock champion, lost his points on two different occasions during the 1950 season. North Carolina driver Lee Petty finished in second place in the strictly stock series in 1949. Petty would have been the Grand National champion the next season as well, had he not been stripped of more than 800 points in July. Although NASCAR's penalties for appearing in "outlaw" events angered drivers, other organizations also engaged in similar practices. Late in 1950, NASCAR proved to be the beneficiary of the AAA's more draconian methods of maintaining driver loyalty. In November 1950, Bill Holland, the 1949 Indianapolis 500 winner, drove in a charity match race in Miami, which prompted the AAA to ban the controversial driver for one year. Holland responded by running IMCA sprint car races and, in 1951, began appearing in NASCAR events. Holland was not especially successful in Grand National, but France squeezed as much publicity as possible out of the former Indy champ's arrival in NASCAR.[3]

The 1950 season also marked the emergence of two of Grand National's earliest stars—Edward Glenn "Fireball" Roberts Jr. and Curtis Turner. Based in Daytona, Roberts began racing in 1947 under the tutelage of Marshall Teague. In 1950, Roberts won his first race and finished second in Grand National points. In a style that NASCAR fans became more familiar with during Roberts's late 1950s heyday, he needed to finish only in fifth place during the season-ending race in Hillsboro, North Carolina to win the championship, but the young Floridian refused to run conservatively. Preferring immediate victory, he blew up his Oldsmobile en route to a 21st place finish. Roberts was friendly and cordial away from racing, but his churlish persona at the track won him few friends. Nevertheless, his 33 career victories established him as an all-time great. Perhaps the finest dirt track driver America ever produced, Virginia's Curtis Turner won one Grand National event in 1949 and then led in an astonishing 12 of the 16 top-tier events sanctioned by NASCAR in 1950. Turner parlayed the money earned as a teenage tripper into a vast timber empire, the proceeds of which bankrolled his intertwined careers of stock car driver and notorious party animal. His infamous antics, such as landing his private plane on deserted country roads whenever the cockpit ran out of whiskey, established Turner as stock's first folk hero. He would also become the first driver to be banned for life by NASCAR.[4]

Along with the creation of a AAA circuit, the efforts to create a 500-mile race to rival open-wheel's showcase event in Indianapolis marked 1950 as a pivotal year in the history of stock car racing. These attempts represented a natural progression for stock racing. If this style of racing hoped to compete on an equal basis with the top open-wheel series, stock needed a premier race of comparable length to the major AAA event. France and NASCAR, having witnessed the toll taken on strictly stock cars in medium-length races in 1949, did not actually take the lead in promoting a 500-mile event. Promoter Sam Nunis proposed holding a September 500-mile event at Atlanta's Lakewood, and the Midwest-based Central States Racing Association (CSRA), better known for sanctioning sprint car races, also hoped to increase its visibility in stock car racing by holding a long event during the season as well. While Nunis's ongoing affiliation with Lakewood provided him with a track for his proposed event, CSRA had no suitable venue for their race. CSRA then became affiliated with South Carolina peanut farmer Harold Brasington, who offered to host the 500-mile event on the track he planned to open in 1950.[5]

Brasington, who ran in Daytona Beach races in the late 1930s, previously attended the Indianapolis 500 and became convinced that stock car racing needed a similar event. For stock cars to hold a race to truly rival Indy, however, it needed a modern track. With no suitable paved track available, Brasington made the fateful decision to build his own. He constructed a 1.25-mile paved (irregular) oval track in Darlington, South Carolina, 10 miles from Florence. CSRA now had a suitable track, but quickly recognized it could not meet Brasington's request for a field of 75 professional stock car drivers. After struggling to complete the facility, Brasington expected to open Darlington with a stock car event of national import and expressed his displeasure with CSRA's inability to fulfill his goal. France then contracted with CSRA for NASCAR to co-sanction the race and provide its stable of drivers. The involvement of NASCAR allowed Brasington to achieve his dream of hosting the most significant stock car race of the year (and, arguably, of all time) and guaranteed that NASCAR would play a prominent role in the event. On September 4, Darlington hosted the first Southern 500.

Perhaps more than any other event, the inauguration of the Southern 500 solidified both the popularity of stock in the South and the wider popular connections between the region and this particular form of racing. The first race at Darlington was a uniquely southern event. To officially open the track, Brasington invited recent Dixiecrat presidential candidate and current South Carolina governor Strom Thurmond and his wife to cut the ceremonial ribbon. Instead of a green flag, the Southern 500 began with the starter waving a rebel flag. Brasington, deeply steeped in the mythology of the Old South, hired Civil War reenactors to circulate through the fans in the infield. Within a few years an official mascot named "Johnny Reb" became part of the proceedings, and management painted rebel flags on the track's walls (they remained until the 1970s). As the only paved track on the NASCAR circuit until the end of the decade, Darlington became the premier destination for American stock cars—it was the Indianapolis of stock car racing. As such, the prevalence of Confederate iconography at the track became integrally linked with stock car racing. With stock's two most famous tracks located in Florida and South Carolina, NASCAR displayed a southern tether that strengthened both its support in the South and popular connections between stock and the region.

The location of stock car racing's most hallowed tracks reflected this regional affinity. During the mid-20th century, other national sports operated with franchises in major urban centers, but NASCAR flourished at obscure rural locations south of the Mason-Dixon Line such as Darlington, Rockingham, Bristol, and Talladega. No major sports franchises operated this deep in the South, so southerners embraced stock partly out of a sense of regional pride. Only in stock car racing and college football (the other southern sports institution) could the South be viewed as competing at the highest national level. The stock car became a representation of southern pride and independence. Manufactured in the North, but run fastest in the South, stock cars became southern. The traditional southern love for speed, honor, and gambling combined to convert the staid family sedan into a blazing symbol of self-determination. Acceptance of stock cars in the Southeast clearly buttressed Southern Agrarian Stark Young's admonition that "we can accept the machine, but create our own attitude toward it."[6]

For many in the southern elite, Darlington also reinforced notions concerning the social status of stock car racing. Although middle class fans of the sport did represent a significant portion of the 30,000 attendees of the first Southern 500, these respectable spectators perched in the grandstand became immediately overshadowed by the roistering fans in the infield. Many of the infield dwellers camped out for several days before the race in an effort to "reclaim their wildness." Darlington's infield rapidly devolved into a bacchanalian celebration of working-class southern white culture predicated on fast cars, guns, alcohol, and sex. Brasington's Civil War soldiers possessed only a small portion of the fire arms found in the area inside the racing oval. Copious amounts of alcohol led to enormous numbers of fights. The violence later prompted the construction of an infield holding cell. Licentious behavior, also often fueled by alcohol, became a hallmark of the Darlington infield as well. Prostitutes, sometimes working out of hearses and former ambulances, freely circulated through the crowd. In an environment with few restraints on personal behavior, the working class denizens of the infield found release from the frustrations of low-paid, blue collar labor in an orgy of debauchery. Darlington, South Carolina's prior claim to fame had been the so-called "Darlington War" of 1894, where rampaging locals rebelled against new state liquor laws. For wealthy or socially conservative southerners, the Southern 500 infield seemed a frightening return to that event.[7]

Although a lengthy race became a promotional boon for stock car racing, France's concerns over the ability of Grand National cars to withstand the punishment of 500 miles of racing proved well founded. Engine overheating eliminated some cars, but tires stood as the gravest problem for all 75 starters. The compounds they ran simply could not take the punishment of high speeds for extended periods on the hot asphalt of Darlington. Tires deteriorated so quickly that crewmen went into the stands to purchase tires off spectators' cars. Darlington, later dubbed the "Lady In Black," quickly developed a reputation as the most difficult track on the NASCAR circuit, a view still shared by many current drivers. Asked about Darlington after the 1953 Southern 500, Fonty Flock responded with the query, "when are you going to fix this track?" The tire problems would eventually be resolved, but the track's bizarre egg shape, with all the turns of different lengths, continued to pose difficulties for drivers. It is also a one-groove track, meaning that there is only one line a driver can take to traverse the track quickly, which makes for extended periods of single-file racing and few passes. As such, races at Darlington tend to be repetitive revolutions of the track punctuated by cars banging their right sides against the retaining wall (obtaining the infamous "Darlington Stripe" in the process).[8]

Darlington's races, then, offered far less excitement than the track's legendary status would suggest. Southern stock fans thronged the track, not because they would see especially exciting racing, but because of the symbolic value of the events held at Darlington. Brasington and track general manager Bob Colvin created a spectacle for southerners. Although other races on the NASCAR circuit presented themselves as bigger than any regional affiliation—for example, the International 200 or World 600—Darlington events embraced southern connections. For many years Darlington hosted two Grand National events per year, the Southern 500 and the Rebel 300.

In the initial Southern 500, former open-wheeler Johnny Mantz used hard compound racing tires and a measured pace to win the race. With his hard tires, Mantz made only three pit stops, but other racers found themselves compelled to make a dozen or more. Despite the slow top speed of Mantz's 6-cylinder Plymouth, his tire advantage allowed him to finish nine laps ahead of second-place Fireball Roberts (who used 32 tires during the race). After the 6-1/2 hour race, France barred NASCAR technical inspectors from adhering to the typical postrace procedure of tearing down the top five finishers. This deviation from standard practice led NASCAR technical official Henry Underhill to immediately resign, but France's decision did not change. The reason for this sudden alteration to postwar practices stemmed from the fact that France and NASCAR official Alvin Hawkins owned Mantz's car. Most drivers at the time believed France barred the inspections because Mantz's Plymouth would not have passed an inspection. Many at the time also noted that the car had been tuned by Hubert Westmoreland, the former NASCAR nemesis with a well-known propensity for using illegal bootlegger modifications, which gave credence to the notion Mantz's car possessed illegal modifications. With his de facto control of the organization, France possessed the power to change the rules at his discretion. As drivers would soon discover, France's NASCAR rule book could be modified to suit his interests. His arbitrary decisions over the coming decades would earn him the enmity of drivers, car owners, and mechanics alike. Richard Petty succinctly summarized that "anybody who knew France knew that he was a S.O.B."[9]

Despite the problematic nature of both the race and the results, the first Southern 500 proved to be an enormous success for NASCAR. By cosponsoring the event with CSRA, it effectively converted the Southern 500 into a Grand National race. Chastened by its loss of control at Darlington, CSRA returned to focusing on sprint and open-wheel cars in the aftermath of its failure to dominate the Southern 500. Without a similar event to compete with the 500, NSCRA appeared second-rate. The AAA also abandoned plans to sanction a September 500 mile stock car race in the wake of the Southern 500. The Nunis-promoted race at Lakewood was still held, but only as a 200-mile event. For NASCAR, then, the first Southern 500 afforded an opportunity to distance the organization from its competitors. The AAA went forward with plans to expand its stock car series, but NSCRA never again posed a legitimate threat to NASCAR's dominance in the Southeast.

By successfully promoting itself as a serious sanctioning body capable of organizing 500-mile events, NASCAR became much more attractive to sponsors. The financial challenges of motor racing had posed difficulties for drivers since the sport's inception. Factory-backed competitors could minimize their costs, but for those who owned their own cars, racing represented a risky economic proposition. Emblazoning a company's name on the side of a car in return for some sort of remuneration, therefore, became common at all levels of motor sports. For stock car drivers the traditional sponsors ranged from gas stations, garages, and car dealerships (who could provide necessary racing items) to motels and restaurants (who could provide necessary services for drivers). As Grand National rose in stature during the early 1950s, the type of sponsors involved remained constant, but the nature of these firms changed. Top stock drivers parlayed their success into sponsorship by larger regional or national businesses, as local garages and gas stations gave way to oil companies and national auto parts firms. For sponsors, stock cars provided more attractive physical locations for ads than Champ cars. Stock cars possessed significantly more sheet metal suitable for product placement than the smaller open-wheel vehicles. Also, the open spaces on stock cars were overwhelmingly flat, as opposed to the curved exterior of the aerodynamic open-wheelers, so ads placed on a Grand National vehicle looked more like billboards.

National sponsors developed interests in NASCAR as early as the successful 1950 Grand National season. Air Lift Corporation became the first nonregional firm involved with Grand National, but others rapidly followed. In 1951, Pure Oil (later known as Union 76) became the official gasoline of NASCAR (and maintained that status until 2003). Pure Oil also became the first company to sell racing-specific tires to NASCAR drivers. By the end of the decade, Firestone and Goodyear followed suit and also developed presences in Grand National. Mid-decade, Pure Oil and Champion spark plugs implemented contingency money programs, which gave bonuses to drivers who won races while using their products. The appearance of these national sponsors reflected the growing stature of NASCAR. In the Southeast, at least, France's organization had established itself as the leading stock car sanctioning body, and with that leading position it could attract nonregional sponsors who sold products throughout the South. The total financial contributions of corporate sponsors during the 1950s pales in comparison to the deals that developed at the end of the century, but the involvement of these companies kept drivers on the circuit and contributed greatly to the quality of racing on the track during NASCAR's early years.[10]

France's acrimonious relationship with the AAA took on a new dimension in 1952. With the open-wheel organization now running a stock championship series, NASCAR decided it would counter by running its own open-wheel series. Ultimately, France hoped that open-wheel NASCAR drivers could successfully compete at the Indianapolis 500, then switch to stock cars, which would allow him to promote NASCAR as having the finest drivers in the country. France's ideas may have stemmed from the recent involvement of 1949 Indianapolis 500 winner Bill Holland in stock car racing. Regardless of its origins, this ill-conceived plan led to the creation of the NASCAR Speedway Division. The series involved open-wheel cars that used the same specifications as the Champ cars, but with stock car engines. As with strictly stock in 1949, Speedway cars ran a limited schedule (seven races) in 1952. Despite initial excitement at the first few races, Speedway quickly fizzled. With most of the top southern drivers running Grand National events on the same days, few prominent names appeared in the Speedway events, which significantly dampened public enthusiasm. France also discovered something the AAA had been conscious of for decades—open-wheel racing did not draw well in the South. Stock dominated in the area (something France had a part in creating) and open-wheel vehicles with second-tier drivers simply was not going to change that. In 1953, the series included only four races and was discontinued. Despite NASCAR's abandonment of an open-wheel series intended to compete with Champ cars, the AAA continued to view France as an enemy. For example in 1954, AAA officials ejected France from the Indianapolis Motor Speedway garage area, even though he had purchased a ticket.[11]

Along with inaugurating the Speedway Division, 1952 also marked the end of the Grand National career for the last of the early female drivers in NASCAR. Louise Smith, Sara Christian, and Ethel Flock Mobley all ran in the 1949 strictly stock series. Smith, who possessed a reputation for being just as rough-and-tumble as the early male drivers from the South, retired last and ran her final Grand National event in 1952. Fifi Scott made two starts in 1955's West Coast Grand National races, but after her appearance, women disappeared from the circuit. For the next 20 years a woman appeared in a Grand National event only once (Goldie Parsons in 1965). The dearth of women at the top level of stock car racing reflects the general under-representation of women in all forms of motor sports, but stock proved especially prone to gender inequality. Out of the almost 3,000 drivers who have competed in NASCAR's top series, only 14 have been women. Predominantly southern and politically conservative, stock car drivers tended to view women inside a race car as socially unacceptable. NASCAR contributed to this view by banning women from the pit areas for many years. Prominent NASCAR figures such as Richard Petty and Banjo Mathews publicly declared their opposition to women behind the wheel. Most men within NASCAR viewed stock car racing as a masculine preserve and balked at the notion of relinquishing their hegemonic control of the sport. Sylvia Wilkinson summed up the position of women in NASCAR by positing that "there are two groups of women in the stock car world: wives and mothers in one group, whores and race queens in the other." A race queen such as the legendary Linda Vaughn, who began her career at the dawn of the 1960s, could become entrenched in the world of NASCAR, but only in an objectified, ancillary role.[12]

Most of the male objections to female stock drivers during the 1950s revolved around claims that women did not possess the physical strength needed to engage in lengthy races and that the sport was simply too dangerous for women. These claims were inadequate as a justification for excluding female competitors, but the dangers of stock car racing were very real. Driver (and spectator) fatalities occurred in all forms of motor racing, including stock. From its inception, NASCAR mandated seatbelts and safety glass for all vehicles, but allowed for no other safety measures. The issue of safety improvements on Grand National cars posed a serious problem for NASCAR and its attempt to remain wedded to notions of factory stock vehicles. What emerged during the decade was an effort by NASCAR to maintain the stock appearance of Grand National cars, while allowing for incremental safety improvements. NASCAR eventually reversed itself and allowed roll bars, and it also recommended the wearing of stronger helmets and flame-retardant suits. Some parts of the cars could be strengthened, but only if these modifications did not alter a vehicle's outward appearance. Still, Grand National cars remained remarkably dangerous (and especially inadequate regarding tires and brakes), and spectator safety measures at most tracks were crude at best. During the mid-1950s, safety concerns over all forms of motor racing reached a fevered pitch. At Le Mans in 1955, Pierre Levegh's car crashed into a crowd of spectators, killing 80. This tragedy, coupled with fatalities on American tracks, prompted the AAA to announce it would not sanction any form of motor racing after the 1955 season. Deaths in the United States led to an abortive effort to ban all motor racing in this country a few years later. The all-out ban did not occur, thereby saving NASCAR, but safety concerns continued to plague the organization. During the 1960s, the issue of safety prompted two significant drivers' challenges to Bill France's leadership.[13]

The attempt to deflect the AAA's ability to supersede NASCAR as a stock car sanctioning body included not only the abortive speedway division, but also efforts to increase the organization's presence outside the Southeast. During 1949, NASCAR began working more closely with the veteran New Jersey-based promoter Ed Otto, who organized a few modified races and the strictly stock event in Hamburg, New York. A legendary Barnumesque promoter (he greeted everyone with "hello, sucker" and referred to his promotions as "swindles"), Otto brought considerable connections with Northeast tracks with him. NASCAR desperately needed Otto, and Bill Tuthill offered him 20 percent of his NASCAR stock in return for Otto's efforts. Counting the two trips to the Langhorne track (already part of the NASCAR circuit), the Grand National series ran 10 races outside the South during the 1950 season. These races in additional areas brought several new drivers into Grand National from outside the South, including 1950 Grand National champion Bill Rexford of New York (another northern driver would not win the championship until 1989). Otto assisted NASCAR in breaking into the states of Indiana and Ohio and increased the number of races in New York. Although the claim proved to be somewhat premature, one reporter noted that Otto's promotions had made NASCAR "national in scope." Otto's substantial skills as a promoter ensured ample attention for initial Grand National races on more than three dozen tracks in the Northeast, Midwest, and Canada during the decade. With events in both established racing hubs and obscure locations, these races outside the South helped establish the NASCAR brand in markets impenetrable for France.[14]

From the beginning of his organization, France hoped to be the national sanctioning body for stock cars. To do so he needed the assistance of promoters (such as Otto) familiar with areas outside his southern base. France felt compelled to attempt to rapidly expand NASCAR's geographical reach, not just by a personal desire to be national in scope, but also to keep his drivers satisfied. NASCAR's cash payments to end-of-the-season points leaders encouraged racers to abide by the strict rules against racing for other sanctioning bodies. This monopolization of the best talent helped France undercut competing organizations. For drivers, abiding by NASCAR's dictates only made economic sense, however, if competing exclusively under that organization's imprimatur provided for more earnings than racing for all other sanctioning bodies. Under those circumstances, France needed to find enough race dates to keep the drivers compliant. Otto, therefore, contributed to NASCAR's long-term viability by adding nonsouthern dates to the schedule when France could not provide a full season of southeastern events. Otto's efforts to establish NASCAR in the North ultimately failed to make stock car racing as significant in that area as it was in the South, but his promotional work both helped keep drivers loyal and helped lay the groundwork for NASCAR's eventual national growth.

Races outside the Southeast during the 1950s helped build NASCAR, but these events did not augur an immediate nationalization of stock car racing comparable in popularity to that in the South. France's plans to expand outside the Southeast involved working with Otto in the North (Northeast and Midwest) and Bob Barkhimer (and later Johnny Mantz) on the West Coast. NASCAR discovered these regions contained pockets of stock car racing enthusiasts, but not enough to sustain a heavy NASCAR presence. Accustomed to open-wheel racing and with numerous other entertainment opportunities available, the Northeast market resisted Otto's attempts to create an additional base of NASCAR operations. In the Midwest, an area traditionally somewhat more supportive of stock, Otto found himself in stiff competition with other sanctioning groups for the allegiance of the area's stock car fans. IMCA continued to operate out of fairground tracks in the region until the 1970s, which may have siphoned off some potential NASCAR supporters, but the biggest challenge came from the AAA. After renewing its involvement with stock in 1950, the AAA created a stock car championship series of 15 to 20 races per year. The majority of these events occurred in the Midwest. Although the AAA continued to promote open-wheel Champ cars as its showcase series, its determination to maintain a viable stock car circuit hurt NASCAR in the Midwest. The effects of the AAA series on NASCAR were muted somewhat by the regional nature of the circuit and the low prize pools offered because of the limited number of races. For example, in 1954 Grand National champion Lee Petty won $21,101, but AAA champion Marshall Teague pocketed only $13,522. Four Grand National drivers won more money than Teague that year (with one-fifth less than $600 behind him). When the United States Auto Club (USAC) replaced the AAA as the primary sanctioning body for open-wheel racing in 1956, it also continued to support a stock series, but operated it in a very similar, low-paying fashion as the AAA.

The combination of other sanctioning groups, preference for open-wheel, and competition for disposable income from other forms of entertainment forced Otto to scramble to fill seats at his promoted races. Otto relied on tricks he learned as a promoter of midget races during the Great Depression to do so. For a few races, Otto brought in European sports cars to compete with NASCAR's traditional American sedans. He also scheduled two Grand National events in Canada, which marked NASCAR's first international efforts. His NASCAR-promoted events included ostrich and donkey races, a woman who drove around the track blindfolded, daredevils who shot themselves out of cannons, and special women's events known as powder puff derbies. Carnival gimmicks such as these brought in fans, but also forced Otto to develop increasingly outlandish "special attractions" to sustain attendance levels. As such, Otto found it easier to simply replicate the same gimmicks, but at different tracks.

It would be an overstatement to suggest that stock car racing had no support outside the Southeast, but there is certainly some truth in Illinois stock racer Fred Lorenzen's assertion that "the North was not race country." An examination of the northern tracks used by NASCAR in the 1950s illustrates the difficulties the organization faced in establishing a residence in the region. During the 1950s, only 42 northern tracks staged Grand National events. In the same period North Carolina alone possessed 21 tracks that hosted races in NASCAR's premier division. Of those 42 northern tracks, more than half held only one race and another six staged only two. In other words, Otto felt comfortable enough about his chances to make money to return for a third race on only 11 northern tracks. Further, the bulk of these 42 tracks witnessed their Grand National events early in the decade; as frustrations mounted, Otto's northern attempts dwindled. From 1957 until the end of the decade, only 16 northern tracks hosted Grand National races. A disgruntled Otto eventually broke with France in the early 1960s over how to proceed with the development of Grand National races and he sold the Floridian all of his NASCAR stock. During the 1960s, a NASCAR completely controlled by southern interests visited the North for only a few races each season.[15]

On the West Coast Barkhimer faced difficulties similar to Otto's problems on the East Coast. During the decade of the 1950s, 18 western tracks (including historic venues such as Oakland Speedway and Ascot) hosted Grand National races, but only nine saw a second event. One issue that hampered efforts in both the North and West was that many of NASCAR's biggest names refused to travel such long distances to compete. The hassle and expense of dragging a trailer-hitched stock car cross-country in the preinterstate era served as a deterrent to many drivers. According to 1960 Grand National champion Rex White, the prize money available for races in Arizona and California was too low to make the long trip from the Southeast viable. Distance from the southeastern center of NASCAR activities also led western drivers to become disenchanted with the organization. At the beginning of the 1955 season, for example, drivers at two California tracks, unhappy with the far-away management of NASCAR, decided not to renew their NASCAR memberships, and instead joined the new Western Auto Racing Association. NASCAR's policies did not help the situation in the West. They significantly undercut the ability of the West Coast tracks to attract stock's biggest stars and, without marquee names available to them, promoters in the area certainly felt Grand National affiliation offered few benefits. Although NASCAR encouraged drivers to participate in as many races as possible and found ways to compel drivers to preregister for events to assist promoters, it also tacitly recognized the reluctance of drivers to travel cross-country.

During the 1950s, NASCAR booked two Grand National races on a single day every season save 1953. All of these double-bookings involved a West Coast race. NASCAR effectively undermined efforts by West Coast promoters to establish the Grand National circuit in their territory by giving their drivers the opportunity to compete close to home in the Southeast rather than traveling to California or Oregon. With a race in the South available on the same day, a difficult trip to the West Coast made little financial sense for most drivers. Had NASCAR truly wanted to develop a significant West Coast presence, the organization could have avoided the double-bookings, which might have encouraged more drivers to make the cross-country trek. Conscious of the financial windfalls of races in the Southeast, however, NASCAR refused to forego dates in their home region.[16]

Failures to establish Grand National as a significant series in the North and West led to a retrenchment in the South. By the late 1950s, Grand National rarely ventured outside the nation's southeastern quadrant. For example, in 1959 and 1960, NASCAR's premier series involved 44 races per season, but areas outside the South hosted only five races each year. Ed Otto's feverish attempts to book Grand National races in the North during the early 1950s virtually ceased at the end of the decade, with only three northern races in 1959 and two in 1960. The push to book Grand National races across the country effectively died with the 1950s. From the early 1960s until the early 1980s, NASCAR's top division would venture out of the South for only a handful of races each season. By the late 1950s, then, NASCAR was a clearly southern organization. USAC dutifully continued to operate its primarily Midwestern stock circuit, but NASCAR had established its dominance over that series during the late 1950s. A southern organization ruled stock car racing, and for later generations the logical conclusion from this seemed to be that, therefore, stock car racing was southern. A more correct assertion would be that stock car racing *became* southern. The traditional southern values previously discussed helped stock both take root in the South and then flourish there during the 1950s. A host of new social and cultural issues during the next two decades, coupled with NASCAR policies, deepened those connections to create the "southern" sport of stock car racing.

Despite the inability to establish viable beachheads outside its southern base, NASCAR managed to develop closer relations with Detroit automobile manufacturers during the 1950s. To guarantee Detroit's participation in stock car racing, however, NASCAR needed to present its style of racing in as positive a light as possible. Success on the race track could lead to increased sales of passenger vehicles, but involvement with stock car racing was also dangerous, as sales might slump for a particular make or model if the car became associated with racing fatalities. As France keenly wanted manufacturers to play an active role in NASCAR, reducing any possible negatives remained of vital importance. NASCAR's safety advances during the 1950s therefore reflected factors of organizational growth and economics as much as concern for the well-being of drivers. As a former racer himself, Bill France understood the need to keep racers safe, but he also recognized the importance of making manufacturers feel comfortable having their name associated with NASCAR. By moving to make stock cars safer, especially during a period of widespread antiracing sentiment, France helped calm the fears of manufacturers enough to keep them involved with his organization.

France also understood the importance of parity among manufacturers. Allowing one make of car to dominate all others would inevitably drive away other manufacturers (and, potentially, paying spectators as well). France viewed maintaining relationships with as many manufacturers as possible as beneficial for the organization and sought ways to keep all companies both involved and competitive. Until the early 1980s, stock cars were actually factory-produced vehicles gutted and partially rebuilt for competition. As not all Detroit products possessed equal handling or top speeds, NASCAR found itself forced to ban specific motors and models that created an unfair advantage for those teams who used them. These problems of regulating parity lessened in the 1980s with the rise of purpose-built vehicles that could be standardized through NASCAR mandates, regardless of what brand the car allegedly represented, but posed serious difficulties for NASCAR's administrators until then.

Automobile manufacturers' direct involvement with NASCAR fluctuated from periods of heavy participation to eras in which they were (officially, at least) without connections to stock car racing. The 1950s marked the first of the eras of significant manufacturers' commitment to NASCAR. During this decade the automobile industry itself underwent enormous changes. Desires for new automobiles, pent up by World War II, propelled an explosive growth in car sales. The prosperity of the 1950s also resulted in the emergence of notions that suburban families needed two cars to operate efficiently. American automobile manufacturers scrambled both to keep pace with demand and to expand their market share. Both Ford and General Motors (and to a lesser extent Chrysler) undertook massive advertising campaigns in the midst of this car boom. As a result of these efforts, the Big Three controlled 90 percent of automobile sales in the United States by 1953. Underfunded smaller manufacturers, slowly being squeezed out by the larger companies, found themselves left searching for means of staying competitive. Just as similar-size firms did in 1927, some of these smaller companies then latched on involvement with stock car racing as a vehicle for advertising their products. Unlike 1927, however, the major manufacturers followed suit and also availed themselves of the promotional possibilities of stock racing. Bill France initially promoted strictly stock because he felt fans would connect with race cars that looked like their own. American automobile manufacturers hoped they could invert that equation—successful performance on the track by their products would make fans want to make those cars their own.[17]

Struggling Hudson Motors became the first manufacturer directly involved with Grand National. Their Hornet model, introduced in 1951, featured a very fast in-line, six-cylinder engine with dual carburetion and a low center of gravity that combined to make the car both fast and easy to handle. In 1951, Hudson began supplying Hornets to the Grand National team of Marshall Teague. Emblazoned with "Fabulous Hudson Hornet" across their sides, the "Teaguemobiles" driven by Teague and Herb Thomas proved to be formidable stock cars. Teague's conflicts with Bill France hampered the team (Teague lost all of his Grand National points for running in a AAA event), but Herb Thomas still won the season championship. The difficulties with NASCAR management forced Thomas to run a few races in other makes, but five of his seven victories occurred while driving a Hudson. Teague bolted for the AAA stock series in 1952 where his Hudson, tuned by the great Smokey Yunick, won 12 of the 13 events in that series. Hudsons would dominate Grand National in the early 1950s to a degree never again duplicated by any manufacturer. They won 12 races in 1951, then 27 of the 34 races in 1952, and 22 of the

37 the next season. Even as Hudson itself staggered toward oblivion in 1954, its cars won 17 Grand National races.

Hudson's involvement in 1951 corresponded with an audacious effort by Bill France to make all manufacturers cognizant of Grand National. As part of Detroit's 250th anniversary celebration, France organized the Motor City 250 at the old Michigan Fairgrounds. France promoted the event as a celebration of Detroit's prominence in the automobile industry and encouraged all brands to participate. As a result of his efforts more than a dozen makes of car competed on the one-mile dirt track, with Tommy Thompson's Chrysler emerging victorious after an exciting duel with Curtis Turner. The smaller manufacturers viewed the race as a showcase event for their products against the more-hyped vehicles of the Big 3. NASCAR public relations director Houston Lawing later noted that "the Hudson people really wanted to win that race." The Grand National cars had previously ventured to Grand Rapids, Michigan in July, but it was the August race in Detroit that brought home to the car companies how important stock car racing could be to them. In the next few years most car company involvement with NASCAR remained at the local dealership level, but a fierce manufacturers' war would develop by mid-decade.[18]

The rise of Hudson helped spark a classic three-way championship competition over the first half of the 1950s. From 1951 to 1954, first and second place in the season standings went to either Tim Flock, Herb Thomas, or Lee Petty. Both Flock and Thomas raced Hudsons, but Petty managed to get more speed out of Chrysler products than anyone else. These men also represented the three basic streams from which early southern Grand National drivers developed: tripping, auto mechanics, and farming. Tim Flock, like his two brothers before him, learned to drive working as a tripper in North Georgia. Although typically far less flamboyant than his brother Fonty, Tim gained his own outre reputation when he competed in several 1953 races with a rhesus monkey named Jocko Flocko (wearing his own driver's suit) as his copilot. Flock won the Grand National title in 1952, driving Ted Chester's Hudson and again in 1955 in one of Karl Kiekhaefer's Chryslers. During the 1951–54 period, North Carolina farmer Thomas won two season titles and finished as the runner-up the other two seasons. He racked up a remarkable 39 victories during those four seasons. Thomas had solid campaigns the next two years driving Chevrolets and Chryslers before a horrific accident in October 1956 effectively ended his career. Petty never finished below fourth in the championship over the entire decade of the 1950s, winning three titles in the process. One of the more complicated early Grand National stars, Tar Heel mechanic Petty was a devout family man and Christian who steadfastly avoided the hedonism associated with early NASCAR; however, he also remained aloof from most other drivers and gained a well-earned reputation for rough driving. Although a fine driver in his own right, Petty is now best remembered as the founder of the four-generation Petty racing dynasty.[19]

France's efforts to enlist manufacturers and Hudson's runaway success pushed all the major car companies to become more actively involved in Grand National by mid-decade. Quite unexpectedly, given its prior low profile in racing, Chevrolet fired the opening salvo in the war between the major manufacturers. Even though Chevrolets could not match the power of other makes, Chevy's new V-8 made its lightweight cars competitive in NASCAR's second-tier Short Track series. These developments actually caught the company itself unawares. Chevrolet then quickly publicized its stock car successes in a series of spring 1955 ads and developed a working relationship with mechanic Smokey Yunick. The Chevys managed only two Grand National wins that season, but one of them was Herb Thomas's prominent victory at the Southern 500. On the basis of 1955's successes, Chevrolet organized a more substantial racing team in 1956.[20]

Chevrolet's early 1955 publicity campaign forced Ford to also increase its commitment to Grand National racing. Much like Chevrolet, Ford did not deeply involve itself in Grand National until 1955, but unofficially it connected local dealerships to race teams as early as 1951. To counter Chevrolet, Ford assembled its own small stock car racing program. Under the leadership of Buddy Shuman, Ford organized a two car team to compete at the Southern 500 in 1955. The cars performed poorly, but Ford's determination to succeed in Grand National did not waver. During the winter Ford assembled a team under the direction of Red Vogt, who replaced the deceased Shuman, that included drivers Fireball Roberts, Curtis Turner, Joe Weatherly, and Ralph Moody.[21]

Several other manufacturers also began to organize factory teams as well. Packard, Mercury, and Dodge all provided some degree of support to Grand National teams. Chrysler, however, stood as the manufacturer to beat in 1955, despite making no direct contribution to any Grand National drivers. In February of that year, Chrysler tried to counter its declining market share by issuing the C300 as part of its "Forward Look" program. Equipped with a hemispheric-head V-8, the 300 (dubbed the "beautiful brute") offered a frightening amount of horsepower. Fortuitously for Chrysler, the 300 caught the eye of Karl Kiekhaefer, who decided he wanted to become involved with stock car racing as a way to advertise his Mercury outboard motors. As the stock operation was viewed as a means of selling Mercurys, Kiekhaefer made sure his brand's name was connected with a first class operation. Kiekhaefer's white cars were always immaculate; he conveyed the cars to races in elaborate and modern haulers, and his crews all wore professional looking matching uniforms (at a time when no one else did). Kiekhaefer pioneered techniques in analyzing weather and track surface conditions in preparing his cars, and he required his crews to keep meticulous notes on how they set up cars for each race. In keeping with his theme of associating only with the best, Kiekhaefer convinced Tim Flock, who left NASCAR in 1954 after a dispute with France, to drive his 300. Flock won an astonishing 18 races en route to the championship. Lee Petty, also driving a 300, finished third behind Buck Baker's Ford.[22]

For 1956, Kiekhaefer assembled a multicar team that, at various times, featured Tim Flock, Buck Baker, Herb Thomas, Fonty Flock, Speedy Thompson, and Frank "Rebel" Mundy. His cars won 21 of the first 25 races of the Grand National season and seemed poised for a repeat of 1955's success until internal dissension derailed the team for much of the summer. Tim Flock and Herb Thomas both quit, with Thomas then competing successfully in a Chevrolet. A late season surge saw Buck Baker win the first of two consecutive Grand National titles. Despite phenomenal success in his two seasons on the Grand National circuit, Kiekhaefer abandoned his team at the end of the season. To his dismay, the team's dominance fueled hatred instead of respect. Fans tired of seeing a Kiekhaefer 300 always winning, and they began booing the team's drivers. Kiekhaefer feared this animosity would adversely affect Mercury sales and consequently severed all connections with NASCAR.[23]

Although internal issues contributed to the Kiekhaefer team's midseason slump, the actions of Bill France also played a role. The Ford team fired Red Vogt, who was quickly hired by Kiekhaefer, early in the season, and replaced him with John Holman, a relatively unknown mechanic. One of Holman's first moves at Ford was to request permission from Bill France to alter some parts on his cars for safety reasons. France, desperate to regain racing parity, permitted Holman to make these dubious alterations, which immediately translated into a more competitive Ford product on the circuit. Buoyed by the changes, Fireball Roberts and Ralph Moody both won several races in factory-sponsored Fords, while Curtis Turner drove his independent Ford to a win at the Southern 500. The Ford team had contracted with one of NASCAR's budding stars, Robert Glenn "Junior" Johnson Jr., but he did not actually race for them that season. Johnson established a name for himself by running successfully in 1955 in his own independent Oldsmobile, which caught the attention of Ford. Johnson agreed to drive for Ford once the team became competitive in 1956, driving an independent Pontiac until then. Before Holman turned the team around, however, Johnson was arrested by federal agents while tending to his father's still in Wilkes County, North Carolina. Later dubbed by Tom Wolfe "The Last American Hero," Junior Johnson resumed his Grand National career after prison and became one of the series' stars of the early 1960s. For Chevrolet, 1956 did not prove as disastrous as it did for Johnson, but their factory team had little to celebrate. Unable to find a way to equalize its cars with Ford and Chrysler, it proved to be another disappointing Grand National season, with only three wins to its credit (two by Herb Thomas and one by Paul Goldsmith).[24]

Although Chrysler dominated the Grand National season, all three of the major automakers managed to find ways to tout their successes. They could do this because in 1956 NASCAR once again expanded its group of sanctioned series. Late in the 1955 racing season, NASCAR, as it did repeatedly during the decade, absorbed a smaller sanctioning body, in this case SAFE (Society of Auto Sports, Fellowship, and Education), which operated a series based on convertibles. For 1956, NASCAR created its own convertible racing circuit. France hoped that the convertibles would attract fans because they could actually see their favorite driver in action as he sped around the track. Spectators may have been excited by this prospect, but drivers and track owners found the series far less appealing. Most of the prominent Grand National drivers refused to participate, with only Curtis Turner making a serious effort in the series. Despite Turner's enormous number of victories in the first two seasons of the new series, little-known Bob Welborn won the championship the first three years. Attempts to generate support for the series included having the convertibles compete on the track at the same time as the Grand Nationals, but this move only demonstrated the inferiority of the convertibles. The result was a slow descent into irrelevance for the series. From a high of 47 races in the inaugural year, the convertibles dropped to 15 races in 1959. In 1960, citing a lack of drivers, NASCAR abandoned the series. For Ford and Chevrolet, the lower level NASCAR series allowed them to claim success in the 1956 season. Chrysler products won the most Grand National races, Fords emerged victorious in the preponderance of the convertible races, and Chevrolet won the most in the Short Track series.[25]

The departure of the Kiekhaefer team seemed to open the door for more success for the factory teams. Ford's tightly organized team was now joined by Chevrolet's Georgia-based Southern Engineering Development Company, under the control of Hugh Babb. Also, Pontiac, Mercury, Oldsmobile, and Plymouth provided some measure of assistance to Grand National teams in 1957. Early in the year, much to Bill France's delight, the factory Ford team (Fireball Roberts, Marvin Panch, and Ralph Moody) traded victories with the Chevrolet-sponsored cars of Buck Baker, Speedy Thompson, and Jack Smith, which seemed to portend an exciting season-long battle. Manufacturer involvement in stock, however, led to dramatically increasing costs for those drivers who wanted to be successful. Without the substantial financial backing of a factory behind them, independent drivers found themselves uncompetitive and began dropping out of Grand National. Fields for Grand National events fell to less than 20 cars, which forced NASCAR to make an effort to increase parity.[26]

In April 1957, NASCAR announced a ban on fuel injection and superchargers, technological advances that had helped give the factory teams advantages. Independent drivers lauded this move, but for the manufacturers the message was that they could no longer use Grand National as a testing ground for new technologies. Outside the sport, officials of the Automobile Manufacturers Association (AMA) became increasingly concerned about the promotion of horsepower and speed that had become de rigueur in car advertisements, fearing this might promote excessive speeds that would lead to increased fatalities and might eventually spark government investigations. France responded to these concerns by declaring that manufacturers could no longer reference NASCAR in their ads. For the car companies, NASCAR had become an expensive diversion that could be neither used for performance development nor publicly promoted. In the midst of an industry-wide slowdown (the next year, for the first time ever, more cars were imported into the United States than exported), the auto makers could not afford to squander advertising dollars and engineering resources on NASCAR. After a Grand National car flew into the grandstands at Martinsville in May and created another round of bad publicity, the automakers moved quickly to dispose of their white elephant factory teams. In June, all manufacturers signed off on an AMA document declaring an end to direct factory involvement in all forms of motor racing and then sold their Grand National cars (typically to their drivers).[27]

Officially, all drivers became independents in June 1957. The AMA ban, however, was widely, albeit surreptitiously, violated until the manufacturers officially returned in the mid-1960s. For example, Ralph Moody and John Holman established a car-building operation that was a Ford operation in all save name. Other drivers found themselves able to walk into dealerships and drive away with new models. Manufacturer participation certainly reduced from the 1956 peak, but it still contributed to the sport. Bill France responded to the departure of factory assistance by raising purses and offering some teams "travel money" to get them to the races. Still, the 1958 season brought smaller fields and slower speeds—developments that suggested NASCAR's momentum might be ebbing. France, however, moved to rebuild NASCAR without direct factory assistance or an extensive northern presence. His new direction for Grand

National involved strengthening the sport's southern base and finding ways to regain speed. For the cars to go faster, they needed asphalt tracks with high-banked turns and long straightaways. As the Eisenhower administration clicked off its final days, Bill France ushered in a new period for NASCAR—the era of superspeedways.[28]

4

SUPERSPEEDWAYS

Beginning in the late 1950s, NASCAR became an organization that evolved purely on the basis of Bill France's vision of the sanctioning body. Although France, as the head of NASCAR, shaped the course of the organization before this point, issues related to finances, stability, and the relationships with promoters and drivers kept him from operating as freely as he would have liked. By the late 1950s, however, France controlled the nation's largest stock car racing organization, a position that gave him considerable leverage in the industry. Over the course of the next decade, he drove out all of NASCAR's other shareholders, engaged in almost incessant conflict with automobile manufacturers in an effort to guarantee that he dictated what would appear on the track, squashed attempts by drivers to exert their power, and oversaw the construction of a host of new tracks. For most stock car fans of the period, the development of new race tracks represented the most obvious of France's machinations. Like the American Automobile Association (AAA) before him, France believed that the status of a racing series could be measured by the tracks on which that series appeared. During NASCAR's first decade, France was forced to rely on dusty short tracks as part of the process of establishing his organization as a viable sanctioning body. At the dawn of the 1960s, however, France initiated a program to move NASCAR from red clay to asphalt. Modern, paved circuits became the norm in the series, and by the early 1970s, Grand National cars no longer raced on any dirt tracks. The crown jewels among the new courses were enormous tracks more than 1.5 miles long known as superspeedways. For France, the superspeedways gave stock car racing an unimpeachable claim to being a modern, highly professional form of racing. Given the connections between NASCAR and the city of Daytona, France not surprisingly chose to construct the first of these tracks there.

Despite Daytona Beach's status as the "birthplace of speed," late 1950s residents of that city increasingly came to view their annual stock car race as a nuisance. As the value of beachfront property rose, support decreased for allowing noisy stock cars to tear up the beach. Pressure from local residents prompted France to announce in early 1954 that a new purpose-built speedway would be constructed in Daytona in time for the 1955 Speed Week. France's announced opening proved wildly optimistic. His planned track fell victim to financial woes, disagreements with local residents concerning the location of the track, and the political movement to ban all motor racing. France managed to clear all of these hurdles but the financial one. In 1958, with everything finally in place and construction underway, France had exhausted all his funds and found himself forced to find outside investors. Chief among his financial saviors stood Clint Murchison, Jr. A hedonistic Texas oil millionaire, Murchison later became the founding owner of the Dallas Cowboys in 1960. Murchison and France initially bonded over their similar conservative political alignments. The NASCAR chief's views led him to develop close connections with other figures on the far right besides Murchison, such as George Wallace and L. Mendal Rivers (who became NASCAR's commissioner in July 1969). With NASCAR under France's complete control, his own political beliefs became interwoven with the organization. The connections between NASCAR and conservatives (most famously with the "NASCAR dads" of the early 21st century) have been spotlighted in recent years, but those ties actually date back to the 1950s.[1]

With funding eventually secured thanks to Murchison's assistance, Daytona International Speedway officially opened in early 1959. France wanted to build a track that surpassed Indianapolis and, although not immediately apparent, the superspeedway in Daytona did eventually accomplish that goal. With a unique "tri-oval" design, Daytona looked like no other track in the country. To ensure high speeds, France banked the 2.5-mile track's turns to 31 degrees. The speeds attainable on the new track frightened even veteran Grand National drivers. Their concerns became more pronounced when, in an attempt to establish a new world speed record for a closed course, Marshall Teague was killed instantly when his open-wheel vehicle flipped and broke apart in February. Two weeks later, the inaugural Daytona 500 ushered in NASCAR's superspeedway era. The race itself proved to be even more exciting than Bill France could have hoped. More than 41,000 spectators watched Joe Weatherly, Lee Petty, and Johnny Beauchamp cross the finish line side—by side. Weatherly was actually two laps down, but the other two were competing for the win. The initial decision gave the victory to International Motor Contest Association veteran Beauchamp, but three days later photographic evidence led to a reversal, and Petty became the first Daytona 500 champion.

The massive, modern facility and fantastic finish created an enormous wave of positive press.

Perhaps France's greatest success with Daytona occurred off the track. In the mid-1950s, he took the lead in creating the Automobile Competition Committee of the United States (ACCUS), with the goal of gaining recognition for that group as the American affiliate of motor sports international governing body, the Federation Intenationale de l'Automobile (FIA). Such recognition would allow ACCUS-sanctioned events to become part of the world racing calendar. As a member of the ACCUS, NASCAR races sanctioned by the FIA became both open to all drivers with FIA licenses and part of the world drivers' championship. Sanctioned by the FIA, the Daytona 500 gained global stature. USAC's membership in the ACCUS also worked to France's advantage. With FIA-sanctioned events open to all drivers holding a license, drivers from both American sanctioning bodies could compete against each other. France, cognizant of the overall superiority of NASCAR's stock drivers over USAC's, believed such head-to-head competition would help prove NASCAR reigned supreme. In the next few years USAC's incompetent efforts to keep the drivers apart also aided France, as it made that organization appear afraid of NASCAR (and brought FIA disciplinary actions against them as well).[2]

The Daytona facility itself also gave France an advantage. Although in competition with USAC, France needed as many events as possible to pay for his huge new track and signed agreements with his rival for two Champ car races at Daytona. In the April event driver George Amick was killed when his car hit an outside retaining wall at more than 170 miles per hour. USAC promptly canceled a scheduled July race and never returned to Daytona. For France this meant he not only owned the most modern race track in the country, but he could keep his greatest rival from using the track without appearing to be engaging in vindictive politics. With a July date freed up, France organized a sweepstakes race (meaning it was open to both Grand National and convertible cars) as the Firecracker 250. At the July race "Little" Joe Weatherly became the first driver to purposefully use the aerodynamic benefits of racing single-file at high speed ("drafting") when he followed Fireball Roberts for 100 miles. In the 1960 Daytona 500, Junior Johnson would turn drafting into a science.

The opening of Daytona gave NASCAR a signature event near both the beginning of the season (the Daytona 500 would not become the first race of the season until three decades later) and as the season wound down (the Southern 500). For Bill France the goal became filling in the months between those two races with similar premier events. Daytona represented the opening salvo in an effort to move Grand National racing away from its roots on dirt tracks and toward paved speedways. In a very real sense, France adopted a strategy that mirrored AAA policies of the past. To make NASCAR more modern, France slowly eliminated the short tracks and horse ovals. These changes, however, did not please everyone involved in the sport. For example, racing columnist Don O'Reilly blasted France for abandoning the sport's roots in favor of the big paved ovals. Local fans also lamented the loss of Grand National events on their home short tracks. Drivers balked at the shifting nature of Grand National for a variety of reasons. Some drivers recognized that only highly subsidized semifactory teams could achieve the speeds necessary to succeed on the superspeedways, which might make them uncompetitive. Drivers who learned their craft on dirt feared those skills would not translate to asphalt. Perhaps most important, many drivers acknowledged that the reckless image of a stock racer was easier to maintain on the slower short tracks; a number of them were simply frightened by the high speeds of the new tracks. Lee Petty later admitted about the first Daytona 500 that "there wasn't a man there who wasn't scared to death of the place." France, though, refused to let these concerns alter his vision for Grand National and pressed forward into the superspeedway era.[3]

Older fans' complaints of the loss of Grand National races in their locales remained muted to a degree by NASCAR's continued support of dirt tracks in its lower series. Pressure on NASCAR was also lessened by the fact that it would take more than a decade to phase out all the dirt tracks. This staged transition to asphalt kept fans across the Southeast from uniting in their opposition to France's plans. The NASCAR chief also helped undercut criticisms by building as many of the new speedways as possible in the South. As the base of stock car fandom, the South represented the most logical region to construct tracks that needed to attract enormous crowds to turn a profit. A smattering of northern superspeedways would come to host Grand National events in the coming decade, but these tracks represented only a small portion of the events in NASCAR's top series, and France carefully kept the nonsouthern tracks geographically spread out. His hope was that keeping the nonsouthern tracks isolated from each other would allow each to pull in fans from a wide region without competing with each other.

In some ways the complaints of the drivers proved the easiest to address. During the 1960s, France crushed two attempts at collectivized actions by drivers by simply showing these men that they were replaceable. If drivers did not like the way France operated NASCAR, they could race elsewhere; and if they chose to cross France by complaining about his policies, he forced them to leave by banning them. France knew that disgruntled drivers had few other options, save driving in the lower-paying

USAC series. Further, the NASCAR leader understood that a steady supply of young and reckless drivers could be counted on to replace nervous veterans. France exerted absolute power within the organization, and he never hesitated to demonstrate (whether to drivers, owners, fans, or manufacturers) that he was NASCAR.

The rise of speed on the new tracks quickly ushered in a new generation of Grand National drivers. The old guard of the 1950s faded away as younger drivers, less cognizant of their mortality, flooded into the sport. Among the veterans of the 1950s, a few did manage to successfully transition to the superspeedways of the 1960s. Fireball Roberts, who never found a top speed fast enough for his liking, became Grand National's leading star in the early 1960s. Roberts's love of speed eventually cost him his life on a superspeedway in 1964. Curtis Turner, the master of the red clay, also proved himself adept on the asphalt, but clashes with France kept him off the track for much of the decade. Lee Petty won his third Grand National championship in 1959 and had a successful season the next year, but then ran only a few races in the next four years. By far the oldest driver on the circuit (he was 46 in 1960), Petty simply could no longer withstand the physical punishment of sustained high speeds for several hours. Petty, however, did not go quietly. He became renowned for filing postrace challenges over scoring irregularities and claims of cheating by other drivers. Petty had a long-running feud with Junior Johnson, who declared in 1960 that "I'll take care of Petty when the right time comes." His rough driving (on short tracks, at least) continued until the end of his career. By 1960, however, a different Petty posed the greatest threat on the track.[4]

Lee's son Richard made his debut driving NASCAR convertibles in 1958. Lee helped outfit his son in Petty Enterprises equipment, but he also made clear that he would treat Richard like any other driver on the track. Richard made his Grand National debut in July 1958 at the one-third–mile paved track in Toronto. He was knocked out of the race on the 55th lap when Lee, battling for the win, put Richard into the wall. The next summer Richard took the checkered flag at Lakewood, only to have his first career victory taken from him after Lee filed a protest over the scoring. Richard's struggles during his first two seasons, however, served merely as an extended apprenticeship for what became the most successful career in NASCAR history. He won his first race in 1960, then went on to win another 100 races during the decade. The first of his seven career championships occurred in 1964. Petty did not retire until the early 1990s, by which time he stood as NASCAR's all-time leader in victories, with 200. Remarkably, "King" Richard finished in the top 10 in points every year from 1960 to 1983. Unlike his father, the younger Petty cultivated a fan-friendly persona that made him the most popular driver on the NASCAR circuit. Richard's blue number 43 became the most famous car in NASCAR history. Modern fans might more readily recognize the black number 3 of Dale Earnhardt, but Petty's car stood as the symbol of NASCAR for almost 40 years. Petty's distinctive shade of blue, initially adopted in the late 1950s because he had to mix white with the blue to have enough paint to cover his first race car, became so deeply ingrained in the psyche of NASCAR supporters that to this day good weather on race day is still occasionally referred to as a "clear Petty blue sky."[5]

Lee Petty's career effectively ended after a serious accident at Daytona in 1961, but Richard's star waxed as his father's waned, and he became the public face of NASCAR during the new superspeedway era. In 1960, Daytona was joined by superspeedways in Atlanta, Charlotte, and Hanford, California. France's plan of pushing Grand National toward modern tracks led to those four speedways hosting nine series events that season. The NASCAR chief's strategy paid immediate dividends when CBS broadcast the Daytona 500 qualifying races on live television, which brought Grand National racing national attention; however, various difficulties made the opening of the new tracks problematic. Marchbanks Speedway in California proved to be the most ephemeral of the three new tracks. The track fell victim to the geographical issues faced by all West Coast tracks of the period. Most Grand National drivers simply refused to make the trek and, bereft of big name drivers, Marchbanks stopped hosting races in the series after 1961. Charlotte and Atlanta became permanent stops on the NASCAR circuit, but their openings also demonstrated the challenges of building superspeedways in the early 1960s. As a result of construction difficulties, Atlanta International Speedway did not host its first Grand National event until July, a full eight months after the track's announced opening. Charlotte's track also witnessed construction-related issues, but financial woes and a power struggle provided much of the off-the-track drama.[6]

Charlotte Motor Speedway opened in 1960 under the partnership of Curtis Turner and Bruton Smith. Both had planned to construct tracks in Charlotte in 1959, then found themselves forced to work together out of financial necessity. For Turner the track represented a vanity project; for Smith, Charlotte was to be a counter-punch to long-time rival France's opening of Daytona. The project eventually suffered from weather and construction delays, financial woes, and erratic behavior by Turner. Charlotte managed to open in June 1960 with the track not yet fully completed. Despite these problems, the ownership attempted to establish the track by organizing the longest stock car race ever—the World 600. The race proved as disastrous as the construction process. During the 600, long stretches of the uncured asphalt broke up, throwing chunks into the radiators of cars. Moreover, wary Grand National fans, aware of the delays and difficulties, had refused to buy tickets, and the grandstands were only half full. Turner, who engaged in bank fraud to cover the race's purse, then scrambled to cover his debts with actions that led to his banning from NASCAR.[7]

Having exhausted more traditional means of obtaining the funds to pay off the track's debts, Turner attempted to establish a system of pari-mutuel wagering on Grand National races. France and others opposed this scheme, which led the desperate Turner to then accept a loan from the Teamsters. In return, Turner pledged to make a good faith effort to convince Grand National drivers to join the Federation of Professional Athletes (FPA), the Teamsters' new attempt to become involved in professional sports. Drivers, angry over low purses and France's dictatorial rule, proved easy to convince. Few of the men on the Grand National circuit had not clashed with France at some point in their career. Turner, Fireball Roberts, Buck Baker, and Tim Flock quickly moved to register the majority of Grand National drivers as new members of the FPA, which prompted swift action from NASCAR. France met with the bulk of the drivers in August 1961, noted he knew how to use a firearm, and then declared no unionized racer could compete in a Grand National event. The threatened ban brought most of the drivers back into the fold, including Fireball Roberts. For their refusal to renounce the FPA, Turner and Flock received lifetime bans from NASCAR.[8]

France's determination to crush the unionization effort stemmed from his traditional southern perspective on management rights. For France, ownership of NASCAR meant only he possessed the power to shape the organization. Driver/worker demands for increased purses and a voice within NASCAR simply could not be tolerated. To keep control France "employed practically every tried and tested method of keeping unions out, from threats and intimidation, to 'yellow dog' contracts, to accusations of communism, to propaganda, to blacklisting." Fireball Roberts noted the FPA "must have grabbed Mr. France where it hurts." France previously squelched North Carolina driver Bryant Wallace's threat to organize drivers, but it was his Piedmont mill owner-style actions against the FPA that led later historians to view NASCAR as the "most southern sport on Earth."[9]

France succeeded in eliminating the FPA threat through his own actions, ingrained southern prejudice toward unions, a public outcry over the tainted Teamsters' role, and drivers' legal status as "independent contractors." His heavy-handed approach helped reinforce to drivers France's control, but it was also unnecessary. Because they independently contracted to compete by handing entry blanks to race promoters, drivers

could not legally unionize. France knew he could legally defeat the FPA
before he met with the drivers, but he chose to personally confront them
with threats "under the iron-fisted banner of NASCAR" as a means of
demonstrating he could meet the challenge personally, without relying
on the courts. By defeating the FPA through his own actions, France had
defended his honor.[10]

Charlotte Motor Speedway was mired in Chapter 10 bankruptcy by the
time France defeated the FPA, but court-appointed executives managed to
keep the track open and host the second World 600 in May 1961. David
Pearson of South Carolina earned his first career Grand National win in
the event. Pearson, out of a rather lackluster field, became NASCAR
Rookie of the Year in 1960, but 1961 was his breakout season. He won
three superspeedway events that year, which established Pearson as a
driver capable of handling NASCAR's transition away from short and dirt
tracks. Later dubbed the "Silver Fox," Pearson won three Grand National
championships during the 1960s, then scaled back his schedule to race
only in the most prestigious events. He eventually won 105 races, second
only to Richard Petty.

Bill France's bumpy conversion of NASCAR occurred during a period
in which USAC still represented a challenge to the Daytona group's hegemony. USAC hurt its own cause by running a limited schedule with
relatively low purses. Also, its efforts to keep NASCAR drivers out of
USAC-sanctioned events led to both bad publicity and run-ins with the
FIA. Amid controversy over sanctioned events at Riverside International
Speedway in 1963, the confident France declared "we aren't concerned
about USAC." As head of the larger of the two groups (in terms of stock
racing), France could afford to be cavalier, but his bravado masked a continued concern about USAC operations. By this point the USAC stock
series had virtually abandoned the South (it typically went to the region only once per year), but it still had the cache of Indianapolis 500
winners running in the circuit. As a means of ensuring unfettered im-
plementation of his personal strategy to defeat USAC, France bought
out Ed Otto in 1963. To assist him in permanently establishing USAC's
second-class status, France developed increasingly close connections
with Midwest Association for Race Cars (MARC), a group established
by former NASCAR official John Marcum in 1953. In 1964, MARC became the Automobile Racing Club of America (ARCA), and the series traveled to Daytona for the first time. France saw ARCA as fulfilling
two distinct needs: undercutting USAC in the Midwest and providing
a training ground for young stock drivers. As such, France arranged for
ARCA events to become part of Grand National race weekends at many
southern tracks. Affiliation with NASCAR brought much needed money

to ARCA, but at the expense of ever establishing itself as a truly independent, national organization. ARCA president Marcum accepted this role and bore no illusions about his organization. In 1964, he quipped that ARCA was "the hamburger circuit." Regardless of its president's views, ARCA served as a viable home for stock drivers either on the way up or sliding toward retirement. During the early 1960s, drivers such as Jack Bowsher, Benny Parsons, Nelson "El Toro" Stacy, Jack Purcell, Tom Pistone, and Charlie Glotzbach all competed successfully in ARCA.[11]

Golden boy Fred Lorenzen also raced in MARC, but he found greater success in USAC in the late 1950s. Originally from Illinois, Lorenzen abandoned the low-paying USAC circuit and moved South to get closer to the center of NASCAR activity. He felt compelled to make this move because, as he later noted, "the North was not race country." In 1961, Lorenzen became a driver for the Holman-Moody Ford team and immediately established himself as a force on the superspeedways. Like Pearson, Lorenzen ran a limited schedule, focusing only on the most lucrative races. He won 27 races over seven seasons before retiring (for the first time) in mid-1967. Although he rarely ran more than 20 races in one season, Lorenzen developed into one of NASCAR's most popular drivers. He mixed speed with good looks and articulate interviews in a way not previously witnessed on the Grand National circuit. *Sports Illustrated* reporter Kim Chapin somewhat derisively called him the "best of the citified button-down stockers," but Lorenzen can now be seen as the prototype for the handsome and media-savvy nonsouthern drivers so highly desired by current NASCAR sponsors. For Bill France, "Fearless Freddie" embodied the new image of NASCAR he tried to cultivate during the 1960s.[12]

Drivers such as Lorenzen, Pearson, Petty, Ned Jarrett, and Rex White spearheaded the youth movement of the early 1960s. Star drivers from the 1950s quickly gave way to the youngsters at the dawn of the superspeedway era. Lee Petty and Herb Thomas both retired early in the next decade. Two-time national champion Buck Baker continued to race through the decade, but increasingly found himself overshadowed by his son Buddy. Tim Flock never ran another Grand National race after his 1961 ban, and Curtis Turner returned to NASCAR in 1965, but as a shell of his former self. Two of the big names from the 1950s continued to thrive in the next decade before succumbing to lethal crashes in 1964. "Little" Joe Weatherly, who began his Grand National career in 1952, won back-to-back national championships in 1962–63, before dying in a wreck at Riverside in January 1964. Six months later, Fireball Roberts died from burns suffered in a crash at Charlotte.

These younger drivers (and surviving veterans) increasingly competed on the long, asphalt tracks Bill France so coveted. By 1965, the Grand

National series boasted five superspeedways, each of which hosted multiple events. After NASCAR abandoned the problematic Marchbanks Speedway in 1962, its position as the fifth superspeedway was taken by the new North Carolina Motor Speedway (typically referred to as Rockingham) in 1965. Thus Bill France's plan of first modernizing facilities in areas of Grand National strength resulted in NASCAR's biggest events occurring in Florida, North and South Carolina, and Georgia. Unlike the wildcat era of the early 1950s, when France would sanction a race anywhere in the country that would have the Grand Nationals, the 1960s saw only limited forays outside the Southeast. To maximize the number of top drivers who would attend the nonsouthern races, these excursions became western and northern "swings," with multiple events scheduled back-to-back to reduce the number of actual long trips a team had to undertake. France's southern strategy helped convince southeastern-based drivers to make the long treks to the North and West Coast, which served to reduce the number of local drivers from those areas who could qualify for the nonsouthern races. As a result, even Grand National races outside the South became thoroughly dominated by southern drivers. During the 1950s, only 41 percent of Grand National competitors hailed from the Southeast; by the 1960s the number increased to 72 percent. Always deeply rooted and supported in the South, the Grand National series became truly southern during the early 1960s.[13]

Grand National managed to build on this base of stock support thanks to the changing environment of the postwar South. Per capita income in the region grew dramatically from 1940 to 1960, which gave increasing numbers of southerners disposable income for race tickets and memorabilia. Rising income also allowed for an expansion of private automobile ownership, which made it easier for southerners to travel to local short tracks or regional superspeedways and also increased the importance of the automobile in the lives of many southerners (which helped fuel an interest in motor sports). Economically, then, the South became more like the North. These economic realities helped facilitate a rise in the popularity of sports in the South that also made the region's sporting culture more closely resemble that of the North. In the 1950s, college basketball and, especially, football emerged as important aspects of southern culture. NASCAR, the only sports organization southeastern residents might truly call their own, became an integral part of southern sports as well.[14]

Stock car racing emerged as a full member of the southern sporting culture, however, almost a decade after the rise of college athletics. Although NASCAR benefited from the growing importance of sports caused by increased income, it blossomed as a truly southern sport at the dawn of the 1960s. Bill France's vision of building on the southern base through

superspeedways succeeded partly through the increasingly favorable economic climate of the South and partly through the embrace of stock by
white southerners during a period of great social upheaval. The changes
wrought by rising income levels and urbanization raised concerns among
white southerners, but the birth of the modern civil rights movement
brought absolute terror. The social structure of the South, predicated
on race and deference, cracked under the combined weight of African
American protest and the federal government's intervention. White
southern defenders of the old order responded with their own form of
protest—massive resistance. In many ways the ultimately rear-guard action of massive resistance represented the death knell of the myth of the
Old South. Notions of chivalrous white knights, happy "mammies," and
African Americans content with their subservient status melted in the
southern heat of fire hoses, bombings, and cross burnings. The destruction of the old social order compelled white southerners to seek out a new
set of myths and values that defined their regional identity. New totems
of "southernness" needed to develop. Headed by a socially conservative
southerner and already established in the South, NASCAR offered a
ready-made new outlet for regional identity.[15]

As Grace Elizabeth Hale noted, "white southerners chose geographical
anchors, whether imagined spaces evoked by narratives or the physical
spaces recaptured through spectacle, literally to ground their racial identity within the mobility of modernity." College football and basketball
games could serve as geographical anchors for spectacle, but these events
proved problematic. Federally mandated desegregation converted the
field, court, and stands into environments for the types of assaults on the
old social order decried by conservative white southerners. Also, working-
class southerners typically did not frequent college campuses. Their traditional habitats were the locations Ray Oldenburg dubbed third places,
sites of informal community gathering such as lunch counters, barber-
shops, high school parking lots, and gas stations. These third places also
represented the types of locations under threat by African Americans de-
manding public equality. Conservative working-class whites in the South
then sought out new "great good places," such as the lily-white infield of
a superspeedway. As a *New York Times* writer suggested, "infield auto-race
viewing in the South has become a cult." Stock car races created what
sports theorist Susan Birrell called "a social ceremony structurally capable
of fulfilling social functions comparable to those of religious ceremonies,
specifically by serving as an arena for the creation of symbolic leaders and
the display of heroic action."[16]

Grand National events were not informal, but they were about community building, however temporary. Going to a Grand National race

created an ephemeral "city." In some rural southern states the gatherings at a superspeedway created "cities" that rivaled the populations of the state's permanent settlements. These gatherings ostensibly represented sporting events, but they also served to establish an identity for working-class southerners. NASCAR infields reinforced values and hegemony under threat in the larger society. For conservative southerners, this meant a defense of white power in the face of federal intervention, the civil rights movement, the "anti-American" actions of student protesters, and the unforgivably traitorous actions of Lyndon Johnson, who turned on his southern brothers to promote African American rights. Stretched across wide, rural swaths, working class stock fans could congregate in traditional third places only in small groups. A Grand National event could bring together tens of thousands of like-minded southerners in an environment legally open to anyone who chose to purchase a ticket (thereby circumventing any governmental intrusions), but so overwhelmingly white and potentially dangerous as to keep out African Americans, "long hairs," and liberal Yankees. Grand National events in places like Georgia became, in effect, regional third places. Not only did the infields offer a safe haven for white southerners, but they could take immeasurable pride in the knowledge that the sporting event going on around them represented the pinnacle of stock car racing. The carousing of Darlington's infield continued, but the presence of cultural signifiers such as the "Johnny Reb" mascot and acres of rebel flags brought in by spectators increasingly established it (and others) as a racially charged space. NASCAR was important to white southerners not just because it was a sport in which southerners competed at the highest level, but because it was the first sport in which to be viewed as the best, northerners had to come South instead of vice-versa. For decades southern professional baseball and football players found themselves forced to trek north to prove themselves, but stock compelled northern drivers to come south to compete in the Southern 500, Rebel 300, or Dixie 400. New York driver Lloyd Moore noted that "we were Yankees heading into rebel territory and we knew it."[17]

From the beginning, motor sports has been an overwhelmingly white preserve. A few African Americans competed at high levels, perhaps most famously the West Coast driver "Rajo Jack," but the AAA put an end to this by officially banning black (and, for good measure, female) drivers from their sanctioned events. "Rajo Jack" occasionally claimed to be Portuguese to circumvent racial barriers, but his ability to compete against the nation's finest drivers ended with the AAA ban. For the best African American drivers, such as Charlie Wiggins of Indianapolis, segregated contests represented their only outlet in motor sports. As such, a few African American racing series, the open-wheel Gold and Glory

Sweepstakes and Afro American Automobile Association being the most famous, flourished during the 1920s. With its traditional connections to southerners and the working class, groups not known for progressive social views, stock operated as an even more racially homogenous form of motor sports than open-wheel. In the immediate postwar period, a few African American drivers, such as Ivy Cook and "Baby Face" Hilton, competed in integrated northern modified events, but most black stock drivers appeared only in loosely organized, segregated races.[18]

Within NASCAR, circumstances for nonwhite drivers were little better. Richard Petty and Gober Sosebee both acknowledged their Native American roots and faced little hostility, although Sosebee was sometimes billed as "Georgia's Wild Injun." Petty wore turquoise jewelry and talked openly about his Cherokee heritage, but, like Sosebee, he was viewed by stock fans as white. Non-native American groups, however, found Grand National far less welcoming. Hispanic driver Franco Menendez raced under the name Frank Mundy and felt so compelled to establish his Caucasian bona fides that he adopted the nickname "Rebel" and competed with a Confederate flag painted on his car. For African Americans, NASCAR posed added challenges. Overwhelmingly white and competing primarily in the South, the Grand National circuit proved especially closed to black drivers. Driver Janet Guthrie, who faced enormous discrimination herself, later commented with only slight exaggeration that NASCAR was the only top-level sport that "meets the standards of an Aryan nation."[19]

Branch Rickey selected Jackie Robinson over more talented African American athletes out of the belief that Robinson's temperament would allow him to withstand the abuse sure to be hurled at the man who broke Major League Baseball's color line. Given both the climate surrounding Grand National and the lax security of most pit areas, only an African American of similar demeanor to Robinson could compete in NASCAR's top division. Virginia tripper Wendell Scott broke NASCAR's color line when, after running "outlaw" races the two previous years, he became the first African American to obtain a NASCAR license. He made his NASCAR debut in a low-level Sportsman division race at Daytona in February 1954, then broke the Grand National color line in March 1961. Like Robinson before him, Scott endured verbal abuse and violent threats. Robinson received death threats in the late 1940s, but Scott faced legitimately life-threatening situations as racist drivers purposefully wrecked him and, in at least one instance, sabotaged his car before the race. Scott was fully cognizant of the dangers he placed himself in, noting that "I picked the hardest sport for a black man to do good in." To survive in the wooly world of southern stock car racing, Scott adopted a public attitude similar to Robinson's nonthreatening persona. Despite deliberate provocations, Scott never retaliated or publicly denounced white drivers.[20]

Scott's race elicited various responses from stock promoters. At some tracks he was allowed to race as a gimmick, with crowds cheering when Scott was bumped. One track announcer regularly introduced him pre-race as "the world's only nigger race car driver." Other track owners let him race, but only as W.D. Scott to avoid conflict with racist fans who might recognize the name "Wendell Scott." As NASCAR rules permitted individual race promoters to decide who competed in their events, Scott found himself closed out of certain races. Both Bruton Smith and Bob Colvin refused to accept Scott's applications for their races. Bill France's relationship with Scott was more complex. France shielded the driver from especially egregious abuses on occasion, but declined to help Scott in cir-cumstances where it would place France in conflict with someone of au-thority in NASCAR. Colvin and Smith, for example, faced no opposition from France when they barred Scott from competing. France also passed over Scott for Grand National Rookie of the Year in 1961 in favor of a lesser white driver to avoid any possible racial conflict. For legal reasons France could not simply bar Scott from Grand National, but he was clearly not completely pleased with having an African American on the circuit.[21]

The racial dilemma posed by Scott came to a head in 1963. At a December Grand National event in Jacksonville, Scott appeared to have won the race (in a car he purchased from Ned Jarrett). Apparently un-prepared for this possibility, officials did not wave the checkered flag until Buck Baker crossed the finish line, and then awarded him the victory. Hours after the race NASCAR reversed the decision and gave Scott the win, claiming a scoring error caused the mix-up. Most trackside observ-ers, however, recognized Scott's victory as soon as he finished his last lap. NASCAR's decision to initially claim Baker as the winner stemmed from the combustible racial situation Scott's victory would have produced. Grand National's customary postrace ceremony involved the presenta-tion of the victory trophy by the race queen, who then kissed the winner. For Scott, kissing the white race queen represented a potentially lynch-able offense in the South. Fearful NASCAR officials, therefore, waited until all the spectators (and the race queen) left the track before awarding Scott the victory. Scott's 1963 win is still the only victory for an African American in NASCAR's top series. He also remains the only black driver to have competed regularly on the circuit. Other than Scott, only four African American drivers, with a combined total of eight starts between them, have raced at the highest level in NASCAR.[22]

Wendell Scott might have won more races with better equipment, but as a lifelong independent driver he received little assistance. For Scott, there was little chance to ever receive factory support. As he was barred by racist promoters from many of Grand Nationals' most significant races, factories inevitably passed him up for drivers who appeared in all circuit events. Scott's plight as an independent, however, was not especially unique. During the 1960s, Detroit's manufacturers provided enormous support, albeit sometimes abruptly terminated, for NASCAR's top drivers. Independent drivers found it increasingly difficult to compete with teams receiving such assistance. For Bill France, the inequality between independent and factory drivers threatened to drive away the independents he needed to fill race fields.

Of even greater concern to France was the lack of parity caused by different levels of manufacturer involvement in stock. France adamantly believed the sport was best served by having a number of car makes capable of winning any given race, viewing this as a way to attract brand-loyal spectators. Grand National's rules advocating "stock" vehicles, however, worked against this parity, as not all Detroit products were equal. Bill France responded by simply voiding the NASCAR regulations that made all stock products that reached a production run of 1,500 cars legal in Grand National events. To ensure parity, France effectively made up his own rules and did so on the fly. He banned models, motors, and parts whenever he felt they gave a particular manufacturer an unfair advantage. During the 1960s, then, manufacturers discovered what the drivers learned in the 1950s—Bill France was the dictator of NASCAR. Angry and frustrated, Detroit's automakers pulled out of NASCAR on a regular basis during the decade whenever the new rules worked against them. Although France lamented these occasional departures, he believed racing parity to be more important than any car brand. And even more important was his demonstration that Bill France—not drivers, USAC, or automakers—ruled stock car racing.[23]

Despite the 1957 AMA pledge to end involvement with racing, Detroit's manufacturers, conscious of the perceived connection between NASCAR success and sales, surreptitiously continued providing parts to chosen teams. During the early 1960s, Pontiac funneled parts to the teams of Smokey Yunick, Cotton Owens, and Bud Moore, while Plymouth supported Petty Enterprises. In June 1962, Ford announced it would once again become openly involved in racing. Within Grand National circles this came as no surprise, as many were well aware of Ford's postpledge role in assisting the Holman-Moody team. Henry Ford II made clear the reasons behind public involvement by stating, "we want to win races, we know winning races sells cars." Ford's announcement led GM to declare they would continue to abide by the agreement out of concern that overt racing involvement might spark another horsepower war. As part of their renewed commitment to avoid this possibility, GM discontinued its secret supplying of Pontiac parts to Grand National teams. Chrysler, on the other hand, responded to Ford's actions by announcing the company would begin producing high performance parts for stock car racing. For Bill France the renewed (public) involvement of the factories promised an increase in funds for some Grand National teams, but it also raised concerns over the continued viability of the independents. With fresh memories of the damage done in the late 1950s, when one manufacturer gained unchallengeable superiority, France tried to limit the powers of the manufacturers by barring engines with a displacement of more than 428 inches. France hoped this would prevent any factory team from gaining an advantage through the use of a monstrous engine. His announcement also signaled that France intended to reaffirm his control over the sport.[24]

France's concerns over the manufacturers creating unlevel playing fields seemed borne out by the next two seasons. In 1963, Fords dominated the long tracks, while the powerful but aerodynamically wretched Chrysler products ruled the short tracks. For France, the one bright spot in this circumstance was that independent Joe Weatherly, who jumped from team to team during the season, ran consistently enough on all types of tracks to win the championship. The next year Chrysler introduced new hemispheric heads that allowed Grand National cars to reach speeds of close to 180 miles per hour. In a reversal of the previous season, Chrysler's hemis ruled the long tracks, with the better handling Fords gaining the upper hand on short tracks. With criticism already mounting over speeds spiraling out of control, the 1964 season became even more nightmarish for France when both Weatherly and Fireball Roberts died in crashes. Then in September, driver Jimmy Pardue died during tire tests at Charlotte. Under enormous pressure, France moved to placate those concerned about safety in NASCAR. Two weeks after Pardue's death, France announced a ban on overhead cams, high risers, and hemispheric heads. Driver safety also improved during the 1965 season with the introduction of Goodyear's Lifesaver Inner Tire (often called the "inner liner") and fuel cells that kept gas from igniting during wrecks.[25]

Ford applauded France's moves, but Chrysler declared the new rules would make them uncompetitive. After NASCAR refused their appeal for a rules revision, Chrysler announced a boycott of the 1965 season. Their exit paved the way for Ford to dominate in a fashion not seen since the early 1950s glory days of Hudson. During 1965, Ford products won 48 of the 55 Grand National events. In one remarkable stretch, Fords prevailed in 32 consecutive races. Many of NASCAR's biggest drivers bowed out rather than race in equipment inferior to the Fords. Richard Petty, David Pearson, and Bobby Isaac all fell victim to the Chrysler ban and began the

Grand National season following other pursuits. The combination of Ford domination and the sidelining of some of the sport's biggest names proved poisonous at the turnstiles. Attendance dropped across the circuit and promoters clamored for changes. Mid-season, France announced hemis would be allowed to compete if placed in the heaviest of Chrysler products and, in a move that reeked of desperation, Curtis Turner would be reinstated. Although ineffective in most of his starts, Turner still drew fans and displayed some of his old talent when he won at the newly opened track in Rockingham. With Turner and, at least partially, Chrysler back, the season ended on a high note.[26]

Unfortunately for Bill France, Ford felt slighted by the Chrysler-friendly rules changes and during the winter of 1965–66 announced that it would race its own new engine in 1966. Angered by Ford making this declaration without their prior notification, both NASCAR and USAC immediately banned the new engine, which, in keeping with what had become an all too familiar pattern, led Ford to announce a boycott of the 1966 season. France viewed Ford's boycott as simply childish and refused to negotiate with the company as he had with Chrysler. With Ford drivers competing without either new equipment or factory money, Chrysler regained the manufacturer's edge. Driving a Dodge owned by Cotton Owens, David Pearson racked up 15 victories on his way to the season championship. Although France refused to budge on his Ford ruling, the lack of competition for the Chryslers led him to allow independent drivers of other makes to bend the rules in an effort to make them more competitive. The flexibility of France's rule book reached its pinnacle in an infamous series of events before the August Dixie 400 in Atlanta. Prerace inspectors banned LeeRoy Yarbrough and David Pearson, in Dodges, for minor rules infractions, but passed through cars built by Junior Johnson and Smokey Yunick. Johnson's Ford, dubbed the "Yellow Banana," had been cut and chopped into an aerodynamically sound vehicle that violated numerous NASCAR regulations. The car had been altered so much that simply looking at the vehicle should have led inspectors to ban it. Yunick brought Curtis Turner to the track in a hand-built 7/8ths model of a 1966 Chevy, which was also allowed to race. Chrysler drivers objected, but there was nothing they could do about the inspections. And Ford, shaken by France's resolve, returned to Grand National later in the season without its new 427 OHC engine.[27]

Despite preseason saber rattling by Chrysler, after two years of disputes, 1967 witnessed a Grand National season without significant manufacturer issues. It was also the year Richard Petty earned the nickname "King Richard." His Petty Enterprises Plymouth proved unstoppable for most of the year. When the season ended Petty earned a Grand National record

27 victories, including a remarkable mid-year streak of 10 consecutive. Thirty-year-old Bobby Allison finished a distant fourth in points, but won the second-most number of races (6) and established himself as a driver on the way up. Unlike Petty, who raced for Petty Enterprises his entire career, Allison struggled to find the right team. His constant battles with owners and mechanics eventually led him to simply establish his own team. Originally from Miami, Allison based his team in Hueytown, Alabama, and assembled a formidable array of drivers consisting of relatives and local friends that became known as the "Alabama Gang." From 1967 through the 1970s, he (along with late bloomer Cale Yarborough) stood as Petty's greatest rival on the circuit.[28]

In 1968, the Grand National series witnessed a classic three-way duel for the championship between Pearson, Petty, and Bobby Isaac, but this was not the only important NASCAR title being contended. Bill France reorganized the lower levels of NASCAR once again, bringing in a new series and reworking an old one. The growing popularity of "pony" cars (small muscle cars of the Mustang and Camaro variety) led him to create the Grand Touring series for vehicles of this size. France's decision also stemmed from his desire to undercut the similar (and successful) Trans-Am series of the Sports Car Club of America. In its initial season, Mustangs, Camaros, Cougars, Firebirds, Darts, and Javelins were eligible to compete in Grand Touring. During the inaugural 1968 season, a number of Grand National's biggest names would compete in the series, with the title ultimately going to veteran Dewayne "Tiny" Lund. For the 1970 season, the series became the Grand American (a name France borrowed from the top circuit of the rival United Stock Car Racing Club), but by then the series had devolved into a two-man battle between Lund and Pete Hamilton. With the loss of factory money in 1971, only 11 Grand American events were held. Lund won his third Grand American championship that season, competing mostly against older drivers at the end of their careers such as Buck Baker and Jim Paschal. In 1972, Grand American collapsed after four races. Also in 1968, France converted the old Sportsman Division into a more modern Late Model Sportsman Division, which would be dominated in its early years by Alabama Gang member Red Farmer. In the early 1980s, Late Model Sportsman would be converted into the Busch Grand National Division, the NASCAR equivalent of Major League Baseball's AAA leagues.[29]

The late decade tranquility (however temporary) on the factory front corresponded with another boom in superspeedway construction. While Bill France planned to construct a new track in Alabama, an unexpected northern partner emerged with his own plans for additional tracks. Lawrence LoPatin, a Detroit commercial contractor who had previously helped construct Windsor Speedway, opened his enormous Michigan International Speedway (MIS) with a USAC-sanctioned open-wheel race in October 1968. LoPatin, however, soon fell out with USAC, and Bill France quickly moved to align NASCAR with him. In the fall of 1968, France and LoPatin signed an agreement calling for two Grand National races per year at MIS for the next 10 seasons. Viewing track ownership as a lucrative by-product of his construction operations, LoPatin established American Raceways Incorporated (ARI) as the parent company of his proposed stable of tracks. LoPatin then began construction on Texas International Speedway (opened in 1969) and bought controlling interests in the established tracks at Riverside and Atlanta. He also proposed building Eastern International Speedway near Southhampton, New Jersey, which was scheduled to open in 1970, but was never completed. LoPatin's arrival came at a juncture when Bill France needed allies. The NASCAR chief's actions had alienated the manufacturers, and his plan to transform Grand National into a series competing only on modern tracks slowed as the battles between auto makers affected attendance at existing events. France's strategy ideally involved his personal ownership—through his International Speedway Corporation—of as many of the new tracks as possible, but he did not possess the assets to accomplish this goal. LoPatin's arrival brought with it both a welcome infusion of cash and the ambition to build an empire of racetracks.[30]

France's new track in Alabama propelled the final attempt at a drivers' union. His Alabama International Speedway (always referred to simply as Talladega) represented France's attempt to build a facility even more imposing than Daytona. Despite being within 300 miles of several metropolitan areas, the track itself was located in an obscure, difficult-to-travel-to location. The feasibility of Talladega hinged on new roads to get to the track, which France's political connections made possible. In 1968 (and again in 1972), France served as George Wallace's Florida campaign manager, and their friendship led to the allocation of state funds (through then-governor Lurleen Wallace, George's wife and political proxy) to build roads connecting the track site to highways. As a thank you to her, France put "This Program Dedicated to the late Governor of Alabama—LURLEEN WALLACE" on the cover of the Talladega 500's first program, despite the race occurring a year-and-a-half after her unexpected death. When the track opened in 1969, it was the longest oval on the Grand National circuit—a 2.66 mile behemoth that frightened even hardened superspeedway veterans. Talladega's dimensions invited speeds simply beyond the level of safety available with current equipment. Consequently, the first race there led to the final battle between drivers and Bill France in the war over who controlled NASCAR.[31]

Richard Petty, the face of NASCAR, shocked fans twice in 1969. First, he left Chrysler, the manufacturer synonymous with Petty Enterprises, to drive a Ford. Second, he organized the last drivers' challenge to France. In August 1969, Petty convened a meeting of top Grand National drivers before the Yankee 600 at MIS. Petty and the others believed the financial windfalls of NASCAR did not adequately trickle down to the drivers, nor did they—the men who risked their lives in the races—have enough voice in track design and scheduling. This group then created the Professional Drivers Association (PDA) as a union for all Grand National drivers who shared their concerns. Recognizing the mistakes of Curtis Turner's similar effort, the PDA operated in secrecy until the bulk of Grand National drivers became members. They also avoided affiliating with any existing unions. Before the September Southern 500, the PDA went public with both its existence and demands. Again, cognizant of Turner's mistakes, Petty pointed out the group had no interest in boycotts or strikes; they simply wanted recognition from NASCAR and a discussion of their concerns. France, again operating like a paternalistic mill owner, declared he would not meet the PDA demands and noted that NASCAR already provided a very good living for drivers. If they felt wronged, as "independent contractors," they were free to seek employment elsewhere.[32]

The opening of the new track at Talladega, occurring at the peak of this impasse, tested the resolve of both sides. Talladega, with longer straights and higher banking than Daytona, threatened to push Grand National cars over the 200 miles per hour barrier, well beyond the speed certified by NASCAR's tire manufacturers. PDA drivers requested the Talladega 500 be delayed until additional testing could be completed. France refused to yield to these demands and declared the race would go off as scheduled. In a legendary move, France—nearly 60 and long past his competitive driving days—climbed into a Grand National car and turned laps at 176 miles per hour to prove the track's safety, then cheekily requested a PDA membership card. After tires began shredding at an alarming rate during qualifying, the bulk of the PDA (and Firestone—who then completely abandoned its NASCAR efforts) boycotted the race and left Talladega. France, determined to once again prove his control, held the race with a smattering of Grand National competitors (of the top drivers only Bobby Isaac, Coo Coo Marlin, and Tiny Lund raced), a handful of ARCA regulars, and a large contingent of Grand Touring racers. Little-known Richard Brickhouse tore up his PDA membership card before the race and then scored his first and only Grand National victory. For France, it signaled his victory over the PDA members, who he knew had no choice but to come back to Grand National.[33]

Talladega represented not only France's victory over the drivers, but also a deepening of the connections between NASCAR and subaltern white southerners. Lurleen Wallace may have been the name on the program, but George was the Wallace who became associated with the track. From their initial meetings in 1965, France and Wallace developed a close friendship. France helped support Wallace's electoral bids through both financial contributions and by scheduling appearances for Wallace at NASCAR events. In the early years at Talladega, race fans witnessed Wallace riding around the track in the back of a convertible, delivering prerace speeches, and presenting the trophy to the winner. Wallace, along with other conservatives Curtis LeMay, Tom Adams, and Hayden Burns, also became a VIP guest at other NASCAR events, most notably the Daytona 500. For the working-class white southerners who made up the preponderance of Grand National crowds at the time, Wallace's presence linked stock car racing to their own conservative political beliefs. In an era when defense of segregation became a rallying cry for right-wing southerners, arch-segregationist Wallace emerged as a hero. His prominence at NASCAR events helped reinforce the "good ol' boy" connotations of Grand National for southerners and northerners alike.

As the final nail in PDA's coffin, France added a "Good Faith" clause to Grand National entry forms in the fall of 1969, which called for drivers to make a good faith effort to attend any race for which they registered. For the 1970 season the clause changed to include language that authorized NASCAR to place another driver in a registered car if the original driver could not or would not compete. The new entry form gave France an enormous amount of power, but it deeply angered drivers and, more important, manufacturers. Whether or not France ever planned to actually hire replacement drivers, Detroit balked at the idea that France could control its factory-backed cars. France then parlayed his victory over the drivers into another effort to demonstrate his sovereignty over the manufacturers as well. In August 1970, he announced that Grand National cars on superspeedways would now be equipped with a speed-limiting carburetor restrictor plate. This move stemmed partially from the fear of continued driver unrest, but it also reflected France's concerns that the aerodynamic monstrosities raced by the factories (such as the ungainly Plymouth SuperBird) diverged so sharply from normal passenger vehicles that they hindered fan identification with the Grand National cars. Ford and Chrysler, already reeling from the rising tide of market-share stealing imports, responded by announcing severe reductions in factory support for Grand National. Chrysler declared it would assist only Petty Enterprises in 1971, and Ford completely abandoned NASCAR.[34]

Of those deeply connected to NASCAR, only Lawrence LoPatin publicly criticized France's handling of the PDA. LoPatin made the critical error of believing his position as ARI president made him powerful enough to disagree with France. Before the 1970 season, ABC signed an agreement with NASCAR to televise parts of four races live and five others on tape delay for $1.3 million. A portion of this money was to go to tracks not hosting televised events. An angry France declined to put any ARI races on the televised list and then refused to give LoPatin's tracks any of the ABC money. LoPatin might have survived France's maneuvers under normal circumstances, but forces beyond his control conspired against him. During the 1970 season, all four of the ARI tracks faced weather-related delays that reduced attendance and eliminated all profits. By mid-year LoPatin was unable to put purse money in escrow, as NASCAR required, and he quietly resigned his position at ARI.[35]

At the dawn of the 1970s, Bill France found himself in complete control of an organization well on its way to fulfilling his dream of a series operating solely on modern paved tracks. He had defeated threats by drivers, promoters, and rival organizations. Grand National also received more positive publicity than ever before. Newspapers across the country routinely carried race results, and national television broadcast Grand National events. The pullout of manufacturers, however, brought with it the looming possibility of economic difficulties for drivers, teams, and Bill France. Fortunately for France, the U.S. Congress unwittingly provided NASCAR with a financial savior. Bill France's southern organization was about to begin a fruitful 30-year relationship with the traditional staple crop of the South—tobacco. NASCAR's modern era had begun.

5

TOBACCO AND TELEVISION

In 1971, after his victory at the Dixie 500 in Atlanta, Richard Petty became the first NASCAR driver to win $1 million in his career. That same year Buddy Arrington became the last Grand National driver to be arrested for tripping. The end of moonshine connections and the birth of racing millionaires in the same season perfectly encapsulated the evolution of NASCAR. Over the course of the 1960s, Bill France's plan to shift the sport toward modern facilities and long races moved NASCAR toward the mainstream of advertising, sponsorship, and telecommunications, while still retaining its southern base and appeal among working-class whites. These advances served as the prelude to the birth of NASCAR's modern era. During the 1970s, NASCAR, under the leadership of another member of the France family, became an increasingly important part of America's sporting and television cultures, developed close connections with some of the country's largest corporations, and left the red clay ovals. Before the decade ended, the once marginalized stock car racers became honored guests at the White House.

The 1970s, however, appeared far less rosy for NASCAR when the decade began. A plethora of problems seemed to threaten the progress the organization made during the tumultuous 1960s. American Raceways Incorporated's collapse made Grand National appear to be faltering in support. The Professional Drivers Association (PDA) brought forth the specter of labor unrest. Efforts to use restrictor plates to reduce speeds alienated both drivers and manufacturers. Detroit's auto companies announced the end or dramatic scaling back of their commitments to Grand National. And "Big" Bill France, who virtually built NASCAR, appeared to be slowing down through a combination of age and fatigue. France remained active within the organization, but official control of NASCAR fell to his far less experienced son. All of these issues coalesced into a perfect storm of difficulties that made for a very rough 1971. Petty's seven-figure achievement made for good press, but few other positives emerged during the season.[1]

Much of the difficulties of 1971 stemmed from continued unrest among drivers. Although the PDA no longer posed a serious threat, discontent among individual drivers and teams created unceasing complications for NASCAR officials. Most problems between racers and NASCAR developed out of the sanctioning body's introduction of restrictor plates. Before the 1971 season, NASCAR adopted rules that established plates with varying size openings for different motors. France recognized that the plates could be used as a means of leveling the playing field among NASCAR's various makes and models. In keeping with his long-held views on parity, France believed even competition between different car brands kept fans coming to the tracks. The problem, however, was how to guarantee the rules did not penalize one make or engine more than others. NASCAR changed the plate rules over the course of the season, but never found the perfect combination to please all competitors. These difficulties were compounded by the widely held belief that virtually every team was violating the rules in some way. Anger over the carburetor rules led some teams to abandon parts of the season, a situation that served to magnify the reduction of cars as a result of the factory pullouts. Such dire conditions prompted NASCAR to begin including Grand American cars, whose own series was truly dying, in Grand National races to fill out the fields.[2]

As bad as 1971 became, it would have been an even greater economic disaster if not for the arrival of a financial savior. In 1965, amid growing outcries over health risks, the U.S. Congress passed the Federal Cigarette Labeling and Advertising Act, which required that warnings be placed on all cigarette packages. The perceived ineffectiveness of the 1965 act prompted the passage of an additional piece of legislation in 1970. The Public Health Cigarette Smoking Act established new, more strongly worded warnings and also, as of January 1971, banned all cigarette advertising from media forms supervised by the Federal Communications Commission. This new act left tobacco companies, who invested hundreds of millions of dollars annually in radio and television advertising, scrambling to find news ways to promote their products.

Based in Winston-Salem, North Carolina, the R. J. Reynolds Tobacco Company (RJR) made the momentous decision to approach Junior Johnson about sponsoring his Grand National car. For Johnson, this was a welcome turn of events, as he found himself no longer able to compete once Ford stopped supporting his team, but he also recognized that RJR could do far more than just sponsor one team. In a remarkably altruistic act, Johnson put RJR officials in contact with Bill France, who then negotiated with them to develop a dramatic new form of motor sports advertising. Where previous sponsors put their name on a car or race, RJR would link its name to all the biggest races in the Grand National series, along with becoming the name sponsor of the new Winston 500, a $165,000 event at Talladega. Unlike contingency money offered by previous sponsors in return for a driver winning while using the company's product (for example, Bell helmets) or having the sponsor's name stickered on his car, the RJR money would be available to all drivers. RJR established a $100,000 pool to be paid to drivers leading the points standings at various intervals of the season, with half the money going to the top 20 drivers at the conclusion of the year. Points for the new Winston Cup, however, accumulated only as the result of success in races over 250 miles. The tobacco company felt it gained nothing in associating its brand with short and dirt track races, and it refused to affiliate with those events.[3]

RJR money helped keep teams going in 1971, but it also spelled the death knell of the dirt tracks. France's plan to convert Grand National to an all-paved series had already drastically reduced the number of both short and dirt races, and RJR's determination not to be involved with those types of races sped up France's strategy. In 1972, France agreed to make the entire Grand National circuit the Winston Cup. Before enrolling as the title sponsor of stock car racing, however, RJR demanded changes to the series. First, it required a dramatic reduction in the number of Grand National races. Instead of the 50 or so events common in Grand National since the 1950s, RJR requested only one race per week, which allowed each race to become more of an "event." This reduction pushed NASCAR to shuffle some of the dates traditionally associated with specific tracks and to simply abandon other tracks. RJR did not desire to be associated with the primitive dirt tracks, and France obliged by ending Grand National connections with the red clay. After the September 1970 event at State Fairgrounds Speedway in Raleigh, Grand National cars never again competed on dirt. For 1972, NASCAR purged all tracks shorter than 0.5 miles in length and all races of less than 100 miles. Perennial Grand National venues such as Hickory, Kingsport, and South Boston found themselves abandoned by NASCAR as RJR shepherded stock car racing into its modern era. For its efforts in modernizing stock car racing, NASCAR presented RJR with the NASCAR Award of Excellence for 1972. RJR undertook other projects to change the operation of stock car racing as well. Those tracks that managed to survive the purge found themselves compelled to paint their retaining walls red—and white—the Winston colors. Tobacco money also went to some tracks to modernize their facilities, especially garage areas and spectator bathrooms. Race queens dated back to the origins of motor sports, but RJR developed a new series queen to handle a variety of public relations tasks and to be in victory lane after the races. In 1971, Marilyn Chilton of North Carolina became the first Miss Winston Cup. RJR also commissioned Petty Enterprises to build "Winston Number One," an exact replica of a Grand National car that toured car dealerships and shopping malls throughout the Southeast. "Winston Number One" inaugurated the show car era of NASCAR. In the coming years, replica show cars, spackled with sponsors' names, would become an integral aspect of NASCAR's advertising strategy.[4]

RJR's arrival meant that tobacco joined George Wallace as part of NASCAR's embrace of embattled southern symbols. Cigarettes and segregation, however, represented only part of NASCAR's conservative climate. Rebel flags could be found both waving above the campers that filled track infields and painted on the walls at Darlington. One reporter noted in 1970 that Bill France "could help the South rise again" thanks to the Confederate imagery found at NASCAR tracks. And at a time when other professional sports desperately tried to avoid becoming involved in the political imbroglios that wracked the country, NASCAR stood firm in its promotion of traditions that endeared stock car racing to its blue collar fans. In 1971, with public opinion of the military at an all-time low, France changed the name of the Firecracker 400 to Medal of Honor Firecracker 400. France made this move in the midst of NASCAR's financial malaise, confident that stock car fans overwhelmingly supported the Armed Forces. Later that same year Neil "Soapy" Castles painted "Free Lt. Calley" on the rear quarter-panel of his Grand National car to show his support for the officer convicted in connection with the My Lai Massacre. Although general public opinion demonized William Calley, Castles faced no criticism on the Grand National circuit.[5]

Along with defense of the military, NASCAR also moved to more explicitly exhibit the Christian component of the organization. "Brother" Bill Frazier, who began offering race day religious services out of his trailer-mounted chapel in the 1960s, became the official "chaplain of stock car racing" in 1972. Along with gaining NASCAR's stamp of approval, tracks began piping Frazier's sermons through their public address systems so that the entire crowd, not just the drivers assembled around him, could hear his Baptist services. As events of the early 1970s made clear, NASCAR's conservative demographics existed long before 21st century media discovery of "NASCAR dads." RJR clearly understood these connections as well. At roughly the same time it became Grand National's featured sponsor, the company changed its longstanding Winston advertising campaign. Winston Cup would be sponsored not by the cigarette that "tastes good, like a cigarette should," but by the brand that offered "Down Home Taste." The combined effort by France and RJR to promote

NASCAR as wholesome, patriotic, and conservative paid huge dividends later in the decade as the nation continued to drift rightward.[6]

As part of the transition from pioneer to modern era, "Big" Bill France stepped down as president of NASCAR. Just before the 1972 season began, he announced he was abdicating in favor of his son "Little" Bill France. The younger France had previously served as NASCAR vice-president for six years before the appointment. Despite no longer serving as president of NASCAR, "Big" Bill stayed on as an advisor for many years and remained president of International Speedway Corporation (ISC). The transfer of power occurred without incident, thanks in part to the elder France's purchase of the stock owned by Louis Ossinsky, who died in 1971. With no other shareholders involved in NASCAR, the France family's control became absolute. Politically, the retirement of "Big" Bill did little to alter the company, but his son proved far more intent on exploiting NASCAR's television possibilities over the course of the next decade.* A third generation is now in charge of NASCAR, maintaining its status as the only major sports organization that is a family business. Under "Little" Bill the France empire expanded to include ISC ownership of several additional tracks, the Motor Racing Network (which handles NASCAR's radio broadcasts), and Americrown (which provides catering services at NASCAR tracks).[7]

The first full Winston Cup season of 1972 also marked the beginning of one of the most successful driver-team relationships of the 1970s. In 1972, David Pearson began driving for the Wood Brothers team, winning 6 of his 14 starts. He split time with United States Auto Club (USAC) regular A. J. Foyt that year, then became the Wood Brothers' sole driver until 1979. Together they won 43 races over the course of the decade. In 1976, Pearson and the Woods won NASCAR's "Triple Crown" of the Daytona 500, World 600, and Southern 500. The "Silver Fox" won at Daytona by nursing his crumpled car across the finish line at less than 30 miles per hour after tangling with Petty on the last lap of what is sometimes presented as the greatest race in NASCAR history. Pearson was one of a long line of premier drivers hired by the brothers, who were also credited with developing the modern pit stop. The roster of drivers in their famous number 21 included Curtis Turner, Junior Johnson, Joe Weatherly, Speedy Thompson, Marvin Panch, Fred Lorenzen, Dan Gurney, and Cale Yarborough. With a younger generation now in charge, the Wood Brothers team continues to field a car in NASCAR's top division, which they have done continuously since 1950.

---

*Unless specifically noted otherwise, all subsequent reference to Bill France relate to "Little" Bill.

Pearson's "Triple Crown" season also marked the return of women to NASCAR's top series. In 1976, open-wheel veteran Janet Guthrie made five Winston Cup starts driving the Kelly Girl car for owner Lynda Ferreri. Guthrie went on to make 33 Cup starts over four seasons. In 1977, she became the first woman to qualify for both the Indianapolis 500 and Daytona 500. That same season she was joined by two European road racers (Christine Beckers and Lella Lombardi) in the Firecracker 400, the first time three women had started a top-tier NASCAR event since the early 1950s. Guthrie noted that she faced a "great deal of hostility initially" and, if anything, dealt with adversities not confronted by the female NASCAR drivers of the 1950s. Women like Sara Christian and Ethel Flock Mobley had both familial connections to stock car racing and ties to the world of tripping, which eased their entry into the sport. Louise Smith, as a southerner herself, clearly understood the milieu of southern stock and presented herself as a hard-bitten competitor who was, in many respects, just one of the guys.[8]

Guthrie and the women who tried to break into NASCAR in the 1970s, however, posed a more serious threat to the masculine world of Winston Cup. Guthrie hoped to build a career in stock car racing, which threatened the incomes of veteran drivers. Brought in by Bill France for publicity, the European drivers did not even have Guthrie's limited experience in Winston Cup. Although they drove quality machines tuned by Junie Donleavy, drivers feared accidents might arise from their mistakes on the big oval in Daytona. Confronted with harbingers of an assault on the traditionally male preserve of stock car racing, some drivers lashed out. David Pearson, fearful of Title IX spreading to the racetrack, proclaimed that Guthrie "should be home making babies." Southern press outlets proved equally condescending. One 1977 article headlined a Guthrie story with "dating is no problem because she is a racer." Guthrie also ran afoul of the rule at some Winston Cup tracks that disallowed women from entering the garage area, effectively banning her from getting in her own car unless NASCAR made special dispensations. Allowing Guthrie in the pits, however, did not end all resistance from those in control of stock car racing. She repeatedly encountered officials who engaged in petty slights to undermine her efforts on the track. Despite the adversities, Guthrie became the first woman ever to lead a lap in Winston Cup. She gave up stock car racing in 1980.[9]

The tumult created by the arrival of Janet Guthrie in Winston Cup paled in comparison, however, to other issues that threatened to halt NASCAR's growth. NASCAR, as with all other American motor sports of the time, found itself struggling to deal with the energy crisis of the mid-1970s. Gasoline shortages forced NASCAR to reconcile its continued racing of gas-guzzling Detroit sedans at a time when Americans faced rationing of a kind not seen since World War II. Also, NASCAR officials of the time proved simply inadequate in halting the almost ubiquitous cheating. The widespread knowledge of this cheating angered the few rule-abiding teams (and those who could not cheat as well as the better financed operations) to the point of contemplating departure from Winston Cup. For Bill France, the first few years on the job proved exceptionally difficult.

In response to the Yom Kippur War, the Organization of Petroleum Exporting Countries (OPEC) announced an oil embargo of the West in October 1973, which sent shockwaves through an American economy already crippled by stagflation. President Richard Nixon, who adopted oil policies earlier in the year that partly kindled the energy crisis, responded by asking all Americans to conserve energy, including a request that all gas stations close on Sundays. To formulate additional policies, Nixon issued an executive order that created the Federal Energy Office (FEO) in December. The FEO then encouraged all Americans to reduce their energy consumption, especially energy used for leisure pursuits. For motor sports, the effects of the oil shock became cataclysmic. The Stock Car Club of America (SCCA) canceled both the Can-Am and Trans-Am series for 1974. Distance races such as the 12 Hours of Sebring and 24 Hours of Daytona also fell by the board, and USAC found itself short of cars for the Champ Trail. Even some tracks closed, such as the already financially troubled Texas International Speedway. The sanctioning bodies, in a spirit of cooperation rarely seen, hastily organized the National Motorsports Committee to lobby on auto racing's behalf in Washington. With "Big" Bill France acting as its energy point man, NASCAR showed its commitment to conservation by reducing the length of all races by 10 percent and by reducing practice and qualifying periods. These measures prevented direct governmental sanctions on stock car racing, but also contributed to a disastrous season.[10]

After Christmas 1973, economists noted a sharp downturn in driving for social or recreational activities, including attending races. Already forced to conserve fuel, stock car fans balked at making expensive trips to a track only to see a shortened event. As well, with Winston Cup races primarily occurring on Sundays, impulse attendance became nonexistent as potential spectators could not buy gas on that day to get to the tracks. Compounding the difficulties in attracting fans was Winston Cup's new points system, which allocated points based on purse sizes. As an upshot of this system, the rich Daytona 500, only the second race of the season, basically decided the championship. NASCAR officials soon recognized that effectively ending the battle for the championship in February hurt fan interest, but a revision of the point system could not be undertaken until the season officially ended.[11]

NASCAR weathered the energy storm of 1974, but financial woes continued to plague many teams. Part of the difficulty stemmed from the organization's confused points system. Despite a 1975 revision to make the system more equitable, the wealth disparity among teams continued to pose challenges. The withdrawal of the factories actually made success more difficult to attain for the former independents. With manufacturers involved in Grand National, smaller teams occasionally found themselves the beneficiaries of "trickle down" parts and could also purchase used equipment from factory drivers. Without the factories, larger teams had fewer parts to spare or sell, and all new equipment obtained by small teams had to actually be purchased. NASCAR attempted to obviate the horsepower advantage of well-funded teams through the restrictor plates, but every mandated engine change meant all teams had to purchase new equipment, which served only to further undermine the status of small teams. The ever-shifting carburetion regulations stabilized by 1976 as smaller engines became the norm in Winston Cup, but small teams still found themselves at a disadvantage.

Unrest sparked rumors of a rival stock car racing organization in early 1976, with Charlotte Motor Speedway's Richard Howard at the center of the controversy. NASCAR responded by creating new incentive programs to keep drivers loyal. Smaller teams became eligible for "Plan B" money to be paid out to high finishers at each track. For the more prominent drivers, whom NASCAR was far more concerned about losing, it created the new "Winners' Circle" fund. Money from this fund went to the top eight drivers in return for pledges to compete in all Winston Cup events. This kept drivers tied to NASCAR, thereby reducing the influence of rogue promoters and keeping track owners loyal, as NASCAR could now guarantee that the biggest names would show up for its events without having to resort to the old gray area practice of paying "deal money" to drivers.[12]

Financial considerations such as "Winners' Circle" and "Plan B" hinged on success on the track, which encouraged illegal efforts by almost every team. Efforts to establish parity, through either restrictor plates or homogenization of engines, also contributed to rampant cheating during the mid-1970s. Richard Petty sardonically noted that the plates led to "more cheating than usual." As teams lost their financially driven horsepower edge, they had to break the rules to maintain their advantage. Although cheating always represented one aspect of succeeding in stock car racing (witness Glenn Dunnaway in the first strictly stock race), illegal practices reached a fevered pitch during the early years of "Little" Bill's presidency. Although financial issues related to survival in the series loomed large in this development, a perception that the younger France did not possess the iron will of his father may have also contributed to the increase in cheating. Drivers quickly discovered that illegal behavior would still not be tolerated, but the threat of punishment did little to deter drivers and owners who believed all their competitors bent the rules. For those who closely followed the series, the discovery of expandable gas tanks on the cars of several top teams during qualifying at Talladega in 1977 was no surprise. Conditions became so bad that later that season prominent team owner Roger Penske abandoned his Winston Cup efforts, citing the "no cheating" provisions of his contracts with sponsors as precluding him from being able to field a competitive car. Although tightening of the inspection process curtailed the worst abuses by the early 1980s, cheating continues to be viewed as a natural part of Winston Cup.[13]

One of the drivers caught with an illegal fuel cell at Talladega was Cale Yarborough, a former semi-pro football player from South Carolina. Although he began running Grand National in 1957, Yarborough had little success until he began driving a limited schedule for the Wood Brothers in the late 1960s. After the factories left NASCAR, Yarborough competed primarily in USAC Champ cars for a few seasons, then returned to Winston Cup full time in 1973. In mid-1974, Junior Johnson purchased the Richard Howard Chevrolet that Yarborough drove and the team became increasingly competitive. Beginning in 1976, Yarborough won three consecutive national championships driving for the crafty Johnson (who noted, "the name of the game is cheat-and-eat"). Yarborough had two more successful points seasons before adopting a more limited racing schedule in 1981. In February 1979, as the defending champion, Yarborough would participate in one of the most infamous events in NASCAR history, when he engaged in a fistfight with Bobby and Donnie Allison on the backstretch at Daytona. Seen live by a national television audience, their brawl generated enormous publicity for stock car racing.[14]

During Yarborough's championship seasons, Holly Farms became his primary sponsor, a clear reflection of the changing nature of NASCAR during the 1970s. The entrance of RJR ushered in a dramatic increase in the range of companies willing to become involved with NASCAR. The era of car dealers, garages, and local restaurants serving as chief sponsors waned as RJR introduced new advertising techniques. Reynolds rewarded its loyal customers (grocery, gas station, and convenience store chains) by feting them at Winston Cup events, which began a domino effect in which those firms brought representatives from their customer companies to the races as well. Recognizing the masses of potential consumers in the crowds (in 1976, NASCAR became the most attended motor sports series in the world), these companies also began sponsoring teams. The old connections between NASCAR and automotives did not end (STP made headlines in 1972 by forging a relationship with Petty Enterprises), but beer companies, soft drink manufacturers, and restaurant chains became increasingly involved. RJR steadily escalated the point fund money over the decade; Busch Beer began paying pole winners in 1978. National sponsors brought much-needed dollars to many teams, but in many ways this served only to replicate the old factory backing system. Winston money went to winners and the biggest companies wanted to sponsor only successful drivers, so the small teams (still often referred to as "independents") once again found themselves at a disadvantage. NASCAR's "Plan B" arose in the midst of a situation in which frontrunners used money from Coca-Cola and Purolator, while back-markers made do with sponsorship from The Excuse Lounge and Scotty's Fashions.[15]

For small teams to make enough money to continue competing, they needed revenue streams outside of direct sponsorship. Increased purses helped to an extent, but they tended to perpetuate disparities, as bigger, more successful teams earned more money. A new, equitable means of accumulating capital, however, developed during the 1970s. The decade witnessed the birth of a relationship between NASCAR and television, a union that would catapult Winston Cup into the circle of elite American sports during the 1980s. Still overwhelmingly southeastern in orientation, NASCAR would not have been attractive to some prominent companies without television contracts, which gave Winston Cup (and its sponsors) a national audience. Buffeted by a series of controversies and travails during his first decade in charge of NASCAR, "Little" Bill France still managed to ensure the success of Winston Cup through his efforts with stock car racing's twin benefactors—national sponsors and television.

Under NASCAR's revenue distribution system, a portion of the money collected through television broadcast rights went to both the track and all the drivers who competed in the televised event. A small fund was also set aside to be paid to those tracks without televised races. Such a system helped keep the tracks solvent and also assisted the independents. Each driver received an equal share of the television money, which allowed small teams to gain much-needed funds without losing additional ground to the premier outfits. The influx of television and sponsorship money led to a dramatic jump in the amount of money available to drivers. For example, Richard Petty raced from 1958 until 1971 and become the first driver with $1 million in career earnings. In 1975, only four years after becoming NASCAR's first millionaire, he became the first driver to reach $2 million. Even crew members, typically the last people involved with a race team to see any money, benefited from the introduction of wealthy financial benefactors. When coal tycoon Harry Ranier decided to become involved in Winston Cup as a "hobby" in 1977, he lured Herb Nab away from Junior Johnson's team with a crew chief package that included a base salary of $50,000 per year, an amount that would have put Nab on the drivers' yearend leader board during the 1960s.[16]

Television created new economic opportunities, but it also brought with it new responsibilities for drivers. Before the rise of network television coverage in the late 1970s, most drivers interacted only with reporters and columnists affiliated with the print media. The comments of drivers, therefore, went to the fans only after being tidied up by writers and editors, and rancorous tones registered only if those involved with the newspaper or magazine noted the driver's anger. Drivers who made ill-advised comments in the heat of the moment could also track down a reporter later and redo an interview to avoid seeing embarrassing statements in print. Although feuds occasionally bled into print, the system worked to effectively mute both unrest and driver personalities. By skillfully selecting which exact quotes to use, a print journalist could level the playing field between articulate drivers and mumbling ones who never went to high school. In a newspaper, the gap between a polished Fred Lorenzen and a poorly educated Bobby Isaac became much narrower than in reality.

Television, however, changed all of this. Interviews broadcast live or taped for later showing meant that driver comments could not be changed when they cooled down. Personalities also became much more vivid to those outside of the garage areas. In the new television era, drivers needed to be able to communicate effectively without the later assistance of the writers; they had to get it right the first time. For many of the older drivers, this represented a difficult transition. Their success had hinged on the ability to drive and adjust a race car; media relations did not factor into the equation of NASCAR success. Television forced these men to adapt not simply because the networks expected them to coherently respond to questions, but because sponsors expected them to do so as well. An eloquent driver received more air time; therefore his sponsor received more publicity. Well-spoken (and preferably attractive) drivers became an increasingly important commodity as television developed closer links to Winston Cup.

Among the crop of young drivers coming up in the mid-1970s, no racer better reflected the fame-making capabilities of television than Darrell Waltrip. Originally from Kentucky, but based in the Nashville area, Waltrip first appeared in Winston Cup driving his own car in 1972. Waltrip combined the roles of driver and self-publicist in ways not previously seen in NASCAR. He was Ed Otto with a lead foot—a persona tailor-made for stock's burgeoning television era. Characteristically, during the 1973 season he mouthed-off to NASCAR officials, who responded by awarding Rookie of the Year honors to a lesser driver. In 1975, Waltrip shockingly won two races with his own equipment, which led to his hiring by the prominent DiGard team mid-year. Save for a shortened 1990 campaign, Waltrip would finish in the top 10 in points every year from then until 1992, winning three national championships in the process.

Success on the track and his aversion to silence off it led to Waltrip becoming sponsored by Gatorade in 1976, a fruitful relationship that continued until the 1980s. He quickly earned the nickname "Jaws" for his ability to swallow up both opponents and air time. "Big" Bill France appreciated Waltrip's ability, but also wished he would "shut his mouth and drive." Waltrip's 1979 postrace comment "I've got to thank God, Gatorade, and Goodyear for the way we ran today" did not sit well with the old guard of NASCAR, but it epitomized where the sport was heading. Not surprisingly, his flamboyant behavior eventually polarized Winston Cup fans. One group came to love him as a brash winner, and the other hated Waltrip as a loud-mouth who won too much. Unwilling to recognize the role of his own actions in creating this rift, Waltrip noted simply that "everybody loves—or hates—a winner."[17]

Although television efforts to give other drivers a personality might sometimes appear forced, Waltrip needed no assistance in alienating a segment of NASCAR nation. His divisiveness reflected an important aspect of television's ability to give drivers character—the medium could create villains. This sort of color helped create ratings in a sport without home teams for television viewers to watch and support. NASCAR needed the equivalent of the despised New York Yankees coming to town to boost viewership, and a driver like Waltrip could play this role for them. By the early 1980s, signs bearing the message "anyone but Waltrip" began appearing at Winston Cup events. Akin to seeing the "heel" get his comeuppance from the fan favorite in a professional wresting match, viewers at home cheered for Waltrip's defeat. He emerged as the "man stock car fans love to hate" at a juncture when increased television exposure facilitated such visceral responses from NASCAR followers. By the 1980s, NASCAR had reached a status already achieved by professional football and baseball; more fans watched its events on television than in person. Brand loyalty, whether to makes of car or primary sponsors on those vehicles, created only so much affinity among fans; driver personalities—beamed directly into homes—helped propel Winston Cup to new heights.[18]

During the 1970s, television not only helped to keep teams on the Winston Cup circuit and to establish driver personas, it also helped take a still primarily regional sport national. The pronounced southern declension of stock car racing visible during the 1980s had its roots in the increased national visibility afforded by television in the previous decade. As racing reporter Bob Myers noted in 1988, "the medium [television], perhaps more than anything else, is responsible for the explosive growth and popularity of the sport . . . [and] will expand and enhance the spread of stock car racing nationally." During the 1970s, the networks evinced an ever-expanding interest in NASCAR as the sport of stock car racing repeatedly demonstrated its ability to attract viewers. Stock's growing popularity can be easily deduced from both the growing number of Winston Cup events televised and the escalating amounts networks agreed to pay for the rights to broadcast races. In the bottom–line-driven world of network television, increased outlays of both air time and money are acceptable only if supported by ratings, and NASCAR programming consistently attracted viewers.[19]

NASCAR's relationship with network television began in 1960, when CBS aired short segments from Daytona's Speed Week, with Grand National highlights airing on the network's *CBS Sports Spectacular* program in the following years. In 1961, ABC followed suit with similar highlight coverage on *Wide World of Sports*. Realizing the potential of stock, ABC then made its 1970 deal with "Big" Bill for multiple races each season. For NASCAR, the ABC contract represented the birth of real network coverage of Grand National, as it mixed live "look-ins" with highlights and tape-delayed segments. The next year ABC broke new ground with the first live flag-to-flag coverage of a Grand National event, broadcasting the entire Greenville 200 during *Wide World of Sports*. Also in 1971, TelePrompTer offered a multicamera live presentation of the Daytona 500 to closed-circuit outlets (previously they had provided a lower quality telecast of the race). Despite the broadcast's success, the Greenville 200 experiment would not be replicated until the 1979 Daytona 500. As a relatively short event, the Greenville race could be completed within the confines of *Wide World of Sports'* 90-minute time slot, but most Grand National races lasted far longer. The networks balked at devoting the four to five hours necessary to show a typical Grand National event. For NASCAR this reluctance posed a serious dilemma, as the networks could be convinced to show live flag-to-flag coverage, but only of shorter events, at exactly the same time as RJR offered substantial funding, but only with the abandonment of the shorter events. RJR's bigger check eventually won out, and NASCAR parsed the short tracks from the schedule while continuing to work with ABC on non-flag-to-flag coverage.[20]

Winston Cup's presence on television entered a new era in 1975 when races began appearing on two networks. ABC, which had continued to show parts of races for the first half of the decade, contracted for exclusive rights to the Daytona 500 for the next three years. CBS also entered the fray that year by signing its own three year contract, in this case for five races per year. While ABC retained rights to the showcase Daytona 500, CBS's contract gave it the prestigious Winston 500 and World 600. The subsequent expiration of those two contracts led to a pivotal event in the growth of Winston Cup. CBS managed to wrestle the Daytona 500 away from ABC and then announced it would broadcast live flag-to-flag coverage of the entire 1979 event. Because of television's role (and a remarkably dramatic finish), the 1979 Daytona 500 is sometimes promoted as the greatest race in NASCAR history. It is also often credited as establishing stock car racing as a national sport. A host of other factors actually contributed to NASCAR's rise, but the 1979 500 represented an inescapably signal event in stock car racing history.[21]

A stunning series of events, all beyond CBS's control, coalesced on the day of the 1979 Daytona 500 to generate an opportunity for television to showcase Winston Cup at its finest. To its credit, CBS did make every attempt possible to create a top of the line sports broadcast. It brought to Daytona the same production crew that worked the 1979 Super Bowl, hired the best announcers it could find, and covered the track with 19 cameras (including one inside Benny Parsons's Oldsmobile); its efforts won an Emmy for the broadcast. The race itself, especially the finish, was filled with high drama magnified for television viewers by the first-class production. On the last lap of the race, leaders Donnie Allison and Cale Yarborough tangled on the backstretch, crashed into the third turn retaining wall, then slid into the infield unable to continue. Their wreck allowed a trailing pack of three cars to zoom by, with Richard Petty beating Darrell Waltrip to the finish line by a scant one car length. The finish offered a perfect coda to the human interest story pushed by CBS throughout the telecast—the aging star Petty desperately needed a victory and, therefore, violated his doctor's orders to compete at Daytona a scant three months after having half his stomach removed. Even better for CBS, the cool-down lap after the checkered flag saw Bobby Allison stop his car where his brother and Yarborough wrecked to check on Donnie, only to be accosted by the South Carolina driver. Yarborough believed Donnie Allison's blocking actions on the last lap represented a violation of gentlemanly honor, which led him to become involved in a short two-on-one brawl with the Allison brothers. CBS cameras caught the entire fracas live.[22]

By itself, the race's conclusion marked the race as a NASCAR classic, but the role of television made the 1979 Daytona 500 one of Winston Cup's most important races. The announcement of live flag-to-flag coverage generated a great deal of prerace publicity, and, for NASCAR fans unable to attend, this alone made the race special. The real significance of the race, however, was that a large audience of previously non-NASCAR fans watched the broadcast. A massive storm blanketed much of the East Coast that day, which kept many sports fans, who might have otherwise attended live events, trapped at home to watch television. Also as a result of a weather-induced late start, the race ran a bit long and therefore bled into the time slot of CBS's next program. Sports fans tuning in to see the beginning of the Seattle-Washington NBA game found themselves watching the dramatic events of the Daytona 500's finish. Although the "snow storm" viewers typically receive the most attention from those who view the 500 as an important step in building the NASCAR fan base, the "NBA" viewers were perhaps even more important. Overall, the race earned a 10.5 rating (roughly 16,000,000 viewers), but during the last 30 minutes of the broadcast (the part of the race occurring in the NBA time slot), the rating jumped to an astonishing 13.5. Those who witnessed the race while snowed in either had at least a passing preexisting interest in NASCAR or found themselves significantly intrigued by the heavy promotion of a pioneering live race broadcast to watch the broadcast. Those who tuned in to watch the NBA, however, were sports fans that cared nothing for motor sports (or, at least, the stock car form of the sport). NASCAR never would have reached this group had not a fantastically dramatic finish occurred at a point in which the NBA was supposed to be on CBS. Conversion of new fans fueled Winston Cup's growth during the 1980s, and the 1979 Daytona 500 coverage on CBS helped expose millions of previously nonstock sports fans to NASCAR.[23]

The success of the 1979 Daytona 500 represented the culmination of a decade of growth that saw the entry of national sponsors and network television into Winston Cup. Although outside factors helped push both sponsors and television toward NASCAR, actions by the France family served as the primary conduit of these groups to Winston Cup. Increasing both money and media coverage was a perennial goal of NASCAR's leadership, and much of what developed during the 1970s should be credited to the efforts of those in charge of the organization. NASCAR's ability to attract an audience of 16 million viewers, however, also reflected ongoing social and cultural events outside the sanctioning body. Over the course of the decade, NASCAR, as a southern-linked sport, benefited greatly from changing public perceptions of the South and the related growth of interest in southern cultural forms. Within the world of motor sports, NASCAR's popularity received a significant boost from the implosion of USAC.

USAC's collapse benefited NASCAR in two ways. First, it ceased to pose, however minor, a threat to NASCAR's control of stock car racing in the United States. And second, it allowed NASCAR to become the dominant motor sports sanctioning body in general. The tide of auto racing made a permanent turn in 1976, when NASCAR became the most attended racing organization in the world. The cold reality of the numbers, however, merely buttressed what most observers recognized several years earlier, that stock car racing had passed open-wheel to become the country's preferred form of motor sports. The USAC organization managed to muster up little defense against this rising tide of NASCAR stock car racing. Its own stock series went from being a viable alternative to NASCAR in the mid-1950s to decaying to the point of irrelevance in the 1970s. As the USAC stocks staggered toward oblivion, the series began reducing the number of annual events, which had always been fewer in number than Grand National. Typically, USAC sanctioned around 20 stock races per season, but, as NASCAR waxed in the 1970s, the total waned to 15 in 1975. The number of events then dropped almost annually before sinking to single digits in the early 1980s. USAC finally pulled the plug on the moribund stock series in 1984. The final season consisted of only two races.

By always viewing stock as secondary to the more important Champ cars, USAC left its stock series defenseless against the growing Daytona organization. As the tentacles of NASCAR stretched across the country, the USAC stock series found itself squeezed into a small territory in the Midwest, which made USAC claims to operating a national series laughable. The USAC stock series also suffered as a result of the splintering of the organization itself. In 1977, USAC founder Tony Hulman died. The next year, most of the organization's other top officials perished in a plane crash, which left USAC effectively leaderless. A power struggle subsequently ensued between surviving USAC officials and the owners of the most prominent Champ teams, who organized as Championship Auto Racing Teams (CART). Tellingly, the battle between USAC and CART was over the future direction of open-wheel racing—stocks did not matter. A complete fracturing of open-wheel racing resulted from this fight, with both USAC and CART offering competing open-wheel organizations. Bitterly divided, the two small open-wheel organizations simply could not compete with a large, unified stock car group. The open-wheelers then assisted NASCAR in maintaining its dominant position by remaining separated into two groups into the 21st century.[24]

USAC's overall decline versus NASCAR during the 1970s also partly reflected the product on the track. Finances played a key role in the departure of CART, but the two factions within open-wheel also sparred over venues. CART supported the notion of shifting increasing numbers of Champ car events to road courses to give the series more of a Formula 1 feel, but those who remained loyal to USAC stressed oval track racing.

CART recognized something that the USAC leadership, who primarily came from oval-track sprint car backgrounds, failed to either admit or recognize—stock cars put on a better show than Champ cars on ovals. Champ cars might have represented the highest level of racing engineering in the United States, but technology under the hood could not compete with the exciting banging and bumping of stock cars. The wild finish of the Daytona 500, with Yarborough and Allison trading paint until finally wrecking each other, simply could not happen with fragile Champ cars. Contact between cars was an integral part of stock car racing—at some short tracks it was the only way to pass. In Champ cars, contact meant a call for the wrecker. To the detriment of the organization, however, USAC remained doggedly connected to oval track racing during the 1970s. From 1971 to 1976, all Champ car races occurred on ovals. With Winston Cup events now televised, racing fans could compare the two forms of oval track racing side-by-side—and the majority chose to support stock cars.

Champ cars also fell victim to the general economic issues facing all American motor sports during the 1970s. As the most expensive form of racing, Champ car teams required a continuous infusion of money to remain competitive, but they found themselves confronted with an economic slowdown that made obtaining those funds increasingly difficult. During the 1960s, 80 or more drivers started at least one race on the Championship Trail, but that number shrank to around 50 in the difficult climate of the 1970s. Many drivers left the circuit (and many who hung on were not truly competitive) because they simply could not find enough sponsorship to field a first-class team. Champ car drivers found themselves confronted with a cruel irony. The quest to make their cars as fast as possible led to the adoption of ground-hugging aerodynamic vehicles that represented the pinnacle of American racing technology, but their tiny outer shells left little room for sponsorship. Making the cars faster cost money, but by making them faster they reduced their ability to attract funds. Winston Cup cars, on the other hand, served as virtual moving billboards with vast expanses of flat sheet metal to lard with sponsors. For a bottom line-driven company, sponsorship of the series with the most spectators and the best on-car advertising possibilities proved irresistible. During the early years of NASCAR, Champ car drivers lampooned Grand National vehicles as "taxi cabs" on a track, but by the 1970s, those same Detroit behemoths overshadowed the smaller Champ cars in every way possible.

The decline of USAC and open-wheel racing occurred within a national climate already drifting toward stock car racing. During the 1970s, NASCAR both benefited from and contributed to the rising national importance of "southern" cultural forms. Stock car racing, country music, Burt Reynolds, and southern cooking all became celebrated and successful as part of the transition in general attitudes toward the South. The destruction of legal segregation, the emergence of a two-party system in the region, and vast economic gains brought on by industrialization made the South more attractive to nonsoutherners than at any point since the Civil War. Southern successes brought about an in-migration that boosted income levels, suburbanization, and growing national political power. Reflecting the area's new political strength, in 1976 Jimmy Carter became the first southern resident elected to the presidency since Zachary Taylor. Consequently, the South found itself not only increasingly integrated with the rest of the nation, but also part of the political, economic, and cultural mainstream. This was a convergence process that did not necessarily please all southerners. As John Edgerton wistfully noted in his 1974 book *The Americanization of Dixie: The Southernization of America,* "for good and ill, it [the South] resembled the rest of America more and more with each passing year." Symbolic of this erosion of regional separations, the backward "South" became the modern "Sunbelt."[25]

The southernization of America helped make stock car racing a truly national sport. Both southern and politically conservative, NASCAR resonated with a national mood that increasingly embraced "country" cultural forms and disillusionment with liberalism. Stock car racing, in effect, became national because it was regional. A similar transformation can be discerned in country music during the 1970s. Similar to NASCAR, in that it was wedded to tradition, the South, and a conservative political ideology, country music prospered during the decade because it attracted increasing numbers of noncountry, nonsouthern listeners. As Thomas Sugrue and John Skrentny noted, "ethnicity in the 1970s was, to a great extent, performative." Outside the South a phenomenon sometimes dubbed "Redneck Chic" brought country music, pickup trucks, and stock car racing to suburbia. Geographer Richard Pillsbury, the first academic to seriously study stock car racing, sadly proclaimed that "stock car racing is losing its Southern regional identity with the onslaught of national attention" in 1974, but his fears proved only half-correct. NASCAR did lose some of its southern identity over the course of the decade, but going national allowed the sport to survive and prosper. This national success stemmed partly from television exposure, partly from exciting racing, and partly from stock car racing being southern at a time when that regional affiliation became a positive. Charlotte Motor Speedway executive Howard "Humpy" Wheeler, one of NASCAR's most astute observers, accurately posited that NASCAR drivers served as the perfect heroes for a rightward-drifting country because the racers "love mother, kids, good lookin' women, baloney sandwiches, and America." Contrary to Pillsbury's concerns (and impossible for him to have predicted), stock car racing retained vestiges of its roots because the nonsoutherners who became fans in the 1970s wanted it to remain southern.[26]

NASCAR connected to a burgeoning interest in the South not just as an overwhelmingly southern sport but also because it was part of an interconnected world of southern cultural forms. Burt Reynolds, the top male box office draw of the 1970s, built his career through a string of films that linked southern men, redneck fun, and fast cars. Reynolds made his ties to NASCAR explicit in the abysmal *Stroker Ace* (1983), in which he played a hard-luck Winston Cup driver who clashes with his sponsors. Stock car racing possessed even deeper connections with country music. Musicians such as Del Reeves, Patsy Cline, Charlie McCoy, and Jeannie C. Riley often appeared at races either to sing the national anthem or simply as fans. Country music and stock car racing directly intersected with the 1975 RCA album *NASCAR Goes Country*, which featured Richard Petty, David Pearson, Bobbie Allison, and others performing versions of country hits (plus a bizarre version of "99 Bottles of Beer" sung by Darrell Waltrip). More famously (and successfully), Marty Robbins tied the worlds of country music and stock car racing together. The Academy of Country Music's "Artist of the Decade" for the 1960s, he played a moonshine-connected racer in *Hell on Wheels* (1967), then began competing in Grand National and Grand American events the next year. Robbins drove his "Devil Woman" Dodge in select premier events every year until his death in 1982.[27]

During the late 1970s, southern lifestyles also became increasingly prevalent on network television. Programs such as *Carter Country* and *The Misadventures of Sheriff Lobo* continued, to a degree, to offer bumpkin southern characters of the *Hee Haw* and *Petticoat Junction* variety, but other shows reflected the new attitudes toward the South by presenting more nuanced views. *Dallas*, for example, showed that a traditional revenge and sex-fueled soap opera could be effectively translated to the South. For stock car racing, however, the key program became *The Dukes of Hazzard*. Based on the 1975 feature film *The Moonrunners*, the show featured a litany of clichéd southern characters, but also presented many of them as fair-minded, patriotic, and stalwart examples of Jacksonian anti-intellectualism. Bo and Luke (a Vietnam vet) Duke served as good-natured protagonists eliminating crime and corruption from Hazzard County. They battled evil with brains, brawn, and a Dodge Charger stock car named the "General Lee" (replete with a rebel flag on its roof). To complete the connections with southern stock, the Duke boys' back story involved incarceration for tripping, and their Uncle Jessie continued to distill moonshine.

The show's writers positioned the Dukes as classic southern outlaw-heroes that appealed to television viewers in all parts of the country. As trippers and stockers, they helped connect the outlaw-hero image to Winston Cup drivers. In a similar vein, Tom Wolfe had dubbed Junior Johnson "The Last American Hero," but the outlaw-hero persona would be perfected by NASCAR's biggest star of the 1980s, Dale Earnhardt.[28]

NASCAR's growing importance in this prosouthern environment can be seen by the ways it was treated by American presidents. Richard Nixon, as part of his larger "southern strategy," invited Grand National champion Richard Petty to the White House. Petty obliged by bringing his car and his crew for a photo-op in front of the presidential residence. Although Nixon invited Petty inside the presidential residence for a short visit, the entire event appeared perfunctory. Jimmy Carter, however, proclaimed himself a NASCAR fan while still governor of Georgia and invited not just Petty, but (fulfilling a campaign promise) all the leading drivers to the White House in September 1978. In stark contrast to the uncomfortable Nixon, Carter's White House welcomed the drivers and cars to a lavish dinner followed up with a Willie Nelson concert in the backyard. Donnie Allison commented to one reporter, "a bunch of old race cars circled in the driveway of the White House, that's what America's all about." With the president busy overseeing the Camp David Peace Accords, First Lady Rosalynn actually served as the event's host. The president's absence relieved many of the NASCAR guests who preferred to keep their distance from Carter, despite the president's status as a stock fan and southern evangelical. During the post-dinner reception "Big" Bill France made his feelings clear by noting "I didn't vote for Carter in the last election . . . frankly, I've always been a [George] Wallace man . . . and if he hadn't been shot I think we would have been here four years earlier."[29]

Despite the disdain for Carter evinced by France (and Petty, who referred to Carter as "the peanut"), the appearance of Winston Cup's leading drivers at a White House banquet held in their honor clearly reflected stock car racing's expanding national visibility. That importance became even more obvious when Ronald Reagan, as part of a southern campaign swing, appeared at the 1984 Firecracker 400 in Daytona. Sitting presidents traditionally throw out the first pitch at a Major League Baseball stadium on opening day of the season, but none had ever previously attended a Winston Cup event. Stock car racing had effectively become as central to American sports culture as baseball. Whereas Nixon and Carter brought NASCAR to them by inviting drivers to the White House, Reagan felt Winston Cup important enough for him go to NASCAR. Two years later he reinforced his connections with NASCAR by officially pardoning Junior Johnson for his moonshine conviction.

6

THE AGE OF EARNHARDT

The expansion of the late 1970s continued for NASCAR into the next decade. Having gained momentum against all other sanctioning bodies in the previous decade, NASCAR emerged as the undisputed leader in American motor sports during the 1980s. United States Auto Club's collapse led to the abandonment of their stock car series, so Winston Cup no longer had any other national challengers. Furthermore, the chaotic circumstances surrounding Champ cars meant that Championship Auto Racing Teams offered little competition. NASCAR faced its own difficulties because of its reliance on products of the tottering American car industry, but it managed to overcome these issues through vigilant efforts to ensure parity and by reducing the organization's dependency on Detroit through the use of increasing numbers of purpose-built cars. Under "Little" Bill France's leadership, NASCAR managed to consolidate its position through both increased television exposure and the assistance of a legion of new national sponsors. Many of stock car racing's biggest names retired during the 1980s, but a cluster of new stars emerged to replace them. Reflective of Winston Cup's development into a truly national series, a number of the young drivers who surfaced during the 1980s hailed from outside the Southeast.

The greatest star of the 1980s, however, emerged from the traditional stock car racing hotbed of North Carolina. Second-generation NASCAR competitor Dale Earnhardt established himself as a formidable modified driver in the early 1970s, then began his Cup career in 1976, but managed only the occasional ride through 1978. In 1979, his first full Winston Cup season, Earnhardt won one race en route to becoming NASCAR's Rookie of the Year. He won the first of seven national championships in 1980, then fell victim to team-related financial issues the next season. In1982, Earnhardt's career took a significant turn when he became part of Bud Moore's Ford team. Under Moore, Earnhardt competed in the car that initially made him famous—a blue-and-yellow number 3 sponsored by Wrangler. By that point he had also developed a reputation for fearless driving on the track, which earned him the nickname "Ironhead." Earnhardt learned to temper his risk-taking, but his insatiable desire to win led to numerous altercations with other drivers, who often felt he had purposefully wrecked or damaged their cars. In 1984, he took the number 3 Wrangler Jeans Machine to Richard Childress Racing, who began setting the car up specifically to handle Earnhardt's hard-charging style. While driving for Childress, Earnhardt won his final six national championships. By the time of his death in 2001, Earnhardt's number 3 car was painted black and sponsored by Goodwrench. The change reflected the evolution of Earnhardt—"Ironhead" in blue had become "The Intimidator" in black.

Earnhardt's confrontational style (and frequent wins) might have marked him out as another Waltrip—a successful competitor hated by the fans; however, the reverse actually developed. Earnhardt became a huge fan favorite and developed into Winston Cup's biggest star for the next two decades. His popularity stemmed from a public persona that was a combination of genuine personality and carefully cultivated image. Earnhardt relished being viewed as the sullen loner who could intimidate his opponents simply through their knowledge that he would wreck them in order to win. In many respects, Earnhardt perfected the outlaw-hero character. He did so, however, with far more assistance from the media and sponsors than Earnhardt liked to admit.

His stock initially rose thanks to a massive marketing campaign undertaken by Wrangler. As Earnhardt's primary sponsor, Wrangler used his image in a magazine advertising series that promoted Earnhardt as "One Tough Customer." Thanks to his "confidence and independence" Earnhardt drove "hard and fast" on the track, but still found time to devote himself to "hunting and fishing and having a good time." A ninth-grade dropout married three times, Earnhardt was someone his blue-collars fans could identify with, so his success took on added meaning *because* of his tribulations. Converted into a fearsome, self-reliant winner who asked for no quarter, Earnhardt became the advertising equivalent of the Marlboro Man. Earnhardt even looked like an Old West gunfighter with his bushy mustache, steely blue-eyed squint, and firmly-set jaw. Wrangler made this connection explicit with the program cover of the 1982 Wrangler Sanfor-Set 400 at Richmond. Under the caption "headin' for a showdown," Earnhardt, replete with white cowboy hat and six-gun, is shown squaring off against four other gunslingers (Petty, Waltrip, Bobby Allison, and Neil Bonnett), with only the Wrangler Jeans Machine separating them. Symbolically, Earnhardt became the lone gunfighter who could square off against the rest of the world and still emerge victorious. Whether they were beaten-down, blue-collar workers or the newly attracted demi-rednecks, many NASCAR fans found the imagery irresistible.[1]

Earnhardt's popularity, however, did not typically extend to other drivers. Many within Winston Cup found him personally boorish and a dangerous cretin on the track. His relentless drive for victory invariably led to conflicts, wrecks, and fines from NASCAR. Not surprisingly, Earnhardt developed heated rivalries with many of the other prominent drivers of the 1980s. These conflicts typically developed from on-track incidents, for which—rightly or wrongly—Earnhardt normally shouldered the blame. In a typical comment, Darrell Waltrip, after tangling with Earnhardt, hysterically claimed "he meant to kill me." Reflective of traditional southern notions of honor, Earnhardt possessed nothing but disdain for those who complained to the media instead of standing up to him, noting "some of those competitors talk about my driving style, but look at the way they act, like a bunch of babies crying their eyes out." In 1987, NASCAR attempted to curb the escalating number of incidents by sending overly aggressive drivers to the garage area during the race (a practice dubbed by drivers as being sent to the "penalty box"), but to little overall effect. Unchastened by threats of punishment, Earnhardt maintained his hard-charging tactics until his death in 2001.[2]

Earnhardt's status also benefited from the fact that many of the veterans, such as Petty, Pearson, and Yarborough, either began running limited schedules or no longer operated truly competitive teams. With many of the older, more popular drivers bowing out, Winston Cup increasingly became the purview of young drivers and Darrell Waltrip (whom virtually everyone despised). This youth movement helped Earnhardt in that it brought to the fore many new drivers who fans found highly unlikable. Fan complaints of these new drivers emerged from NASCAR's spread beyond their southern stronghold. The organization's increased national visibility helped attract ever larger numbers of nonsouthern drivers. During the 1980s, less than half of all Winston Cup drivers originally hailed from the South. Many young drivers moved up to Winston Cup by first competing in the Midwest-based American Speed Association touring stock car series. Although some of these drivers had southern roots, such as Mark Martin, many came from states not traditionally associated with Winston Cup, such as Wisconsin and Missouri. For older NASCAR fans, this represented an unacceptable Yankee invasion.

The ramifications of these shifting driver demographics became clear in 1989 when Rusty Wallace became the first nonsoutherner to win the national championship since 1950. Although Alan Kulwicki passed fan muster thanks to an appreciation of the challenges he faced as an independent driver, many of the northerners who came to Winston Cup in the 1980s found the spectators to be far less forgiving. Perhaps most hated was Geoff Bodine, who repeatedly clashed with Earnhardt. Bodine proved to be as hot-headed and willing to bang fenders as Earnhardt, which guaranteed some measure of fan disapproval, but he combined that with being from New York to create a truly toxic mix. Also, Bodine's initial attempt to enter Winston Cup in the late 1970s involved rumors of his receiving financial support from the Teamsters, which only added to his unpopularity. For fans normally disinclined to support Earnhardt because of his aggressive style, "Ironhead" became acceptable thanks to his position as a bulwark against drivers viewed as interlopers. These complicated relationships led television executive Patti Wheeler, who possessed firsthand knowledge of NASCAR rivalries, to declare that Winston Cup in the 1980s represented the "ultimate male soap opera."[3]

The growing presence of nonsouthern drivers, whether fan favorites or not, reflected NASCAR's transition to a national organization. Bill France's efforts outside the South, however, did not always bear fruit. The NASCAR North series became the organization's most spectacular nonsouthern failure during the 1980s. NASCAR North, in operation under Tom Curley and Ken Squire since 1979, seemed remarkably successful in the early 1980s. In 1985, the tour had sponsorship from Coors, ran 30 races, paid out more than $1 million to drivers, and even had an event televised by the USA Network. That same season, however, headstrong team owners began challenging the rules interpretations of series officials, and a cluster of scoring mistakes led both to confusion over who actually won the series and ugly lawsuits. With officials in Daytona being pulled into the costly and chaotic mess in the North, NASCAR abandoned its sanctioning of the series in October 1985. An element of the series carried on without NASCAR sanction, but with far less success. NASCAR North's collapse demonstrated something many drivers did not want to admit—without an undisputed, strong-arm leader, a racing series faced grave dangers. The tactics of the France family often alienated, but they also kept Winston Cup moving forward.[4]

Regardless of their view of Earnhardt or the northern invaders, Winston Cup fans of the 1980s found themselves able to watch increasing numbers of NASCAR events on television. Along with its contracts with the networks, NASCAR became involved with cable television in 1981. In 1979, the Entertainment and Sports Programming Network (ESPN) began broadcasting round-the-clock sports coverage. To fill its schedule, ESPN executives scrambled to develop relationships with the NCAA and a host of fringe sports. During the early 1980s, the network established some measure of stability and began courting higher-level professional sports. By the end of the 1980s, ESPN broadcast events from the top levels in professional baseball, basketball, and football, but the first major professional series to become affiliated with the network was NASCAR. The networks balked at airing lengthy NASCAR races, but programming-hungry ESPN relished filling the important Sunday afternoon time slots with an exciting live event.

The initial offerings of 1981 proved so successful that ESPN immediately began expanding its coverage of auto racing. In 1982, the number of motor sports events broadcast on ESPN jumped to 40. By the end of the decade, the network's annual total surpassed 200 races. For NASCAR this relationship allowed it to show flag-to-flag coverage of nonpremier events on national television, something that seemed impossible at the time to arrange with the networks. When ESPN began showing live Winston Cup races, only slightly more than 20 percent of American households had cable, but by the end of the decade, that number had more than tripled. ESPN grew with the expansion of cable (and eventually changed American sports more than anything since the elimination of the color line), and NASCAR's relationship with the network immensely helped stock car racing.[5]

Perversely, part of the allure of ESPN's first year of Winston Cup coverage stemmed from the poor quality of racing that season. After years of threatening to do so, in December 1980 NASCAR announced a major rules revision that banned the traditional large Detroit products and replaced them with mid-sized sedans (with a maximum wheel base of 110 inches). The smaller cars proved difficult to control, especially in packs, and had a nasty proclivity for going airborne when sliding sideways. As a result, these twitchy cars led to more accidents and out-of-control spins. For example, ESPN's first full flag-to-flag live event of the season was the Atlanta Journal 500, where only half the field still ran at the end. Although other factors contribute to the popularity of motor racing on television, crashes are often cited by viewers as one of the attractions of the sport. ESPN's relationship with Winston Cup occurred at a juncture where the cars themselves (and Dale Earnhardt in particular) caused large numbers of viewer-attracting accidents. Although 1981 stood as a very dangerous year for drivers, it was also the optimum moment for NASCAR to connect with cable television.[6]

The quality of racing improved during 1981 (and in the next few years) as a result of the confluence of several factors. First, NASCAR repeatedly tweaked regulations to make the cars perform more satisfactorily. Winston Cup mechanics also learned how to optimize the performance of the smaller cars. The shift from larger cars to ones with a shorter wheelbase (dramatically shorter when compared to vehicles from the early 1970s and before) marked a revolutionary change in the sport, and a rough transitional period naturally developed from such a significant alteration. As at other junctures in the history of stock car racing, these mechanical difficulties receded over time. Finally, Winston Cup teams found themselves able to rely on assistance from the manufacturers. After a decade out of stock car racing, Detroit's auto companies officially reentered NASCAR.

By the early 1980s, the Big 3 faced growing consumer apathy for their products, vigorous challenges from Japanese manufacturers, and a shrinking market share. Chrysler's brink-of-bankruptcy status garnered most of the attention, but Ford and GM struggled as well. Detroit responded with a two-pronged attack. First, it attempted to counter the imports by producing more fuel-efficient, smaller cars to offer an American alternative to the imports. Second, it strove to exploit the sectors of the automotive industry least colonized by the Japanese companies. Ostensibly this strategy meant developing the obverse of their new economy cars; Detroit would stake a claim to superiority in the realm of high performance. To prove this claim, American manufacturers reconnected with a variety of auto racing forms. Some types of racing put Detroit products in direct competition with imports (although more often European rather than Japanese), which ran the risk of adding to their woes if the American cars performed poorly. NASCAR, however, had been all American since the 1950s. Detroit could compete solely against itself in Winston Cup. Although that type of insularity did not afford Detroit's manufacturers the ability to directly measure their products against the imports, it did allow them the opportunity to square off against each other to determine the best American cars. For Detroit auto executives looking to regain market share, taking sales from other American companies served the same purpose as taking them from the Japanese.

Despite the official withdrawal of Detroit from NASCAR at the beginning of the 1970s, some contact had actually continued. In particular, Ford kept back-channel connections with the Wood Brothers and Bud Moore by making racing-alloy engine blocks available to them in the mid-1970s. Even within Ford itself, however, these actions were little known and represented the machinations of only a small group of executives. Reflective of the secrecy surrounding these actions, the blocks had to be imported from Ford plants in Australia. General Motors' Product Performance department continued to operate throughout the 1970s and, not coincidentally, GM vehicles dominated Winston Cup for most of the decade. Although, like Ford, at least partially sub rosa, GM's involvement in motor sports helped make the decade a golden age for Chevrolet and Oldsmobile (which NASCAR allowed to run with Chevy engines) stock cars. Of the Big 3, Chrysler stood as the manufacturer most fully withdrawn from stock during the 1970s. Petty Enterprises remained as loyal as possible (they still ran 1973 Dodges in the 1977 season), but increasingly experimented with other makes in an effort to remain competitive. A heightened sense of competition born out of a need for survival, however, would bring the secretive operations of Detroit into the full light of day during the next decade.

Ford's racing activities went public in 1980 with the creation of the Special Vehicles Operation, with a mandate to reestablish Ford's high performance credentials. Ford's return, however, proved disappointing. Years behind GM in working with stock cars, even the wheelbase reduction of 1981 did not level the playing field. Ford's hopes were buoyed when Dale Earnhardt moved to Bud Moore's Ford factory team in 1982, but the Thunderbirds remained uncompetitive. Ford's failure became doubly unpleasant because it was being easily disposed of on the track by two GM makes. The early 1980s marked the only period in NASCAR history in which Buick dominated the Cup series. Aerodynamic (by early 1980's standards) Buick Regals won 47 of the 62 Cup races held in 1981–82. To make matters worse for Ford, in 1982 the only non-Buicks to go to victory lane were Chevrolets. Ford's fortunes eventually turned mid-decade when competition between manufacturers spurred a partial revival of the "aero wars" of the late 1960s.[7]

As with the auto manufacturers, a desire to increase sales spurred a new interest in NASCAR on the part of national companies. The sanctioning body's growing television presence served as an enormous economic boon to the sport by attracting companies looking to maximize the efficiency of their advertising money. For sponsors looking to increase their market share, televised stock car racing offered opportunities unavailable with any other sport. Since the late 1970s, these races often included in-car cameras, which allowed for additional advertising to be strategically placed inside the car itself. Also, NASCAR represented the only sport that could guarantee sponsors their brand names would be seen by viewers. NASCAR's appeal to sponsors partly grew thanks to the changing viewing habits of Americans. Along with the spread of cable, television underwent another transformation during the 1980s thanks to the increasing numbers of video cassette recorders (VCR) found in American homes. VCRs allowed viewers to both watch programming on their own schedule and avoid having to sit through commercials. The ability to fast-forward through commercial breaks (a practice called "zapping" by frightened advertising executives) meant that sponsorship dollars might be completely wasted. With NASCAR, however, advertising could not be circumvented through "zapping." The cars themselves, garishly covered with sponsor names, served as the advertising, and drivers quickly learned ways to keep their sponsors happy. Although "Jaws" Waltrip's "God, Gatorade, & Goodyear" comment struck many as inappropriate in 1979, by the mid-1980s zap-proof driver interviews always began with a car's pilot commenting on the "Kodiak Pontiac" or "Coors Ford."[8]

Although the incessant plugging of sponsors by drivers became an annoying cliché to many fans, the drivers understood the importance of such references. With the increased presence of major national sponsors came stiff competition among drivers for their money. Corporate sponsorship of teams altered the criteria car owners used when selecting their drivers. Drivers with personal connections to a particular company became a valuable commodity. A driver liked by a prospective sponsor could get a ride over a better driver unattractive to companies. Such considerations meant that primary sponsors gained increasing say in the choice of drivers. As these sponsors dealt with only the most successful teams, the upper echelons of Winston Cup effectively became beholden to the desires of corporations. As Don Rice, a member of Harry Ranier's team, commented in 1981, "the driver [we hire] depends on which driver can help us with a sponsorship."[9]

NASCAR's increased visibility and growing fandom corresponded with a rise in merchandise sales that made sponsorship of a team even more attractive. The close connections between a driver and his sponsored Ford or Chevrolet allowed for the company's name to become part of the merchandise. Even when the image of a Cup car was not part of the merchandise, sponsors made prominent appearances. Virtually all merchandise involving athletes presents them in their uniform, and NASCAR drivers, in keeping with that tradition, invariably appeared on posters, glossy photos, and T-shirts wearing their sponsor-covered fire suits. With the name of their primary sponsor emblazoned in large letters across the chest of the suit, companies could be assured that their brand was associated with their driver whenever he was seen in public. No other American sport gave companies such a deep and constant connection with their spokesperson athletes. Beatrice Foods chairman James L. Dutt noted that auto racing is "the only sport where a corporate sponsor can actually participate in the field of competition." The potency of sponsoring a Cup team came not just from the ability to "participate," but from the attention NASCAR fans paid to these sponsors. In one 1994 study, a group of NASCAR fans named, without assistance or prompting, more than 200 companies who sponsored Cup cars. NASCAR supporters demonstrated a remarkable awareness of sponsors unmatched by fans of any other sport. For companies looking to invest their advertising dollars as wisely as possible, Winston Cup represented nirvana.[10]

Richard Petty, whose 1972 contract with STP made him the first driver to be closely linked with a specific sponsor for an extended period, entered the 1980s as the most recognizable name in stock car racing, but he also found himself increasingly usurped on the track by the younger stars. His inability to compete successfully prompted his team to engage in practices that developed into the blackest moment of his Cup career, the so-called "Pettygate" incident of 1983. After winning the Miller High Life 500 at Charlotte, a postrace inspection discovered that Petty's Pontiac boasted both an engine a full 20 cubic inches over the Cup limit and illegal right side tires. Either of these infractions could (and previously had) resulted in drivers being penalized several laps or disqualified, but in this case Petty was allowed to keep the victory. Upon learning this, angry runner-up Darrell Waltrip defiantly declared "there is no question I am the winner," but he could do nothing about NASCAR's decision. Although Petty faced a fine and lost more than 100 points as a result of his action, many drivers felt Bill France demonstrated enormous favoritism in not taking the victory away from the popular Petty. "Pettygate" served as a vivid reminder to drivers that the France family owned NASCAR, which allowed them to make the rules. Similar (and valid) complaints of favoritism developed around Fireball Roberts and "Big" Bill France in the 1960s and would emerge over the treatment of Dale Earnhardt in the 1990s, but there was nothing drivers could do to counter the preferential treatment. "King" Richard claimed he knew nothing about the cheating and showed his displeasure with the team by bolting from Petty Enterprises at the end of the season to drive a car owned by California politician Mike Curb. While driving for Curb the next season, Petty reached a new height for Cup drivers when he won the Firecracker 400 with Ronald Reagan present. The win marked Petty's 200th career victory in NASCAR's premier series. Petty's postrace interview demonstrated how thoroughly ingrained sponsor promotion had become in NASCAR. He began with "it's a case of Richard Petty winning 200 races, but he didn't do it by himself . . . first, I guess I've got to thank STP." Although he raced for eight more seasons, fan favorite Petty never won another race.[11]

An important change in the perception of NASCAR demographics helped make automotive sponsors such as STP increasingly unimportant. From the early car-related sponsors of the 1950s to the national brands that crept in during the 1970s, all the companies involved viewed NASCAR as a means of advertising among male spectators. Even during the 1950s, large numbers of women attended Grand National events, but most sponsors typically viewed them as disinterested bystanders dragged to the track by husbands and boyfriends. Car dealerships and performance parts companies perceived men as their target audience and paid little attention to the women crowded into the stands of races. More gender-neutral sponsors, such as cola companies, entered Grand National in the 1970s, but the perception remained that the hyper-masculinity of car culture meant that only the men in attendance actually followed the action on the track. During the 1980s, however, increasingly sophisticated studies undertaken by advertising agencies employed by major corporations uncovered what many close to NASCAR already understood—that the preponderance of the women in the stands at Cup events did not simply follow their husbands to the track, they actually followed the sport. Not only were women fans of stock car racing, but, by the late 1980s, they constituted approximately half the fans in the stands. The revelation of a completely unexploited group of consumers associated with a sport that itself allowed for unique advertising possibilities resulted in a new courting of female motor racing fans by some of the most prominent U.S. companies. So-called "women's" sponsors such as Crisco, Tide, Eureka vacuums, Ultra Slim-Fast, and Lifebuoy soap began appearing on the sides of Cup cars.

Folgers coffee became one of the earliest of the "women's" sponsors involved with Winston Cup. Parent company Proctor & Gamble began sponsoring a Folgers car in 1985, then became the title sponsor of Tim Richmond the next year. Ohio driver Richmond represented a sponsor's dream. Incredibly handsome and outgoing, Richmond had a flamboyant personality that guaranteed attention for himself and his sponsor. It also, however, led to continual conflict between Richmond and the NASCAR organization. At the height of his career, Richmond acknowledged that many of his problems with NASCAR stemmed from actions that marked him as "a liberal in a very conservative sport." About as far from the stereotype of a stock car driver as possible, Richmond represented exactly the sort of driver needed by the new "women's" sponsors. With Folgers on—board, he won seven races in 1986 and had the best year of his career.[12]

Richmond's success, however, proved short-lived. He parlayed his fame and looks into an out-of-control hedonism reminiscent of Curtis Turner that eventually proved fatal. In December 1986, Richmond learned he had contracted AIDS, which many within NASCAR attributed to his frequent contacts with prostitutes. Given the then-current perceptions of the connections between AIDS and homosexuality, Richmond recognized the dangers to his career in the conservative world of NASCAR if he acknowledged his illness and admitted only to having pneumonia (which was true). He made a miraculous comeback in the middle of the 1987 season, winning his first two races before his illness cut his return short. Rumors that his erratic behavior stemmed from drug abuse prompted Bill

France to institute NASCAR's first ever drug testing policy for the 1988 season. Richmond attempted one final comeback early that season, but failed his drug test when NASCAR found high levels of over-the-counter medications in his system. Richmond filed a lawsuit in protest, which was eventually settled out of court, but he never competed in another NASCAR event. He finally succumbed to AIDS-related complications in August 1989, and only then did most in the sport learn the truth of Richmond's condition.[13]

Richmond was one of a constellation of younger stars all born at roughly the same time. The class of 1955–1956 included Richmond, Rusty Wallace, Ricky Rudd, Terry Labonte, Dale Jarrett, and Bill Elliott. This group of drivers became the backbone of the sport during the mid-1980s, with many continuing to be successful deep into the next decade. Rudd began his Cup career in 1975, but did not notch his first victory until 1983. Dale Jarrett followed his father Ned into Winston Cup beginning in 1984. Jarrett, however, peaked later than the rest of this group and won the national championship in 1999. Wallace, as previously mentioned, became the first nonsouthern to win the title in 30 years when he became Winston Cup champion in 1989. A renowned road racer, Wallace eventually scored 55 career Cup victories. Texan Terry Labonte won the Winston Cup championship in 1984, then again in 1996. The last of this group to remain active, Labonte was still qualifying for Cup races in 2009 at the age of 52. Along with age and success, all of these drivers also proved to be adept and persuasive spokesmen for the new era of television and national sponsors.

Of the group, Bill Elliott became the most popular and, arguably, the most successful. Elliott became a perennial winner fan favorite by mixing victories and an "aw shucks" Georgia country boy charm. One commentator described him as a "redheaded Huck Finn who speaks with a drawl as Southern as grits." Fans embraced Elliott in part because of the way he rose through the NASCAR ranks. When he first began competing in the late 1970s, he was part of a true family team. The Elliott clan proved remarkably adept at maximizing the performance of their low-budget operation, then received a huge boost when Harry Melling's factory-affiliated Ford team hired Bill. The Dawsonville, Georgia driver won NASCAR's most popular driver poll an astonishing 16 times. His popularity was so great that when Konami released the first NASCAR-sanctioned video game in 1990, it was named *Bill Elliott's NASCAR Challenge*.[14]

Elliott's ties to Ford paid off mid-decade when they introduced a new Thunderbird that could finally compete with the Chevy Monte Carlo. Driving an aerodynamic T-bird, Elliott captured the new "Winston Million" in 1985. As part of its ever-increasing funding of NASCAR,

Winston announced that beginning with the 1985 season it would pay $1 million to any driver who could win three of the four biggest events on the Cup schedule. Elliott earned the million as part of a remarkable season in which he won 11 races. All of his wins, however, occurred on superspeedways and his inability to compete successfully on shorter tracks allowed the far more consistent Darrell Waltrip to win the championship that season. Waltrip's title illustrated the peculiarities of the Winston Cup system, which rewarded steady high finishes over victories. Elliott finished second by more than 100 points despite winning more races than all the other drivers in the top seven combined. Although Waltrip had to run hard until the last race of the 1985 season to earn his championship, the peculiarities of the points system periodically created champions who clinched their titles by running conservatively ("stroking" in racing parlance) during the latter part of the season. Criticisms of cautious late season driving will eventually lead to a major overhaul of the championship points system in the early 21st century. Elliott eventually won his own national championship in 1988, nipping Rusty Wallace by a scant four points.

Two other prominent young drivers emerged during the decade to carry on racing dynasties. Kyle Petty entered professional racing with a stir, winning the first race he ever entered, an ARCA event at Daytona in 1979, then made his Winston Cup debut later that year. In 1981 he began running a full schedule under the auspices of Petty Enterprises. Petty left the family organization in 1984 to drive for the Wood Brothers for the rest of the decade, with limited success. Although neither as popular nor as successful as his father Richard, Kyle served as an important example of the transformations in NASCAR. Although linked to NASCAR's past through his name, Kyle proved to be a far different sort of Petty. While Richard frequently displayed his support for conservative Republicans, Kyle emerged from his father's shadow as a ponytailed liberal. In the new era of "women's" sponsors and national television, even members of the historical Petty line could let their hair down. In stark contrast to Kyle, Bobby Allison's son Davey continued in the tradition of the "good ol' boys" Alabama Gang. Also unlike Kyle, Bobby Allison made his son earn his own way in racing, working his way up through the dirt track ranks. After a successful run in ARCA, the younger Allison debuted in Winston Cup in 1985. Two years later he earned a full-time ride for Harry Ranier and then stayed on when Robert Yates subsequently purchased the team. Opposites on the track as well as off, Kyle Petty managed to win only 8 Cup races over a 30-year career, while Allison picked up 19 in only seven full seasons. Allison nearly won the championship in both 1991 and 1992 before dying in a helicopter crash in July 1993.[15]

At the end of the 1988 season Cale Yarborough, Benny Parsons, Buddy Baker, and Bobby Allison all retired. At the same time David Pearson, who had not actually competed since 1986, officially declared the end of his racing career. Time had clearly caught up with the entire group as none of these drivers finished in the top 20 in points in 1988, even though all, save Yarborough, ran a full schedule. Baker made an ill-advised attempt at a comeback in the early 1990s, but none of the others ever competed in Winston Cup again. Allison had been involved in a horrific crash at Talladega in May 1987 in which his car went airborne, then disintegrated as it shredded a retaining fence. Five spectators were injured by debris. In response NASCAR mandated a return of the carburetor restrictor plates first utilized in the early 1970s. After being even more seriously injured at a 1988 race at Pocono, Allison decided to quit racing.[16]

During the 1980s NASCAR developed two new races as a means of showcasing their stars, both old and new alike. In each case, the events emerged out of the combination of increasing sponsorship monies and NASCAR's growing relationship with television. As part of its effort to promote the revamped Busch line, Anheuser-Busch agreed to sponsor a new non-points paying event in 1979. As part of Daytona's February Speed Week, the new Busch Clash would be held for pole winners from the previous season. CBS carried the event as part of its Daytona coverage. Anheuser-Busch also became the title sponsor for the venerable Late Model Sportsman Division, which became a second-tier touring series for smaller cars in 1982 as the Budweiser Late Model Sportsman. In the mid-1980s NASCAR announced that the name Grand National would no longer apply to the Winston Cup series and the Budweiser series became known as the Busch Grand National series. The Busch series developed into an excellent training ground for the development of young drivers. Borrowing the all-star game concept from other sports, NASCAR used RJR money to create a second non-points event in 1985 called The Winston. The Winston arose at the perfect time for NASCAR as it allowed the organization to feature its younger stars head-to-head against veterans more familiar to the viewing public. Such a race gave the new drivers valuable exposure that eased the late 1980s transition brought on by the retirement of prominent Winston Cup figures. The Winston also sparked one of the events that created the rancor between Tim Richmond and NASCAR that led the organization to create a drug testing policy seen by many as directed specifically against him. At The Winston's 1987 group photo shoot, the irascible Richmond surreptitiously exposed his genitalia, which forced NASCAR to recall posters made from the photograph.[17]

Television, national sponsors, showcase race monies for the top drivers, and expensive technological advances led to the death knell of the independents. Self-financed driver-owners with cars tuned by their shade tree mechanic friends simply could no longer compete competitively. The fate of the independents had been obvious since the early 1970s, with NASCAR's Plan B merely delaying the inevitable, but the enormous jump in costs during the 1980s hastened their demise. With the rise in Winston contingency, sponsor, and television monies came a rise in the amount of capital needed to field a successful team, and the independents did not have those sorts of resources. NASCAR required tracks to pay all the drivers who qualified for Winston Cup events, but the top-heavy pay-outs overwhelmingly favored the well-financed top teams. The inherent logic of rewarding the successful meant that back-markers received too little to ever successfully challenge the top teams. Issues of financial inequality did not begin in the 1980s, but the smaller purses of previous periods compressed the separation to keep the top and bottom teams closer. For example, in 1972 (at a point when independents already complained about costs) the driver who earned the least prize money with 20 or more starts was Neil "Soapy" Castles, with $18,760 for the season. Bobby Allison led all earners that year with $348,939. Using the same parameters for the 1985 season, Trevor Boys sat at the bottom with $76,325, with two drivers over $1 million (and one of them went well over $2 million). Such disparities made it impossible for independents to keep up with the top teams. According to one mid-1980s estimate, a full season on the Cup circuit cost a team $80,000 to $90,000 for tires alone. In 1988, veteran mechanic Smokey Yunick posited that "the lowest-buck operation would still need $500,000 to $750,000 to run the Series for a year." A top team could easily burn through $2 million in one season. Mid-pack independents like Boys, then, inevitably lost money competing in NASCAR.[18]

The rising price of remaining competitive reflected the expense of keeping up with NASCAR's technological developments. Just as the financial distance between independents and top drivers grew during the 1980s, the technological separation between Winston Cup and Champ cars shrank. Computers were first used in NASCAR in September 1983 when Bobby Allison's DiGard team began using probability data to determine pit strategies. By 1988, computerized equipment represented the norm among top Cup teams, with the independents struggling to keep up. Costs also skyrocketed during this same period with the transition from gutted and refurbished Detroit products to completely purpose-built Cup cars with no actual stock components. Well-financed teams could afford to purchase their own equipment and hire skilled builders to construct their cars, thereby increasing their advantage over the smaller teams. Poorer independents often survived by either purchasing equipment from individuals outside their garage or by obtaining used parts from a larger team. These approaches made expenses more feasible for them short term, but more expensive long term. Additionally, buying used parts from a larger team helped subsidize the wealthier organization as it allowed them to offset some of the expense of their initial purchases. Dogged independents such as Buddy Arrington, James Hylton, and J. D. McDuffie struggled through the 1980s, but a 1992 article on independent Jimmy "Smut" Means accurately referred to him as a "dinosaur."[19]

While the independents struggled to find sponsors, other teams sprang up that did not need outside investors. Millionaire Harry Ranier's 1977 entry into Winston Cup heralded the arrival of a group of wealthy dabblers attracted by the growing stature of Winston Cup. Ranier's foray into stock car racing was accompanied by the arrival of another "hobbyist"— coal tycoon J. D. Stacy. After purchasing the car driven by Neil Bonnett, Stacy immediately alienated many involved in NASCAR by reneging on deals. Crew chief Harry Hyde and driver Ferrel Harris eventually filed law suits against Stacy, who temporarily dropped out of NASCAR after a bomb was found under his personal car in late 1978. Stacy returned in mid-1981 with his headline-making purchase of Rod Osterlund's team that had won the 1980 championship. Driver Dale Earnhardt and most of the crew ran afoul of Stacy and departed, making his $1.7 million purchase of the Osterlund team primarily a deal involving equipment. Despite these setbacks, Stacy poured even more money into NASCAR and shocked many at the 1982 Daytona 500 when he arrived with a two-car team and sponsorship of an astounding five other cars. For some of the sponsorship deals, Stacy had entered into long-term agreements for $1 million per year. These investments led Stacy to believe he actively controlled these teams, which led to enormous friction between himself and the teams. He abandoned his $5,000 per race contracts with Terry Labonte for refusing to remove another sponsor's patch from his fire suit and with Dave Marcis after he pushed an out-of-gas Bobby Allison to the pits during a race at Pocono, which resulted in Allison defeating Tim Richmond in a Stacy-owned Buick. A wave of lawsuits over unpaid sponsorship money forced Stacy out of NASCAR for good in 1983.[20]

California entrepreneur Warner Hodgdon (who first gained public attention by building a giant cross in San Bernardino) engineered an even more spectacular crash-and-burn. Hodgdon sponsored Champ cars in the 1970s, then began buying race tracks. During the early 1980s he obtained controlling interest in the speedways at Bristol, Richmond, North Wilkesboro, Nashville, and Phoenix. Hodgdon then paid to become the name sponsor of races at other tracks. As a result, Winston Cup drivers competed at the Warner Hodgdon 200 at Riverside and the Warner Hodgdon 500 at Rockingham. Hodgdon also developed a friendship with

Neil Bonnett that led the Californian to buy half the RahMoc team with Bonnett as the driver. In November 1983 Hodgdon stunned the NASCAR community with the announcement that he had purchased half of Junior Johnson's team. The independent-minded Johnson agreed to the deal in response to the growing costs of fielding a competitive team, but soon clashed with Hodgdon. Like Lawrence LoPatin before him, Hodgdon quickly learned that owning racetracks does not guarantee success. His efforts to keep his NASCAR holdings solvent led Hodgdon to begin missing payments to interests in both NASCAR and his engineering concerns. Faced with $33 million in lawsuits, Hodgdon filed for bankruptcy in early 1985. These millionaire newcomers discovered what the independents already knew, that it was difficult to actually make money in stock car racing.[21]

The cost-cutting that proved so difficult for the independents to achieve also spurred one of the most significant alterations in the way NASCAR teams operated. Wealthy teams that owned all the equipment necessary to build their own cars began to field second cars as a way of maximizing the usage of their resources. For the independents, this development hastened their already impending demise. Independents who purchased equipment from better funded teams found themselves competing with additional cars loaded with better (or at least equal) parts. The expansion of the top teams into multi-car outfits pushed other owners to expand as well, which further squeezed out independents. By the late 1990s, the multi-car team stood as the norm in Winston Cup. Single-car operations, such as Morgan-McClure, struggled on with diminishing returns or abdicated some measure of their independence in return for an alliance with one of the multi-car teams.

Although the modern form of the multi-car team only developed amidst the increasing costs of NASCAR in the 1980s, the concept is as old as the sport. Prior to NASCAR's creation, Raymond Parks operated a multi-car team and Karl Kiekhaefer's Mercury Outboard Motors team ruled Grand National in the mid-1950s, but most owners avoided the additional burdens of trying to manage multiple cars. Holman-Moody sporadically fielded two cars until its demise in the early 1970s, while Petty Enterprises sometimes entered a second car in premier events, but even these two powerhouses did not make a concerted effort to create viable multi-car teams. The prevailing wisdom of pre-1990s NASCAR was that two teams divided an owner's time so much that neither car would be successful. Only amid the spiraling costs of the 1980s did this view began to crack. Junior Johnson made a tentative step toward multi-car teams when he utilized Hodgdon money to field Chevrolets for both Darrell Waltrip and Neil Bonnett during the mid-1980s. However, the two cars operated out of different garages, making them barely teammates. Petty Enterprises also began fielding two cars on a regular basis, but only because two Pettys now competed in Winston Cup. As Richard noted about the operations of his and son Kyle's cars, "the two teams will be separate in every way." While Petty enjoyed being on the track with his son, he also acknowledged the problems of a multi-car operation, telling one reporter before the 1983 season that "it's a real strain on our people to stay prepared."[22]

Charlotte car dealer Rick Hendrick, a relative NASCAR newcomer at the time, became the individual who developed the modern multi-car team concept. Hendrick first entered Winston Cup in 1984, when he was part of an ownership group that fielded a team for Geoff Bodine. With additional sponsorship money available (and some personal issues brewing on the Bodine team), Hendrick added a second car for 1986 and assigned it to driver Tim Richmond and former Bodine crew chief Harry Hyde. Although most observers at the time predicted a disaster (especially given the personalities of the two drivers), Hendrick's experiment garnered a total of nine victories that season. The success prompted an expansion to three cars the next season, with Benny Parsons replacing the ailing Richmond and Darrell Waltrip jumping from Junior Johnson's organization. Hendrick's team prospered thanks to first-class equipment, the willingness of teammate drivers to share important information, and the ability to utilize different race strategies to ensure at least one team car chose the correct one. Much of the residual concerns over the efficacy of a multi-car team dissipated in 1989 when Hendrick cars finished first, second, and fourth at the Daytona 500. Hendrick's success prompted Junior Johnson to field a true multi-car team beginning in 1991, with Jack Roush following suit the next season. Well-funded single-car teams continued to flourish through the mid-1990s, but by the end of the decade the multi-car operations dominated Winston Cup.[23]

Hendrick also played a key role in the development of the first blockbuster NASCAR film, 1990's *Days of Thunder*. Although problematic in its own right, the Tom Cruise vehicle offered a high-budget portrayal of stock car racing superior to prior filmic efforts, which had fallen into three basic categories. The earliest films, such as *Thunder Road* (1958) and *Thunder in Carolina* (1960), had revolved around speed-fiend Southern boys who loved to race and haul moonshine. This style of film reached its pinnacle with *The Last American Hero* (1973), a fictionalized account of Junior Johnson's life. A second group of films utilized stock car racing as the backdrop for country humor. Films of this second type include *Speedway* (1968), *Six Pack* (1982), *Stroker Ace* (1983), and, to a lesser extent, *Greased Lightning* (1977). A final group of films offered cheaply made star vehicles for prominent drivers, such as Fred Lorenzen's *Speed Lovers*

(1968) and *43: The Richard Petty Story* (1974). Prior to *Days of Thunder*, only Howard Hawks, with the inept *Red Line 7000* (1965), had attempted to make a big-budget stock car epic.

The project that became *Days of Thunder* developed out of Tom Cruise's connections with Paul Newman, who had ties to Rick Hendrick. Much of the film utilized Hendrick cars and equipment, and included scenes of actual Cup races with special "camera" cars that qualified for races, then ran in the back of the field to get footage. Many drivers complained of the presence of fake cars on the track, fearful of the added dangers, but, without a union, they had to accept them. Despite the direct involvement of Hendrick, NASCAR, and a few drivers, the film offered a litany of racing cliches, from shade tree mechanics to the incessant banging of cars with each other and retaining walls. Darrell Waltrip noted when the film was released that "there's a lot of Hollywood in it." There was also a lot of the image Bill France hoped to establish for NASCAR. While promoting the film, Cruise posited that those involved with stock car racing are "the type of people that built this country." Images of waving flags, smiling white fans, and rustic farms blended with scenes of careening cars to reinforce the fact that, according to Cruise, "NASCAR is a family sport." The film opened at number one in June 1990 and helped the ongoing process of building the NASCAR fan base as it introduced millions of Cruise fans to stock car racing.[24]

The early 1990s also witnessed a series of departures from Winston Cup that signaled, even more than 1988, a changing of the guard in stock car racing. In June 1992, after two years of illness, "Big" Bill France died in Florida. Twenty years before his death, France had transferred his official title as chairman and CEO of NASCAR to son "Little" Bill, so France's passing did not disrupt the day-to-day operations of NASCAR, but all involved in stock car racing recognized his momentous importance to the sport. Even Richard Petty, who clashed with the iron-fisted France many times, acknowledged that he "didn't agree with a lot of the things he did . . . but what he did for stock car racing in general can't be denied." Petty himself became the other significant departure in 1992 as he launched a year-long "Fan Appreciation Tour" before retiring from driving at the end of the season. When Petty retired, he ranked first in Winston Cup history in starts, poles, wins, laps, laps led, races led, and total miles. Despite not winning a race in his final eight seasons, "King" Richard's popularity never wavered. For the season-ending Hooters 500, Atlanta Motor Speedway had to install additional seats to accommodate the overflow crowd of well-wishers. An estimated crowd of 162,000 jammed the facility to watch Petty finish 35th.[25]

Petty's final career race also witnessed the end to one of the closest points battles in NASCAR history. With six drivers still in contention at Atlanta, Alan Kulwicki finished second in the race and took the championship. Despite his status as a Northern interloper, Kulwicki became a fan favorite because he earned his dues as an independent during the 1980s. He also became famous for driving a backwards "Polish victory lap" after wins. Kulwicki competed in the first five races of 1993 season, but then died in an airplane crash in April. In July, Davey Allison died when he crashed his private helicopter in route to Talladega (original Alabama Gang member Red Farmer was also injured in the crash). At the time of his death, Allison was in fifth place in the Cup standings. These tragic events stripped Winston Cup of two of its brightest young stars, but a new one loomed on the horizon. The 1992 Hooters 500 not only marked Richard Petty's final Winston Cup start, it was also the first for Jeff Gordon.[26]

7

YOUNG GUNS

"Big" Bill France lived long enough to see stock car racing blossom from a ramshackle and marginalized endeavor into the most popular motor sport in the world. Under his watch, 40 years of growth brought NASCAR to a position of prominence in American sports unimaginable in the organization's early years. These successes, however, served as merely a prelude to the expansion of the 1990s. Over the course of the decade, NASCAR developed a network of speedways that demonstrated a truly national scope, signed contracts for the television broadcasting of every Cup race, and finally invaded the citadel of American racing—Indianapolis. This growth, though, came at a price. Appealing to fans and sponsors across the country meant that NASCAR found itself compelled to reduce the number of races at traditional venues in the South, oriented all aspects of events toward television instead of the attending spectators, and shaved off all its remaining rough edges. To the chagrin of many older fans, the wholesome and fan-friendly NASCAR of the 1990s cracked down on rough driving and increasingly embraced unproven, yet telegenic, young drivers over the crusty veterans with greasy fingernails who previously gave stock car racing much of its earthly allure. In the 1950s, Herb Thomas and his mouth full of cracked teeth sufficed for a newspaper ad hawking oil filters, but in the late 20th century world of television spots, seven-figure sponsorship deals, and focus groups, companies wanted a fresh-scrubbed heartthrob such as Kasey Kahne to promote their wares. The potential loss of fans resulting from shifting race locations and drivers, however, was offset by a NASCAR program of connecting with conservatives across the country. NASCAR, to a greater degree than any other sport, positioned itself as a bastion of patriotism and family values.

More traditional fans embraced the "values" aspect of NASCAR, but increasingly found themselves confronted with a dwindling supply of "good ol' boy" drivers to support. In 1993, two young drivers of the old style (Davey Allison and Alan Kulwicki) died in accidents, and in early 1994, Alabama Gang veteran Neil Bonnett perished in a practice crash at Dayona. Traditional southern drivers became increasingly scarce as the number of Winston Cup competitors from the South continued to decline. During the 1990s and early 2000s, the percentage of Cup drivers hailing from southern states dipped to 46 percent; since 1990, Wisconsin has contributed more drivers than South Carolina, Georgia, or Florida. Even many of the remaining successful southern drivers distanced themselves from the moonshine and outlaw myths of early stock. After toiling far back in the standings for much of the previous decade, second-generation North Carolina racer Dale Jarrett emerged as a top driver in the 1990s, winning the championship in 1999. As a son of the South whose father also won a NASCAR championship, Jarrett appeared to be a direct link to stock car racing traditions. Jarrett, however, drove a car owned by NFL coach Joe Gibbs as part of a team that stressed the born-again Christian status of its members. Well spoken and friendly, southerner Jarrett could win a race without being booed by the fans, but he was not the sort of driver who inspired passion among the type of spectators who crowded the infields of Darlington or Talladega.[1]

Under these circumstances, more traditional NASCAR fans became increasingly dogged in their devotion to aging veterans. Even the formerly much-reviled Darrell Waltrip managed to become a fan favorite as his career wound down in the early 1990s. Fifty-year-old "Handsome" Harry Gant, active on the Cup circuit since 1973, also rose in popularity (especially after winning four races in a row late in 1991) thanks to his rugged southern looks and Skoal sponsorship. The real hero for many traditional fans in the 1990s, however, was Dick Trickle. Despite enormous success in American Speed Association (ASA) races, Trickle did not earn a full-time cup ride until 1989 (at age 47). In much the same way that Kulwicki transcended his northern roots in the eyes of NASCAR fans, Wisconsin native Trickle developed a cultlike following thanks to his evocative name and hard-bitten lifestyle. Trickle famously had a cigarette lighter installed in his Cup car so that he could smoke during caution laps and was once caught by an in-car camera drinking a beer during a race. Although he never won a single Cup race, Trickle's popularity allowed him to continue to race on the circuit until age 60. In *Days of Thunder*, Tom Cruise paid homage to him by naming his character "Cole Trickle."

Dick Trickle possessed a cultlike popularity, but Dale Earnhardt's connection with the fans of the 1990s represented a mass movement. The "Intimidator" solidified his support among traditional NASCAR fans by winning the championship in 1991, 1993, and 1994. By this point, Earnhardt's success among stock car racing supporters stemmed from the imbrication of his racing style, image as an old school racer, and the fact that (in his early forties at this point) he had achieved the status of elder statesman. In a transitional period in which NASCAR attempted to broaden its appeal through the recruitment of younger drivers from outside the Southeast, Earnhardt became a cherished symbol of old NASCAR to traditional working-class, southern fans. As a result, merchandise bearing Earnhardt's distinctive slanted "3" became increasingly popular. The success of this merchandise reflected one of the distinctive aspects of NASCAR fandom. To a degree not found in other sports, fans of stock car racing associate their favorite drivers with their car numbers. Thanks to its association with Michael Jordan, the number 23 became very popular with basketball fans (and players, witness LeBron James), but every NBA team can assign a player that number. In NASCAR, each number is allocated to one driver (technically it is assigned to the owner), which creates special connections between numbers and drivers. Earnhardt's decals, flags, and shirts often did not even include his name, just the number 3. To those who followed NASCAR, the number was enough. Whether emblazoned with a name or just a number, merchandise became an enormous source of revenue for NASCAR during the 1990s. As with all potential revenue streams, the organization moved quickly to maximize merchandise profits. For example, in order to streamline activities with mega-retailer Wal-Mart, NASCAR opened an office in the department store chain's hometown of Bentonville, Arkansas. By the early 21st century annual retail sales of NASCAR merchandise topped $2 billion.[2]

Earnhardt's early 1990s run of championships ended in 1995, and from that year on he steadily fell back in the championship points race, with a slight rebound in his final full season. His decline can be attributed to age, the disadvantage of racing for an owner (Richard Childress) disinclined to adopt the multicar team strategy sweeping the sport, and the emergence of hungry young challengers. Of all the new drivers of the 1990s, none loomed larger in NASCAR than Jeff Gordon. Gordon's breakout season of 1994 can be seen as the beginning of NASCAR's modern boom in popularity. His ascension heralded not just the transference of top status from the old king Earnhardt to the new one Gordon, but also the rise of the new style of driver-personality that has dominated NASCAR for the last 15 years. Suspect in the eyes of many traditional fans, Gordon and his progeny spurred these stock car supporters to deify Earnhardt. Gordon won the championship in 1995, which ended Earnhardt's string of titles. This alone caused ill will toward the younger driver, but Gordon spawned a hatred among some NASCAR fans comparable only to the late 1970s backlash against Darrell Waltrip. Like Waltrip, Gordon inspired dread in older fans because he augured yet another transformation in the type of drivers in NASCAR.[3]

Gordon's roots lay in California, but he first gained acclaim as an adolescent open-wheel driver on the dirt tracks of Indiana and Ohio. In the early 1990s, Ford began backing him in the Busch Grand National series, with the assumption that the talented youngster would drive a Thunderbird once he made the transition to the Cup series. In an enormous tactical error, Ford declined Gordon's request for a formal commitment from the manufacturer. Cup team owner Rick Hendrick, whose cars are Chevrolets, then swooped in and signed Gordon (and his Grand National crew chief Ray Evernham) to a long-term contract in 1992. As part of Hendrick's successful multicar team, Gordon won three championships over the course of the decade. In 1998, he scored one of the greatest seasons in NASCAR history, winning 13 races and finishing in the top 10 in 28 of 33 starts. This remarkable consistency resulted in only four other drivers finishing within 1,000 points of Gordon at the end of the season. Such successes should have made Gordon immensely popular among NASCAR fans, but his victories served only to alienate a significant portion of stock car racing supporters. In a sport that promotes brand loyalty, Gordon's jump from factory-assisted Ford to Hendrick Chevrolet struck some fans as traitorous—an inauspicious first impression. Supplanting Earnhardt as Cup champion also contributed to this situation, but factors beyond the track made many fans hostile toward Gordon.[4]

Despite Gordon's success in sprint cars and midgets, many NASCAR fans believed he had not earned the right to a full-time Cup ride at age 21. For generations, Cup drivers paid their dues by struggling to work their way up through the dirt track ranks, but Gordon had risen meteorically thanks first to his parents' mortgaging of their own future to support him, and later to Ford money. Although far from wealthy, he appeared to have bought his way to fast success. For blue-collar NASCAR fans who championed Earnhardt as one of their own, Gordon epitomized the advantages unfairly gained by those with money. This inequality continued when Gordon earned a spot in Hendrick's successful Cup organization without having to first take rides with underfunded back markers (as Earnhardt and many others had done). Therefore, traditional southern NASCAR fans perceived Gordon as unproven, wealthy, northern, and spoiled. For them, Gordon represented the absolute antithesis of Earnhardt (veteran, southern, and aggressively self-reliant), and old-style stock car supporters found him, not surprisingly, repellent. When Gordon proved himself by winning his first Winston Cup championship at age 23, Earnhardt fans found themselves confronted with a nightmarish scenario in which a driver they abhorred had become the new face of NASCAR. As Bill

France noted, "some of the fans have a problem with the new kid on the block beating their heroes." For NASCAR fans, an unbridgeable divide emerged that permanently separated those who purchased merchandise with "3" on it from those who bought gear emblazoned with Jeff Gordon's number "24."[5]

Those upset about Gordon's arrival in Winston Cup also latched on the notion that he was "soft." Earnhardt-style fans believed Gordon's level of masculinity compared unfavorably to that of the grizzled "Intimidator." The questioning of Gordon's masculinity stemmed from his driving style, aggressive but not confrontational, and his appearance. Whereas Earnhardt looked like a craggly old gunfighter, *People* magazine named the telegenic Gordon one the world's 50 most beautiful people in 1997. Although not the first handsome driver, Gordon was the first to both consciously focus on his appearance and to try to cultivate a more cosmopolitan image. In the hypermasculine world of traditional stock car racing fans, such behavior could only be explained one way—that Gordon was homosexual. Despite two marriages (including one to a former Miss Winston Cup) and children, anti-"24" forces began bringing T-shirts and signs to Cup races that read "Gordon is gay." The phrase became so pervasive that country comedian Cledus T. Judd even recorded a song with that title.[6]

Many of the homophobic anti-Gordon stock fans pointed to Gordon's own actions as proof of his homosexuality. Although Gordon typically tried to ignore discussions of his sexuality, aspects of his career can be viewed as seemingly deliberate provocations—passive-aggressive endeavors that appeared calculated to inflame Earnhardt supporters by reinforcing the depressing belief that a homosexual is defeating their champion. From the beginning of his Cup career, DuPont served as Gordon's primary sponsor. The chemical company hoped association with NASCAR's newest star would help them promote their line of paints. To that end, Gordon's car sported a garish multicolored paint scheme. As a means of helping drivers find their stalls on pit lane, a member of the crew holds a sign attached to a long pole over their pit box. As part of the DuPont sponsorship, Gordon's pit sign was a square with multiple horizontal stripes of color. The sign closely resembled the rainbow flag adopted by the lesbian-gay-bisexual-transgender (LGBT) community as a symbol of unity and sexual freedom. These LGBT connotations were reinforced by the fact that Gordon's pit crew called itself the "Rainbow Warriors." Also, Gordon appeared to want to become part of the liberal and gay-friendly entertainment world by appearing in movies and on television (in 2003, he became the first NASCAR driver to host *Saturday Night Live*). As final "evidence" of Gordon's sexual orientation, traditional fans pointed to his drinking habits. Despite being part of a beer-and-whiskey-soaked sport,

Gordon released a line of California wines bearing his name. Before releasing the wines, Gordon made clear his products were not for the average NASCAR supporter by noting that "it's a high-end wine that is going to be exclusive to get . . . it's not race related and it's not something we're trying to take to race fans."[7]

Despite a cold reception from an element of NASCAR nation, Gordon's appeal to other fans made him a valuable commodity among sponsors. The 1980s trend of companies unrelated to the automotive industry becoming involved in stock car racing continued into the 1990s and beyond. Gordon's success, as feared by the Earnhardt supporters, ushered in an era in which car owners increasingly sought out telegenic drivers who could attract sponsors. Companies wanted physically attractive racers because sponsorship deals increasingly included the use of drivers in television ads. The crass commercialism of Darrell Waltrip thanking his sponsors in victory lane after races in the 1970s morphed into drivers shilling for companies on national television. A cadre of blandly handsome and nonthreatening young drivers without southern accents emerged as spokesmen for their various sponsors. The Gillette Company went so far as to hire a group of these drivers to appear in their ads. The company dubbed them the "Young Guns," a fitting name for an entire generation of media-savvy drivers. Jeff Gordon posited that sponsors would "rather have somebody that has good looks and a good personality and has the marketability, whatever that may be." Roush Racing executive Geoff Smith, whose job does not require a Gordon-like smoothness in dealing with the media, more candidly acknowledged this by noting that "when you look around the garage, you don't find race-drivers that are dog ugly." Appearance became so important to sponsors that 2005 Cup champion Kurt Busch underwent plastic surgery to reshape his ears.[8]

Humpy Wheeler spoke for many traditional fans opposed to the "Young Guns" when he noted "we still need that rough, tough, good old boy who can mix it up on the track, we don't want 20 guys walking in wearing Brooks Brothers suits and Gucci shoes, drinking tea down in the pit lane." Wheeler's pleas will likely go unanswered as NASCAR continues to promote respectable-looking young drivers as the face of the sport. For NASCAR, however, this presents a dilemma. With a roster of virtually interchangeable "Young Guns" competing for the Cup, it is difficult to generate the sort of fan affiliation involved with personalities such as Richard Petty or Dale Earnhardt. Sponsors, though, want polished and nonthreatening drivers as spokesmen. As with many of the difficulties associated with becoming more national and corporate-driven, NASCAR has sought to chart something of a middle course, while leaning toward placating deep-pocketed sponsors. On the track, aggressive driving is tolerated as long as it does not reach the point of being obviously confrontational (at that point NASCAR begins doling out stiff penalties). Similarly, postrace feuds between angry drivers that escalate to pushing, finger pointing, or getting into each others' (helmet-covered) faces is tolerated, but NASCAR officials typically step in to make sure tempers do not boil over into actual fisticuffs. By condoning these types of encounters (which are quickly becoming as ritualized as baseball brawls and the shoving matches at prefight weigh-ins among boxers), NASCAR allows drivers to maintain representations of honor and masculinity without engaging in the sort of physical violence that might be viewed unfavorably by the corporations sponsoring the drivers. The boundaries of acceptable behavior can be seen in NASCAR's treatment of driver Tony Stewart, who has received numerous penalties and fines for antics that would have merited no disciplinary action in the early years of stock car racing. A replay of the Yarborough versus Allisons fight at the 1979 Daytona 500 ever occurring seems highly unlikely.[9]

Despite complaints from Wheeler and others over the new style of drivers, NASCAR quickly recognized the appeal of the "Young Guns" to female fans and sought out ways to profit from the legions of women supporting the sport. Under the assumption that women buy cologne for their husbands and boyfriends, NASCAR released the Daytona 500 line of fragrances in 2006. This move was partially prompted by the success of Halston's Z-14 cologne after Jeff Gordon began promoting it. To assist women in producing meals for race day, NASCAR put its name on crock pots, potatoes, bacon, and barbeque sauce. As a means of attracting a younger generation of female fans, NASCAR sanctioned the release of a very successful NASCAR Barbie in 1999. NASCAR's most direct move to sell product to adult women, however, occurred in 2006 when the organization green flagged a line of Harlequin Romance novels based on the world of stock car racing. Although the series involved only fictional drivers, the cover art on many volumes features a dark and handsome driver who bore a striking resemblance to Jeff Gordon. By 2009, Harlequin had issued almost 40 novels in the popular series.[10]

The year 1994 marked not only the beginning of NASCAR's modern boom, but also the birth of the Gordon-Earnhardt rivalry. Although Gordon ran a full slate of Winston Cup races in 1993, it was not until the next season that he truly emerged as a significant opponent to Earnhardt. The "Intimidator" won his final championship in 1994, with Gordon winning two races. Although the newcomer finished only eighth in points, he clearly stood as the breakout star of the season. With all six of the drivers separating them in the standings being aging veterans, Gordon became the logical new rival for Earnhardt. For the rest of the decade, these two

battled for NASCAR supremacy. As the ravages of age caught up with
Earnhardt, however, the rivalry increasingly became one fought out in
the media and among fans. Earnhardt helped fuel the competition by derisively dubbing Gordon "Wonder Boy," a name the veteran's fans gleefully
used as well. Despite the fierce partisanship of the two drivers' fans, on the
track the rivalry became decidedly one-sided. Gordon won the Winston
Cup championship three times during the 1990s, but Earnhardt never
won another after his 1994 triumph.[11]

Although Gordon won only two races in 1994, one of his victories that
season occurred in the most significant Winston Cup race since the 1979
Daytona 500. Reflective of both NASCAR's rising importance and the
decline of open-wheel racing, in 1994 Winston Cup ran its first race at
Indianapolis Motor Speedway (IMS). Speedway president Tony George,
locked in a battle with Championship Auto Racing Teams that eventually
led him to establish the rival Indy Racing League (IRL), recognized that
the financial windfall from hosting a NASCAR event would help support his struggle to gain control of open-wheel racing and therefore began
a dialogue with stock's leadership in the early 1990s. Any doubts about
NASCAR's ability to draw fans to the venerable track evaporated when
30,000 fans showed up just to watch stock cars test tires at the speedway
in late June 1992 (a scant two weeks after the death of "Big" Bill France).
The inaugural Brickyard 400 in 1994 drew more than 300,000 NASCAR
fans to IMS. To the delight of many of the local Indiana race fans, adopted son Gordon won the race. For Gordon, his victory at IMS signaled
his arrival in NASCAR; for NASCAR, the Brickyard represented the
culmination of decades of competition with open-wheel racing. Since the
early 20th century, the Indianapolis 500 stood as the premier racing event
in the United States, and open-wheel enthusiasts pointed to the exclu-
sion of stock cars from the track as evidence of the second-class nature of
the "taxi cabs." NASCAR's appearance at what car owner Chip Ganassi
called "hallowed ground" destroyed the last vestige of open-wheel superiority in American racing.[12]

The granting of a race to IMS also became part of a trend toward expanding NASCAR's national appeal by scheduling events at new, nonsouthern venues. NASCAR's schedule remained fairly static from the
establishment of the Winston Cup until the early 1990s, but the organization's drive to expand propelled significant shifts during the last decade
of the century. The NASCAR leadership adjusted the Cup season to create a more regionally balanced schedule by sanctioning events at new
tracks. The tightly packed cluster of tracks in the Southeast proved to be
the biggest losers in this shift. Although long associated with NASCAR,
the tracks at North Wilkesboro and Rockingham both lost their Cup

dates. Almost as shocking as Wilkes County losing its NASCAR events, Darlington lost the right to host the Southern 500 on Labor Day weekend (and completely lost its second date of the season). These traditional Cup events perished so that new races could be held outside the Southeast. This effort at regional balance led to Cup events in Chicago; Phoenix; Miami; Las Vegas; Louden, New Hampshire; and southern California. North Wilkesboro, for example, lost its two dates after being purchased by Bruton Smith's Speedway Motorsports, Incorporated. Smith moved one date to his track in New Hampshire and the other to a new track in Texas. Much like their abandonment of dirt tracks in the 1960s, NASCAR viewed these moves as steps toward modernization, and any loss of support from traditionally minded fans was more than offset by the increased revenue generated by the jumps in attendance provided by the large new tracks. For the France family these profits benefited them doubly. Not only could their NASCAR reap the rewards of these large crowds, but the family-controlled International Speedway Corporation (ISC) owned the new tracks in Florida, California, Arizona, and Illinois.[13]

The great irony of NASCAR's nationalization and abandonment of southern tracks was that it occurred during a period when the organization more fully acknowledged its "southernness." For decades the Bill Frances sought to present stock car racing as something more than just a southern pursuit and downplayed the notion that the Southeast represented NASCAR's backbone of support. With NASCAR finally positioned as a national enterprise, the organization could acknowledge its southern roots without appearing to be merely a regional sport. As Derek Alderman and others noted, NASCAR reached a "transcultural" status in the last two decades. As a transcultural sport, NASCAR is "influenced simultaneously by tradition and transition." The regional affiliation of stock car racing remained in the notion that it is a "southern" sport, but mass commercialization and communication positioned NASCAR within a national popular culture. Older, southern fans lamented NASCAR's altered character, agreeing with Richard Pillsbury's assertion that it has lost its status as a uniquely southern entertainment, but a much larger national audience embraced stock partly out of its connections with the southeastern bootlegger image of masculinity. This transcultural status allows NASCAR to promote itself through affiliation with "southern" traits (conservatism, patriotism, love of family) while still able to promote stock car racing as part of a truly national sports culture.[14]

The Gordon-Earnhardt rivalry that propelled much of the growth of transcultural NASCAR came to an abrupt and tragic end in 2001. After a resurgence in 2000 (he finished second in points), Earnhardt appeared ready to make a run at one last championship in 2001. At the Daytona

500, however, Earnhardt lost his life when his Chevrolet slammed into the outside retaining wall on the final lap of the race. The nature of his death helped cement Earnhardt's iconic status. Not only did he die while competing in the "Great American Race," but his end came as a result of his efforts to block other cars so that the two cars owned by Dale Earnhardt, Incorporated (driven by Michael Waltrip and Dale Earnhardt Jr.) could finish in first and second place. For Earnhardt's fans, such an ending gave Earnhardt's death a heroic mystique; he died assisting others (including his own son). Subsequently, recollections of "Ironhead" wrecking others to get to the front became virtually subsumed by the image of Earnhardt in 2001—aggressive but altruistic. Dying for the cause of victory by his team helped reinforce the perception of Earnhardt as the "Last Confederate Soldier." Iconic to traditional fans in life, Earnhardt assumed legendary status with his death at Daytona. For NASCAR fans, his number 3 gained an artifact status similar to that of the cross for many Christians. After his death fans began silently standing with three fingers raised during the third lap of Winston Cup races in tribute. And while the true believers emblazon his number on every material item imaginable, almost 10 years after his death no Cup driver has dared to race with 3 on his car. In a sport that does not officially retire numbers, 3 has become a de facto one and Earnhardt now looms as the martyred saint of stock cars. As Robert Lipsyte noted, the Earnhardt myth presents him as "a man's man who sacrificed himself to shepherd his flock to the finish line, a hero who in death evoked both John Wayne and Jesus."[15]

Gordon went on to win his fourth NASCAR championship in the tragedy-marred 2001 season, wracking up almost $11 million in winnings along the way. He narrowly edged out the inheritor of Earnhardt's outlaw status—Tony "Smoke" Stewart. An Indiana dirt track legend (he scored an unprecedented achievement in 1995 by winning the title in all three of United States Auto Club's touring series), Stewart won the IRL championship in 1997 before switching to stock cars. In 1999, he became Cup series Rookie of the Year by winning three races in a car owned by Joe Gibbs. Stewart's meteoric rise culminated in the first of his two Cup championships in 2002. Like Gordon, although for very different reasons, Stewart polarized NASCAR fans. Whereas some stock fans blasted Gordon for being soft, Stewart earned the ire of many for being too rough. The hot-tempered Stewart's drive to win led him into frequent conflict with other drivers, NASCAR officials, and reporters. He earned reprimands and sanctions from NASCAR, his team, and primary sponsor Home Depot. Stewart's fender banging antics on the track (and on pit road and postrace "cool down" laps) led to well-publicized feuds with Gordon, Kurt Busch, Matt Kenseth, and Clint Boyer. Stewart's actions pushed the normally circumspect Gordon to publicly declare that Smoke was a "bonehead." Although his image as Winston Cup's resident bad boy brought kudos from some who decried the "increasingly vanilla world of NASCAR," Stewart turned off many fans because, like Earnhardt in the early 1980s, his aggressive style meant that at some point he tangled with their favorite driver. In recent years, however, support for Stewart has swelled for several of reasons. With growing numbers of unproven "Young Guns" appearing, traditional fans have gained an appreciation for the way Stewart proved himself before obtaining a Cup ride. Stewart's notoriously hedonistic lifestyle of womanizing and gluttony (he is infamous for being out of shape) has also made him a hero of the rowdy track infield denizens. And his refusal to drive a Toyota when Joe Gibbs Racing switched from Chevrolets after the 2008 season earned Stewart the respect of diehard brand supporters in the stands. Stewart reinforced his throwback status by organizing his own team after departing from the Gibbs organization.[16]

Although Stewart drove like the "Intimidator," much of the support garnered by the senior Earnhardt was transferred to his son Dale Junior. Earnhardt *fils* became a perennial winner of NASCAR's most popular driver poll after first taking the title in 2003. His popularity developed out of his familial connections, fan-friendly sponsorship, and his ability to maintain the allegiance of older fans while appealing to a younger generation. For most of his career, Budweiser, the beer of choice in red states, served as Dale Jr.'s primary sponsor. Traditional NASCAR fans also took comfort from the younger Earnhardt's affiliation with Wrangler, his father's first big sponsor. Unlike Dale Jr., however, the "Intimidator" would have never allowed his car to run an event with the Dave Mathews Band as a cosponsor. Such actions give Dale Jr. great cache with younger fans who want to support a driver with cultural reference points similar to their own without resorting to affiliation with one of the "Young Guns." His fantastic popularity can be attributed to Dale Jr.'s ability to connect with the entire spectrum of NASCAR fans—traditional, traditional-leaning youth, and "heart-throb" supporters. Success with NASCAR nation, however, does not automatically translate to victories on the track. During his first five full seasons in the Winston Cup, Dale Jr. showed flashes of brilliance and established himself as a consistent contender. Since turning 30, however, Earnhardt's successes have dwindled. In the second five years of his career, Dale Jr. managed only three victories. In 2008, he joined the highly successful Rick Hendrick team, thereby eliminating the ability of his supporters to claim inferior equipment contributed to Earnhardt's struggles, but his results place him as only the fourth best driver on the team.[17]

To the chagrin of NASCAR, the latest member of the Earnhardt dynasty did not become the dominant driver of the 21st century. Rather, as with

Gordon in the 1990s, a driver unpopular with fans—Jimmie Johnson—
emerged to win four consecutive championships. Some of Johnson's problems with NASCAR nation can be traced directly to actions on the track.
For example, Johnson's crew chief, Chad Knaus, has been punished several times by NASCAR for cheating. The inevitable backlash against a
dominant driver also contributes to fan dislike of Johnson. Much of the
animosity toward Johnson, however, stems from the perception that he
is a clone of Jeff Gordon. Like Gordon, Johnson is from California and
landed his first Cup ride with the Hendrick team. Also, *People* magazine
included Johnson in its 2000 list of "sexiest men alive/men in the fast
lane." Johnson compounds his problems by living in Manhattan with a
model and driving a Hendrick car that is co-owned by Gordon. For many
traditional fans, Johnson's connections to Gordon place him beyond the
pale of supportable drivers, despite his obvious skills.[18]

The emergence of "Young Guns" and nonsouthern racers, however,
has not altered one traditional characteristic of NASCAR drivers. Stock
car racing remains a sport with no African American competitors. In
recent years Hispanic drivers Juan Pablo Montoya and Aric Almirola
competed in NASCAR's premier series, but no African American has
regularly run in the NEXTEL Cup since Wendell Scott retired in the
mid-1970s. NASCAR's cautious response to this situation reflects the
dilemma faced by the organization as it tries to navigate between appealing to a national audience while not completely alienating the conservative southern base that supported the sport in the past. The difficulty in
accomplishing that delicate balance can be seen in comments made by
NASCAR president Mike Helton in 2006. Just one day after telling a
reporter that "the old southeastern redneck heritage that we had is no
longer," complaints from traditional fans forced Helton to soothe their
concerns by telling another reporter that "NASCAR is absolutely as concerned about keeping its roots intact as it is about growing the sport."
The furor created by Helton's statements passed quickly, but a similar
mixed message from NASCAR contributes to continual debate over one
of the most controversial aspects of stock car events—the presence of
numerous rebel flags.

"Little" Bill France's son Brian, who became NASCAR's chief executive officer in 2003, told a CBS reporter that "it's not a flag I look
at with anything favorable," but then facetiously declared "I can't tell
people what flag to fly." While NASCAR might face legal opposition
to the unilateral banning of rebel flags at all events, tracks owned by
the France-controlled ISC could easily ban them but have not. The
NAACP's subsequent request that NASCAR ban rebel flags at races elicited no response from the sanctioning body. NASCAR's silence, even

when confronted with a threatened NAACP boycott over the flag, reflected the organization's efforts to appease conservative white fans, who buy far more tickets than African Americans. Even France's measured statements on the issue brought a torrent of protests from southern fans desirous of maintaining the rebel flag's prominence at stock car races. For some white southern fans, the flags obviously represented more than just links to a Confederate past; like attendance at stock car races and defenses of rebel flags in other aspects of southern life, they helped reinforce notions of social order. Rebel flag-filled stock car events can be viewed as examples of the "geographical anchors" of white southerners outlined by Grace Elizabeth Hale. In a direct response to France's comment and the threat it seemed to pose, the Sons of Confederate Veterans adorned a billboard outside the ISC-owned Darlington Raceway with a rebel flag and proposed their own boycott if the flags were banned. These threats clearly resonated with NASCAR, which has since continued to avoid conflict with this element of NASCAR nation by permitting rebel flags to be displayed at all events. The continued presence of rebel flags reflected comments made by African American crew chief Bill Shutt who noted that, despite nationalization, "this sport was born and bred and developed in the Deep South . . . and it's still there."[19]

Similar to NASCAR's response to the battle over rebel flags, the organization's efforts to enlarge stock car racing's nonwhite fan base appeared to be half-hearted attempts geared merely toward avoiding more public denunciations from civil rights groups. NASCAR began the Drive for Diversity program in 2004 to identify and support young minority drivers, but the program has been both fraught with problems and heavily criticized as being underfunded. The lack of financial support for the Drive for Diversity meant that few potential minority drivers knew of the program, and that those who were involved were being trained with poor equipment. Although the Drive for Diversity has placed drivers in low-level weekly events, no one involved with it has made the jump to one of NASCAR's top two series. Also, questioning of NASCAR's level of devotion to diversity arose in 2008 with African American Mauricia Grant's $225 million lawsuit against the organization. Hired in 2005 as a technical inspector for the Nationwide Series, Grant was fired in October 2007. She then filed the lawsuit claiming that pervasive racial harassment created a hostile working environment and that her termination stemmed from complaints she made about her treatment. In December 2008, NASCAR reached an out-of-court settlement with Grant by paying her an undisclosed amount. Nationwide Series car owner turned television commentator Brad Daugherty, the most prominent African American directly involved with stock car racing, noted that he was "a little disappointed by how far the sport has come as far as inclusion" and that "the changes have only been incremental."[20]

The "whiteness" of NASCAR nation may distress advocates of cultural diversity, but it generated considerable excitement among early 21st-century political operatives. With a voting public almost evenly split between Republicans and Democrats, political strategists from both parties constantly search for untapped pockets of voters with whom to connect. During the 1990s, the two parties made overtures toward "angry white guys," "soccer moms," "office park dads," and "waitress moms" in an effort to give their respective party the slight edge over the opposition needed to take power. The fantastically close presidential election of 2000 served to reinforce the necessity of tracking down and narrowcasting a message to every last potential voter. Inspired by Ruy Teixeira and Joel Rogers's book *America's Forgotten Majority*, strategists became enamored with appealing more directly to the white working class. The rural or "exurb" residing, noncollege educated, progun and military males known as "Reagan Democrats" in the 1980s suddenly became an important political demographic. With both parties unhappy with half of the phrase "Reagan Democrats," these voters became, thanks to a coinage by Democratic pollster Celinda Lake, "NASCAR dads." Although the lumping together of millions of stock car racing fans under the umbrella term "NASCAR dads" clearly reflected a degree of unfair stereotyping— despite outsider impressions to the contrary, an Earnhardt fan would, for example, claim to adhere to values very different from those of a Jeff Gordon supporter—the recognition that NASCAR grandstands are packed every week with a large number of conservative middle or working class whites does possess validity. And, despite the widely held belief in liberal media bias among this demographic, the media scrutiny of "NASCAR dads," especially during the 2004 presidential election season, resulted in coverage that typically presented these fans as they see themselves. One study found that the bulk of news accounts of "NASCAR dads" presented them as distinguished by their "patriotism, loyalty, and family and religious values—all deeply resonant symbols post-9/11/2001."[21]

To the dismay of Democrats desirous of attracting NASCAR voters through appeals to the economic self-interests of working class whites, the majority of stock car fans proved to be more inclined toward the Republicans on the basis of social and national security issues. In recent years Democrats John Edwards, Mark Warner, and Bob Graham have sponsored race cars, but Jimmie Johnson's sardonic comment that NASCAR "seems to be Republican-based" reflected merely a modern recognition of a decades-old struggle facing liberals. Long before the phrase "NASCAR dads" became part of the political landscape, stock car racing's leadership and supporters showed a marked support for the Republican Party. This can be seen, for example, in the comments made after the drivers' trip to the Carter White House and in the shower of boos and "we want Bush" chants that rained down on Bill Clinton during his ill-advised 1992 campaign visit to a NASCAR event. "Big" Bill France may have voted with the Democratic Party, but his allegiance belonged to the conservative southern wing—the "Reagan Democrats" first attracted to the Republican Party via Richard Nixon's southern strategy.[22]

One of the greatest difficulties confronting Democratic efforts to woo NASCAR fans stems from the leadership of the sanctioning body itself. "Big" Bill France's conservative political views can also be discerned in the actions of succeeding generations of the France family. Thanks to the actions of the Frances, stock car racing is the most politically encoded sport in the United States. The political trappings adopted by NASCAR's leadership stress family values, patriotism, support for the military, and Christianity—issues more associated with the Republican Party. Given the political leanings of the France family, this conservative tint to the sport is not surprising. But unlike other conservatives within the leadership of sports organizations, the family's absolute power within NASCAR gives them unfettered control of the environment that surrounds stock car races. They can organize prerace spectacles and rituals to promote their beliefs without concern for the sensitivities of other stakeholders. By creating an environment celebrating conservative values, the France family effectively creates a conservative sport difficult for liberals to penetrate.

The France family carefully cultivates the notion of NASCAR as a sport representative of "American" values. For the Frances, those values mean family-friendly entertainment, patriotism, and respect for religion. Not only is NASCAR the only major American sport that includes a precontest prayer, but it is also the only sport to require inclusion of the performing of the national anthem (and the prayer) as part of its television coverage. Reflective of the blurring of patriotism and support for the military that is part of NASCAR's system of "American" values, military color guards always present the flag during the performance of the national anthem, and fly-overs by Air Force or Navy jets often occur at the conclusion of the singing. Humpy Wheeler took these connections to a new extreme in 1991 with the staging of a mock Gulf War battle at Charlotte Motor Speedway. In recent years the United States military has recognized both that many of the fans at stock car events are among their target demographic for recruitment and also that NASCAR's support helps create an atmosphere highly conducive to the recruitment of new soldiers. To that end, all branches of the military have allocated millions of dollars to sponsor cars in various NASCAR series. Randy Fuller, Air Force liaison for motor sports, noted that "with NASCAR we are already among one of the most patriotic crowds."[23]

Although all sports involve a preevent performance of the national anthem (even if it is not required to be part of their regular television broadcasts) and public support for the military by athletes increased post-9/11, NASCAR's official prerace prayer is unique. The prayer is part of what some scholars have dubbed NASCAR's "theocratic nationalism," which blends patriotism, God, and consumerism into a potent concoction. Motor Racing Outreach, funded by drivers and sponsors, offers a plethora of raceday religious activities that culminate in all drivers, crewmen, NASCAR officials, and much of the crowd bowing their heads in prayer before the race. Only Christian clergy ever perform the prerace prayer, but there is little in the content of the prayer to connect it with any specific denominational beliefs or dogma. An almost standardized thanking of the military and request for divine protection of soldiers, however, always appears in the prayer. As the prayers usually include a reference to that day's race, the recent conversion of traditional race names to events named for their sponsor creates a questionable confluence of religion and consumerism. Whereas in the past a prerace prayer would have requested protection for the drivers in the "Firecracker 400," today's corporate NASCAR results in prayers for the "Coke Zero 400 Powered By Coca-Cola." This "God as product endorser" evolution became truly surreal at Watkins Glen in 2009 when Reverend David Fife began his prerace prayer with "thank you once again Lord for this opportunity to run the Helluva Good Sour Cream Dips at the Glen."[24]

Regardless of their actual political persuasions or religious beliefs, NASCAR fans across the country found it increasingly easy to follow their sport thanks to the expanding amount of television coverage of stock car racing. During the 1990s, six different television networks signed deals to broadcast Winston Cup races, which resulted in every event on the circuit being broadcast nationally. By the end of the decade these television deals brought in $100 million annually. Beginning with the 2000 season, NASCAR consolidated the series' television rights (which had previously been negotiated by individual track owners) to leverage networks to increase the amounts paid to broadcast Cup races. This unified package resulted in a six-year contract with four networks for a total of $2.4 billion. An eight-year extension signed at the end of 2005 raised television revenue to $560 million per year. These staggering figures reflected the high ratings Winston Cup events garnered. Networks were attracted by both the then-current ratings and the prospect of ratings going up over the course of the contract. Viewership did, in fact, escalate under the first consolidated television deal. From the beginning of NASCAR's boom in popularity in 1994 until 2003, the number of households watching Winston Cup events increased by an astonishing 140 percent.[25]

Networks hoping to cash in on the popularity of stock car racing created enormous blocks of NASCAR programming on weekends. By the early 21st century, all Cup races were broadcast live nationally, as were the majority of Saturday Grand National (now Nationwide) events and Friday night Truck Series races. Cable channels also began offering live coverage of Cup (and sometimes Grand National) qualifying and the "Happy Hour" practice period. Also, various prerace and weekly stock car news shows pepper the weekend television schedule. Thanks to this massive amount of stock car-related programming, a fan of the sport could spend an entire weekend in front of the television with only short periods in which he or she could not watch NASCAR. Fans desirous of a constant stream of NASCAR updates also benefited from what one ESPN executive called "a continuous, seven-day presence" on that network's family of channels. The explosion of NASCAR programming even surprised some who had spent decades promoting the sport. Veteran driver Rusty Wallace, who transitioned from competitor to broadcaster, noted "I never thought I would see live [NASCAR] television every week."[26]

NASCAR's increased presence on television renewed concerns over tobacco sponsorship. As part of a program to lower its profile in the face of lawsuits, RJR bowed out as title sponsor of the Cup series. Columnist Viv Bernstein called the move the tearing down of "tobacco's last major billboard." In 2004, NEXTEL signed a 10-year contract to replace Winston. The terms of this contract were not publicly disclosed, but estimates are that NEXTEL will pay approximately $75 million per year. Thanks to the shifting landscape of the wireless industry, the series had to change its name to the Sprint Cup in 2008. By severing ties with a tobacco company, NASCAR eliminated one of the chief criticisms of the organization— that it promoted smoking. NASCAR also felt pressure from groups who believed RJR's title sponsorship violated federal regulations banning tobacco advertising on television. Dumping the Winston name also silenced those who blasted NASCAR for allegedly promoting underage tobacco use in the organization's various campaigns to attract young fans. In a curious sponsorship money-driven move, however, NASCAR dumped tobacco at roughly the same time it began allowing distilled spirits companies to advertise their products on Cup cars. Anti-drinking-and-driving forces loudly complained about this move, but to no avail. In the past few seasons Jack Daniel's, Jim Beam, Crown Royal, and other brands have served as primary sponsors on Cup cars.[27]

NEXTEL's involvement as title sponsor corresponded with a significant shift in the way NASCAR determines the Cup series champion. After numerous tweaks, the points system used by NASCAR stabilized in the 1970s and remained relatively static until the early 21st century. Outcry over the final few races of the 2003 season, however, prompted NASCAR to adopt a new points system akin to a playoff. The criticisms of the 2003 campaign stemmed from the actions of eventual champion Matt Kenseth, who mathematically locked up the championship early and then coasted through the final events of the season. Kenseth's early victory eliminated much of the drama from the tail end of the season, and he was derided for "stroking" in the last few races of the year. Fearful that a repeat of this debacle might contribute to lowering television ratings, NASCAR responded by inaugurating the Chase for the Cup in 2004. Under the new Chase format, NASCAR separates the top 10 drivers (top 12 beginning in 2007) from the rest of the Cup competitors with 10 races left in the season, which makes the "chasers" the only drivers who can possibly win the championship. By resetting the points totals of the eligible drivers at the beginning of the Chase, NASCAR ensures a close points battle until the end of the season. The Chase has proven popular with fans, but it has not managed to overcome the most serious problem confronting the late stages of the Cup season—those races have to directly compete with the National Football League, the undisputed king of Sunday sports programming.[28]

Along with a new crop of (primarily nonsouthern) drivers, tracks, and points systems, 21st-century NASCAR fans also found themselves confronted with significant alterations in the vehicles driven by their favorite racers. In a move that shocked and appalled many traditional fans, Toyota became the first non-American manufacturer to fully enter NASCAR. Cognizant of the hostility in store, Toyota Racing Division (TRD) undertook a staged entrance to cushion their arrival in the Cup series. It quietly entered NASCAR in 2000 by supplying engines for the weekly Goody's Dash Series. In 2004, Toyota began fielding vehicles in the more important NASCAR Truck Series, which was born in 1995 as the SuperTruck Series. NASCAR hoped the racing trucks would become a touring Friday night series to train young drivers before they moved up to the second-tier Grand National series. The trucks also afforded NASCAR the ability to grant events to some of the new tracks, such as those in Kansas and Kentucky, that did not obtain Cup dates. The new career trajectory, however, exemplified by the "Young Guns"— moving directly to the Cup series upon earning a NASCAR license— immediately undercut plans to make the trucks a proving ground for youngsters. Instead, the Truck Series became the purview of a group of career truckers (such as Ron Hornday Jr., Jack Sprague, and Dennis Setzer), Cup series failures, and a few moonlighting Cup regulars. The jolt of Toyota's entrance in 2004 represented one of the few times the Truck Series garnered much attention. After success with the trucks, TRD entered the Grand National and Cup frays in 2007. Old guard fans bemoaned Toyota's arrival in the "American" sport of stock car racing, but the blowback proved relatively muted. The low voltage of anti-Toyota sentiment reflected the success of Toyota's strategy of gradual entrance in NASCAR, the growing acceptance of the brand thanks to its large number of factories within the United States, and the increasing belief among conservative NASCAR fans that China (rather than Japan) should be blamed for the loss of American manufacturing jobs.[29]

Toyota's entry into the Cup series may have also passed without greater comment because their arrival corresponded with an even more controversial move by NASCAR. In an effort to keep drivers safer, reduce costs, and encourage closer racing, NASCAR began using the Car of Tomorrow (COT) during select events of the 2007 season. Along with a host of safety innovations, the COT also slowed drivers down thanks to its aerodynamically unfriendly boxiness. Most drivers viewed the new car with disdain, but they also recognized they would have to come to terms with the COT. As Tony Stewart ruefully noted, "we're stuck with it." In a dramatic break with tradition, the COT's ungainly shape applied to all manufacturers. While the COT retained the distinctive grills of the various manufacturers, viewed either from the back or in silhouette, all brands looked the same. A third generation of the France family had effectively abandoned the encouragement of brand loyalty among fans that "Big" Bill France viewed as an essential aspect of stock car racing's appeal.[30]

Although NASCAR remains second only to the NFL in popularity, the steady growth since the 1950s appears to have reached its plateau. Beginning in 2006, television ratings started to slip. Ratings for the 2009 season were down 21 percent from the peak of 2005. Although its guaranteed television contract temporarily immunizes NASCAR from the effects of this downturn, declining ratings will undoubtedly result in a reduction in the amount the organization can demand in its next contract. Given its control of ISC, the France family has felt an immediate pinch from the concomitant drop in attendance at Cup events. Impossibly high admission prices coupled with the recession forced ISC to slash the cost of tickets in an effort to fill stands for the 2009 season. Economic difficulties can be felt on the track as well. The high cost of operating a competitive team becomes increasingly prohibitive in an environment of shrinking sponsorship dollars and struggling auto manufacturers. The upshot of this financial struggle is the emergence of "start-and-park" teams in Cup races.

These unsponsored cars qualify for races, then drop out in the first few laps to avoid having to buy a second set of tires (or the equipment expenses associated with wrecks). Thanks to guaranteed money for cars that qualify for races, the "start-and-parks" earn enough to proceed to the next race on the schedule. Although NASCAR claims to enforce rules against teams that retire from a race without a legitimate excuse, in reality the organization turns a blind eye to the "start-and-parks" because without them, Cup races could not meet the requirement of 43 cars. As sponsorship became more difficult to obtain over the course of the 2009 season, the number of "start-and-park" teams increased. By mid-season, more than half-a-dozen of these cars dotted the starting lineups of Cup events.[31]

NASCAR's declining television ratings and attendance and the inability to attract a full field of competitive cars may signal the sport has reached an impasse. NASCAR must now decide whether to press ahead with efforts to try to continually expand stock car racing or if retrenchment is in order. Perhaps more important, a decision must be made as to what type of supporters NASCAR wants to placate. Old-style blue-collar fans increasingly feel alienated by the clean and safe drivers they cannot relate to and by the abandonment of manufacturer affiliations. Conversely, new fans of the more business-oriented style of NASCAR find the beer-swilling fans and rebel flags reflective of a sport that has not yet become fully polished. Like the Republican Party, NASCAR finds itself forced to find ways to meld praying and flag-saluting social conservatives with a more open and educated corporate wing. The shared love of stock car racing can maintain only a finite amount of cohesion between the two groups of fans. In the last few decades the NASCAR leadership moved to appease the new style fans under the assumption that expansion was key and that more traditional supporters would remain loyal despite changes. The faltering of recent years, however, brings this logic into question. Some longtime observers of the sport are now arguing that NASCAR's future success rests on abandoning one of these groups of fans in order to earn the undying loyalty of the other. Humpy Wheeler recently noted that NASCAR needs to decide if "we [are] moonshiners, country music, banjos, and Route 66 or are we merlot and Rodeo Drive." As it has been in NASCAR for 60 years, only the France family can make that decision.[32]

NOTES

INTRODUCTION

1. Edward Ayers, "What We Talk About When We Talk About the South," in Ayers, et al., eds., *All Over the Map: Rethinking American Regions* (Baltimore: Johns Hopkins University Press, 1996), 62–82; David Potter, *The South and Sectional Conflict* (Baton Rouge: Louisiana State University Press, 1968), especially chapter 6.

CHAPTER 1

1. For purposes of this study, "open-wheel" will be used as a shorthand term to describe the style of racing that dominated American motor sports outside the South. Open-wheel encompasses a number of different car types, all of which competed with stock for public attention at various times. Most commonly, open-wheel is used to describe the expensive, low-slung racers also referred to as Indy or Champ (for AAA Championship Trail) cars, but it also applies to sprint cars (known as "big cars" mid-century) and midgets. Where especially necessary, I will specifically denote which type of open-wheel vehicle is being referenced.
2. Betram Wyatt-Brown, *Southern Honor: Ethics and Behavior in the Old South* (New York: Oxford University Press, 1982), 25–87; Richard F. Hamm, *Murder, Honor, and the Law: Four Virginia Homicides from Reconstruction to the Great Depression* (Charlottesville: University of Virginia Press, 2003), 62; Frank E. Vandiver, "The Southerner as Extremist," in Vandiver, ed., *The Idea of the South: Pursuit of a Central Theme* (Chicago: University of Chicago Press, 1964), 43–55. For a discussion of the continuation of high rates of violence in the South into the NASCAR era, see Sheldon Hackney, "Southern Violence," *American Historical Review*, 74 (February 1969): 906–925.
3. Allison quoted in Kim Chapin, *Fast as White Lightning: The Story of Stock Car Racing* (New York: Dial, 1981), 54.
4. W. J. Cash, *The Mind of the South* (New York: Alfred A. Knopf, 1941), 62.

5. Hanson Hiss, "The Knights of the Lance in the South," *Outing*, 31 (January 1898): 338–344; Ted Ownby, *Subduing Satan: Religion, Recreation, and Manhood in the Rural South, 1865–1920* (Chapel Hill: University of North Carolina Press, 1990), 70–76; James J. Cobb, *Away Down South: A History of Southern Identity* (New York: Oxford University Press, 2005), 41–48; Chris Economaki quoted in Mark Yost, *The 200-MPH Billboard: The Inside Story of How Big Money Changed NASCAR* (St. Paul, MN: Motorbooks, 2007), 80; Sylvia Wilkinson, *Dirt Tracks to Glory: The Early Days of Stock Car Racing as Told by the Participants* (Chapel Hill, NC: Algonquin, 1983), 17.

6. T.H. Breen, "Horses and Gentlemen: The Cultural Significance of Gambling Among the Gentry of Virginia," *William & Mary Quarterly* 34 (April 1977): 239–157; John Rickards Betts, *America's Sporting Heritage: 1850–1950* (Reading, PA: Addison-Wesley, 1974), 4–20; Nancy L. Struna, *People of Prowess: Sport, Leisure, and Labor in Early Anglo-America* (Urbana: University of Illinois Press, 1996), 120–128; Ned Jarrett quoted in Wilkinson, *Dirt Tracks to Glory*, 154.

7. "Laurel Forfeits Franchise by Racing after Sundown," *Washington Post*, November 1, 1911.

8. Hayagreeva Rao, "The Social Construction of Reputation: Certification Contests, Legitimation, and the Survival of Organizations in the American Automobile Industry: 1895–1912," *Strategic Management Journal* 15 (Winter 1994): 29–44.

9. David R. Goldfield and Blaine A. Brownell, "The Automobile and the City in the American South," in *The Economic and Social Effects of the Spread of Motor Vehicles*, ed. Theo Barker (London: MacMillan, 1987), 115. For the Good Roads Movement in the South, see Howard Lawrence Preston, *Dirt Roads to Dixie: Accessibility and Modernization in the South, 1885–1935* (Knoxville: University of Tennessee Press, 1991).

10. Brian Katan, "Racing's Roots in the Virginia Landscape," in *Horsehide, Pigskin, Oval Tracks and Apple Pie: Essays on Sports and American Culture*, ed. James A. Vlasich (Jefferson, NC: McFarland, 2006), 144.

11. Randall Hall, "Before NASCAR: The Corporate and Civic Promotion of Automobile Racing in the American South, 1903–1927," *Journal of Southern History*, 63 (November 1997), 648. Although Henry Ford introduced his legendary Model T in 1908 as a "car for the great multitude," even that model was beyond the economic reach of most Americans. Only in 1912 did this "economy" car's price drop below the average annual wage in the United States. James J. Flink, *The Automobile Age* (Cambridge, MA: MIT Press, 1988), 33–39.

12. Hall, "Before NASCAR," 647; John M. Burns, *Thunder at Sunrise: A History of the Vanderbilt Cup, the Grand Prize and the Indianapolis 500, 1904–1916* (Jefferson, NC: McFarland, 2006), 83–88, 109–115, 128–141; Robert Casey, "The Vanderbilt Cup, 1908," *Technology and Culture*, 40 (April 1999): 358–362. For the best account of the Grand Prize, see Julian K. Quattlebaum, *The Great Savannah Races* (Athens: University of Georgia Press, 1983).

13. For a detailed discussion of early racing at Daytona, see Dick Punnett, *Beach Racers: Daytona Before NASCAR* (Gainesville: University Press of Florida, 2008) and Ed Hinton, *Daytona: From the Birth of Speed to the Death of the Man in Black* (New York: Warner Books, 2001), especially chapters 3–4.

14. Howard L. Preston, *Automobile Age Atlanta: The Making of a Southern Metropolis, 1900–1935* (Athens: University of Georgia Press, 1979), 17–29; "Atlanta Race Ends," *Washington Post*, November 14, 1909.

15. Al Powell, "Fulford-Miami Speedway," in *The History of the American Speedway*, ed. Allan E. Brown, (Marne, MI: Slideways, 1984), 34–37; Don Radbruch, *Dirt Track Auto Racing, 1919–1941* (Jefferson, NC: McFarland, 2004), 77.

16. Ownby, *Subduing Satan*, 56.

17. David R. Goldfield and Blaine Brownell, "The Automobile and the City in the American South," in *The Economic and Social Effects of the Spread of Motor Vehicles*, ed. Theo Barker (London: MacMillan, 1987), 115–129; George B. Tindall, *The Emergence of the New South, 1877–1945* (Baton Rouge: Louisiana State University Press, 1967), 254–288.

18. Ronald Kline and Trevor Pinch, "Users as Agents of Technological Change: The Social Construction of the Automobile in the Rural United States," *Technology and Culture*, 37 (October 1996): 763–795; Michael L. Berger, *The Devil Wagon in God's Country: The Automobile and Social Change in Rural America, 1893–1929* (Hamden, CT: Archon, 1979), 35–39; Reynold M. Wik, *Henry Ford and Grass-Roots America* (Ann Arbor: University of Michigan Press, 1972), 19–22, 34–58; R. E. Olds, "The Farmer and the Automobile," *Colman's Rural World*, 66 (March 20, 1913), 13; Robert E. Ireland, *Entering the Auto Age: The Early Automobile in North Carolina, 1900–1930* (Raleigh: North Carolina Division of Archives and History, 1990), 29–43.

19. Arthur Raper, *Preface to Peasantry: A Tale of Two Black Belt Communities* (Chapel Hill: University of North Carolina Press, 1936), 174–175; Berger, *Devil Wagon*, 44.

20. Leo Levine, *Ford, The Dust and the Glory: A Racing History, Volume 1 (1901–1967)* (Warrendale, PA: SAE International, 2000), 64.

21. Joe L. Coker, *Liquor in the Land of the Lost Cause: Southern White Evangelicals and the Prohibition Movement* (Lexington: University of Kentucky Press, 2007), 37–78; Junior Johnson, "I Never Got Caught A-Haulin'," in *Return to Thunder Road: The Story Behind the Legend*, 2nd ed., ed. Alex Gabbard (Lenoir City, TN: GP Press, 2000), 31. The increased role of the automobile in the moonshine business can be deduced from the rising numbers of vehicles seized by law enforcement during the 1920s. For seizure numbers from one prominent moonshine state, see Daniel Jay Whitener, *Prohibition in North Carolina, 1715–1945* (Chapel Hill: University of North Carolina Press, 1945), 189. Despite the increased use of motor vehicles to haul liquor after the passage of national Prohibition, enforcement of temperance actually had one negative effect on the auto industry. As the president of

the National Automobile Dealer's Association noted in 1920, laws that allowed for the seizure and sale of cars caught hauling moonshine cost dealers
money because the vehicles were often purchased on the installment plan
and, therefore, not completely paid off when seized. "Prohibition Costly to
Auto Industry," *New York Times*, January 6, 1920.

22. The perpetuation of the popular perception that trippers invented stock car
racing can be seen in recent films *Talladega Nights: The Ballad of Ricky Bobby*
(2006) and *NASCAR 3D: The IMAX Experience* (2004). The latter, officially
authorized by NASCAR, begins with a scene that re-creates tripping. In the
more responsible world of print journalism, *Sports Illustrated* helped perpe-
trate this falsehood with their 1998 special issue "50 Years of NASCAR,"
which includes repeated assertions of bootleggers birthing stock racing. For
a counter to this view, see Hall "Before NASCAR," who, however, tends to
downplay the role of moonshine somewhat too much, and Jeff MacGregor,
Sunday Money: A Hot Lap Around America With NASCAR (New York: HarperPerrenial, 2005).

23. "Stills Use Ford Engines," *New York Times*, January 17, 1928.

24. "Star Auto Drivers to Seek Big Prize on Richmond Track," *Washington Post*,
October 7, 1918.

25. "Auto Race Promoter Learns War Is Really—On Wheels," *Washington Post*,
September 18, 1942; Radbruch, *Dirt Track*, 176–178, 244–245; Griffith
Borgeson, *The Golden Age of the American Racing Car*, 2nd ed. (Warrendale,
PA: SAE International, 1998), 9. Ironically now based on strict adherence
to rules and fair play, a far more legitimate version of IMCA continues to
sanction hundreds of dirt track races annually.

CHAPTER 2

1. "Endurance Testing for Autos Revived by Manufacturers," *Washington Post*,
May 1, 1927; "Interest Is Reviving in Stock-Car Racing," *Washington Post*,
June 19, 1927; William Ullman, "Row in Automobile Racing Is Providing
Stirring Debate," *Washington Post*, June 16, 1929.

2. "Young DePaolo Makes Motor Racing Debut," *Washington Post*, April 2,
1927; "Altoona Race Saturday," *New York Times*, June 5, 1927; "De Paolo
Leads Way in 200-Mile Grind," *New York Times*, July 5, 1927; "Labor Day
Stock Car Races Are Planned," *Washington Post*, August 28, 1927; "Rooney
Drives Stock Car Race Winner," *Washington Post*, September 21, 1927.

3. Jack Cejnar, "American Auto Makers Do Not Seek Speed Records," *Clear-
field (PA) Progress*, January 15, 1930; "Triplett Third Victim," *New York
Times*, March 6, 1934; "Lou Meyer Captures Road Race at Ascot," *Fresno Bee
Republican*, April 23, 1934; "Racers Ready in Stock Car Race," *San Mateo
Times*, May 29, 1937; Levine, *Ford*, I: 111–117; Walter T. Chernokal, "Langhorne Speedway," in Brown, *History of Speedways*, 43–47. The AAA also
sanctioned one-off stock events at Roosevelt Raceway (1939), Funk Speedway in Fort Wayne, Indiana (1941), and Richmond, Virginia (1941).

4. "New Cars Are Being Designed Along Racing Lines," *Charleston (WV) Gazette*, April 13, 1930; Bob Myers, "For the Good of the Sport," *Stock Car Racing*, 8 (September 1973): 28–31.

5. "Victories Won by Barringer and Lawrence," *San Antonio Express*, May 19, 1930; "Sunday Speed Card at Riverside Ready," *San Antonio Express*, March 3, 1933; "Stock Car Races at Rogersville," *Kingsport Times*, September 6, 1931; "Leading Stock Drivers Race at Wolf Lake," *Hammond Times*, August 5, 1933; "17 Logansport District Drivers in Races Sunday," *Logansport (IN) Press*, June 24, 1939.

6. Russ Catlin, "Open Wheeling," *Speed Age*, 8 (December 1954): 9; "Speed Drivers Here, June 23," *Charleston (WV) Gazette*, June 9, 1935.

7. "Rose Is Ranked Nation's Best Driver," *Washington Post*, November 29, 1936; Radbruch, *Dirt Track*, 92–94; Wilkinson, *Dirt Tracks to Glory*, 27.

8. Neal Thompson, *Driving with the Devil: Southern Moonshine, Detroit Wheels, and the Birth of NASCAR* (New York: Random House, 2006), 89; Borgeson, *Golden Age*, 11.

9. Preston, *Dirt Roads to Dixie*, 162–167; Robert Penn Warren, *All the King's Men*, restored edition (Boston: Houghton Mifflin, 2002), 5.

10. Joe Cowley, "Lakewood Speedway," in Brown, *History of Speedways*, 38–39; H. A. Wheeler quoted in Wilkinson, *Dirt Tracks to Glory*, 52.

11. Flock's story is frequently recounted, but appears to have first appeared in Chapin, *White Lightning*, 44–47; "Threw Out Liquor As Spirited Race Grew Closer," *Dothan (AL) Eagle*, October 15, 1931.

12. "Non-pro Drivers to Have Their Day at Langhorne," *Huntingdon (PA) Daily News*, May 25, 1939; "1939 Winner in Stock Car Race," *Chester (PA) Times*, July 18, 1940.

13. "Salisbury to See Auto Race," *Burlington (NC) Times-News*, June 15, 1939; "Car Races at Rowan Slated," *Burlington (NC) Times-News*, September 12, 1939; "Gate City Cars Booked in Run," *Burlington (NC) Times-News*, September 5, 1940; "Charlotte Gets Stock Car Race," *Gastonia (NC) Daily Gazette*, June 7, 1941.

14. "Finishing Up Mile Oval for Initial Test," *High Point Enterprise*, October 3, 1940; "Pair of Local Drivers Enter 100-Mile Event," *High Point Enterprise*, August 31, 1941.

15. Anne B. Jones and Rex White, *All Around the Track: Oral Histories of Drivers, Mechanics, Officials, Owners, Journalists and Others in Motorsports Past and Present* (Jefferson, NC: McFarland, 2007), 9–13.

16. Thompson, *Driving with the Devil*, 111. Both Blind Willie McTell and Jim Croce wrote songs about Roy Hall.

17. Radbruch, *Dirt Track*, 248–251.

18. Sylvia Wilkinson, "Red-Necks on Wheels: The Stock Car Culture," in *The American South: Portrait of a Culture*, ed. Louis D. Rubin Jr. (Baton Rouge: Louisiana State University Press, 1980), 131; Dewey W. Grantham, *The South in Modern America: A Region at Odds* (New York: HarperCollins, 1994), 194–195.

19. Levine, *Ford*, I: 128; Don O'Reilly, "NASCAR: From the Inside Out," *Stock Car Racing*, 8 (October 1973): 44; Edgar Otto and Joann Biondi, *Ed Otto: NASCAR's Silent Partner* (Newburyport, MA: Coastal 181, 2008), 153.

20. Thompson, *Driving with the Devil*, 187–188; Henry Heald, "Bill France Does It Again," *National Speed Sport News*, 4 (February 12, 1946): 7; "Red Byron Wins Stock Car Race," *Anniston Star*, February 25, 1946; "Stock Autos to Race at Greensboro," *Burlington (NC) Daily Times-News*, August 1, 1946; "Ed Samples Wins Stock Car Event," *Burlington (NC) Daily Times-News*, April 21, 1947; Jones, *All Around the Track*, 19–23; John Bentley, "Souped-Up and Hot," *Sports Illustrated* 1 (November 1, 1954): 16–21.

21. "Red Byron Wins Stock Car Auto Race," *Anniston Star*, February 25, 1946; "Red Byron Cops Daytona Road Race," *National Speed Sport News*, 4 (April 25, 1946): 4; "Red Byron Bids for Charlotte Stock Car Honors," *Statesville (NC) Daily Record*, June 16, 1949; Thompson, *Driving with the Devil*, 179–185.

22. Wilkinson, *Dirt Tracks to Glory*, 33–37; "Bob Flock Victor in Stock Car Classic," *Illustrated Speedway News*, 6 (August 15, 1947): 1.

23. "Sports Shorts," *Anniston Star*, March 4, 1947; Bobby Nelson, "Bill France to Promote Midgets," *National Speed Sport News*, 5 (June 25, 1947): 3; "Wilkes Racers Look for Crowds," *Statesboro (NC) Daily Record*, July 3, 1947; "Wilkes Racers Ready," *Statesboro (NC) Daily Record*, July 26, 1947; "Stock Car Auto Races August 9 at Greenville," *Florence Morning News*, August 5, 1947; "Stock Car Races at Harrington Monday," *Denton (MD) Journal*, August 29, 1947.

24. Joe Whitlock, "Behind the Legend of the Smoke-Filled Room," *Grand National Illustrated*, 6 (March 1987): 50–57; Allen Guttmann, *From Ritual to Record: The Nature of Modern Sports* (New York: Columbia University Press, 1978), 16.

25. NASCAR, "1948 Rules and Regulations," copy in author's possession; "Meeting Ends for Car Racers," *Indiana (PA) Evening Gazette*, December 19, 1947.

26. Greg Fielden, *NASCAR Chronicle* (Lincolnwood, IL: Publications International, 2003), 19–21; Sam Packard et al., "Four Days in December," *Winston Cup Illustrated*, 17 (February 1998): 74–77.

27. "CSRA Outline Their 1946 Season Activities," *National Speed Sport News*, 4 (April 11, 1946): 5, 12; "New Eastern Stock Car Association of Drivers and Car Owners," *National Speed Sport News*, 5 (December 17, 1947): 7; "ASCA Looks for Big Outdoor Season in '48'," *Illustrated Speedway News*, 6 (December 19, 1947): 4; Frank L. Harvey, "Thunderbolts with Fenders," *Saturday Evening Post*, 221 (August 7, 1948): 20–21, 79; "Southern Entries for Uniontown Automobile Derby," *Connellsville (PA) Daily Courier*, April 21, 1948; "Stock Car Drivers to Race at Palmyra," *Canandaigua (NY) Daily Messenger*, May 22, 1948; "100-Mile Stock Car Race Will Feature Valley Fair Program," *Davenport Democrat and Leader*, August 8, 1949.

28. Thompson, *Driving with the Devil*, 280–282; "Roofing Tacks Hold Up Charlotte Race," *Statesville (NC) Daily Record*, April 4, 1949; Peter Golenbock, *NASCAR Confidential* (Osceola, WI: Motorbooks International, 2004), 27.

29. "First 500-Mile Event for Stock Cars Sept. 4," *Tucson Daily Citizen*, August 7, 1950.

30. Greg Fielden, *Forty Years of Stock Car Racing*, 4 Vols. (Surfside Beach, SC: Galfield Press, 1995), I: 6–10.

31. "Dunnaway Wins Stock Car Race," *New York Times*, June 20, 1949. For an extended examination of rules violations in NASCAR, see Tom Jensen, *Cheating: An Inside Look at the Bad Things Good NASCAR Nextel Cup Teams Do in Pursuit of Speed* (Phoenix, AZ: David Bull, 2002).

32. Dan Pierce, "The Most Southern Sport on Earth: NASCAR and the Unions," *Southern Cultures* 7 (Summer 2001): 9.

CHAPTER 3

1. "AAA Sanctions Stock Car Races," *Walla Walla Union-Bulletin*, March 7, 1950; Richard Minor, "The Sporting World," *Burlington (NC) Daily Times-News*, May 10, 1950; "Making It Official," *Lubbock Morning Avalanche*, November 8, 1950; Fielden, *40 Years*, I: 42.

2. "Racers Ready for Concord Run," *Statesville (NC) Daily Record*, March 4, 1950; "Big Race Set for Lakewood," *Statesville (NC) Daily Record*, July 27, 1950; "Stage Is Set for Lakewood," *Statesville (NC) Daily Record*, July 29, 1950; "Stock Cars Roar Through 80-Lap Grind Today for 2nd Time on Florence Track," *Florence Daily News*, April 16, 1950.

3. Carl R. Green, "Tighter Controls of AAA Drivers Proposed," *National Speed Sport News*, 9 (January 10, 1951): 8; "Barred by AAA Holland Turns to Stock Cars," *Coshocton (OH) Tribune*, May 24, 1951.

4. These two are also linked in that they are among the very few early NASCAR drivers to be the subject of quality full-length biographical works. For Roberts, see Godwin Kelly, *Fireball: Legends Don't Fall From the Sky* (Daytona Beach, FL: Carbon Press, 2005). For Turner, see Robert Edelstein, *Full Throttle: The Life and Fast Times of NASCAR Legend Curtis Turner* (Woodstock, NY: Overlook Press, 2005).

5. Fielden, *40 Years*, I: 19–20.

6. Stark Young, "Not in Memoriam, But in Defense," in Twelve Southerners, *I'll Take My Stand: The South and the Agrarian Tradition* (Reprint, Baton Rouge: Louisiana State University Press, 2006), 355; Wilkinson, *Dirt Tracks to Glory*, 111.

7. Pete Daniel, *Lost Revolutions: The South in the 1950s* (Chapel Hill: University of North Carolina Press, 2000), 93.

8. Fielden, *40 Years*, I: 32–34; Richard Minor, "The Sporting World," *Burlington (NC) Daily Times-News*, August 29, 1951; "Fourth Annual '500' Big Parade of Pageantry, Thrills, Courage," *Florence Morning News*, September 8, 1953; Richard Pillsbury, "Stock Car Racing," in *The Theater of Sport*, ed. Karl B. Raitz (Baltimore: Johns Hopkins University Press, 1995), 293.

9. Tom Kirkland and David Thompson, *Darlington International Raceway, 1950–1967* (Osceola, WI: MotorBooks International, 1999), 17–18; Thompson, *Driving with the Devil*, 328–329; Levine, *Ford*, I: 199–200; "Auto

That Won Darlington Race on Display Here, *Burlington (NC) Times-News*, September 16, 1950; Richard Petty quoted in Otto, *Ed Otto*, 114. France met Mantz earlier in 1950 when both were competing in the Carrera Panamericana, the legendary 2,000-mile Mexican road race.

10. Mark Yost, *The 200-MPH Billboard: The Inside Story of How Big Money Changed NASCAR* (St. Paul, MN: Motorbooks, 2007), 58; Rex White, *Gold Thunder: Autobiography of a NASCAR Champion* (Jefferson, NC: McFarland, 2005), 45.

11. Steve Pappas, "NASCAR," *National Speed Sport News*, 9 (November 14, 1951): 9.

12. Wilkinson, *Dirt Tracks to Glory*, 15, 92–93; Jones, *All Around the Track*, 146–148; "Louise Smith," *Sports Illustrated* 104 (April 24, 2006): 29; Anne Amerson, *The Best of "I Remember Dahlonega": Memories of Lumpkin County, Georgia* (Charleston, NC: History Press, 2006), 75–76; Douglas A. Hurt, "Dialed In? Geographic Expansion and Regional Identity in NASCAR's Nextel Cup Series," *Southeastern Geographer* 45 (May 2005): 127.

13. "Sport: Daredevil Driver," *Time* 60 (December 8, 1952): 8.

14. Steve Pappas, "Florida Rules the Auto Racing World," *Panama City News-Herald*, July 12, 1953; Otto, *Ed Otto*, 56–57.

15. Fred Lorezen quoted in Wilkinson, *Dirt Tracks to Glory*, 109.

16. "Lu Gandolfo, "Snags in Auto Racing Plans Are Outlined at Meeting," *Modesto Bee and News-Herald*, February 4, 1955; "Barkhimer Rose from Race Driver to Promoter," *Oakland Tribune*, February 13, 1957; White, *Gold Thunder*, 128, 130, 135. White expressed a similar reluctance to travel to the Northeast.

17. John B. Rae, *The American Automobile Industry* (Boston: Twayne, 1984), 99–116; Robert Sobel, *Car Wars: The Untold Story* (New York: E. P. Dutton, 1984), 8.

18. Houston Lawing, "Thompson in Chrysler Captures Detroit 250," *National Speed Sport News*, 9 (August 15, 1951): 3, 22; Richard Minor, "The Sporting World," *Burlington (NC) Daily Times-News*, October 3, 1951; "Darlington's Southern 500 Field Limited to Six of Any One Make of Car," *National Speed Sport News*, 10 (August 6, 1952): 7.

19. Flock stopped racing with the monkey after Jocko broke loose from his chain and attacked him during a May race in Raleigh. Unable to pull the monkey off him, Flock had to make an unscheduled pit stop, which cost him second place. Jocko died shortly after the end of his racing career.

20. Paul Van Valkenburgh, *Chevrolet—Racing? Fourteen Years of Raucous Silence! 1957–1970* (Warrendale, PA: SAE International, 2000), 9–11.

21. Levine, *Ford*, I: 209–13.

22. Charles K. Hyde, *Riding the Roller Coaster: A History of the Chrysler Corporation* (Detroit: Wayne State University Press, 2003), 170–177; Peter Golenbock, *American Zoom: Stock Car Racing—From the Dirt Tracks to Daytona* (New York: MacMillan, 1993), 62–63.

23. Peter Golenbock, *The Last Lap: The Life and Times of NASCAR's Legendary Heroes* (New York: Macmillan, 1998), 59–64.

24. Tom Wolfe, *The Kandy-Kolored Tangerine-Flake Streamline Baby* (New York: Farrar, Straus, and Giroux, 1965), 121–166.

25. Sandy Grady, "Stock Cars," *Speed Age,* 10 (February 1957): 57–58; For the convertible series, see Greg Fielden, *Rumblin' Ragtops: The History of NASCAR's Fabulous Convertible Division* (Surfside Beach, NC: Galfield Press, 1990).

26. Al Thomy, "Del Roy Establishes Atlanta Race Stable," *National Speed Sport News,* 15 (January 16, 1957): 5.

27. Levine, *Ford,* I: 231–44; Fielden, *40 Years,* I: 255–258; "Auto Weaknesses Revealed in Tough Stock Car Grinds," *Salisbury (MD) Times,* January 23, 1957; Flink, *Car Culture,* 193–195.

28. "Stock Car Racing Booms Despite Speed De-Emphasis," *Benton Harbor News-Palladium,* July 14, 1960; Van Valkenburgh, *Chevrolet,* 27–30; Levine, *Ford,* I: 245–250; White, *Gold Thunder,* 111.

CHAPTER 4

1. Hinton, *Daytona,* 82–85; "Congressman Rivers Takes NASCAR Post," *Washington Post,* July 20, 1969.

2. Kenneth Rudeen, "They Laughed When NASCAR's Stock Cars Took to the Road at Elkhart Lake," *Sports Illustrated* 5 (August 20, 1956): 81–82; "New U.S. FIA Committee Now Ready to Do Business," *National Speed Sport News* 15 (December 4, 1957): 3; Frank M. Blunk, "Racers Get Together," *New York Times,* February 8, 1961; *New York Times,* "International Group Penalized USAC for Suspending Driver," *New York Times,* June 24, 1964; Chris Economaki, "USAC Stripped of All FIA Races but Indianapolis," *National Speed Sport News* 32 (June 24, 1964): 3.

3. Don O'Reilly, "Inside Auto Racing," *Illustrated Speedway News* 24 (October 27, 1964): 8, 10; Petty quoted in Fielden, *40 Years,* II: 11–12.

4. "Racer, Miffed Over Big Loss, Threatens Rival," *Florence Morning News,* April 1, 1960.

5. Bob Groover, "Competition?," *Florence Morning News,* April 15, 1972. Richard's far less successful brother Maurice also competed in Grand National from 1960 to 1964, then became Richard's crew chief.

6. Fielden, *40 Years,* II: 11–16; "USAC Calls Off Race in Atlanta," *Washington Post,* July 2, 1961; "Plan to Save Charlotte MS Before Jurist," *National Speed Sport News* 31 (January 9, 1963): 2.

7. Edelstein, *Full Throttle,* 126–164.

8. "Rebel 300 in Hot Controversy," *Florence Morning News,* May 10, 1960; Bob Hoffman, "Exhaust Fumes," *High Point (NC) Enterprise,* July 21, 1960; "Pari-Mutuel Auto Racing Rejected," *Washington Post,* August 9, 1961; Venlo Wolfsohn, "Turner Trying to Form Race Car Drivers Union," *Washington Post,* August 23, 1961; Edelstein, *Full Throttle,* 165–177.

9. Pierce, "Most Southern Sport," 16–21; "Bob Hoffman, "Exhaust Fumes," *High Point* (NC) *Enterprise,* August 14, 1960; "Drivers' Careers at Stake," *High Point* (NC) *Enterprise,* August 11, 1961.

10. Bloys Britt, "Stock Car Racing—Is It Sport or Business," *High Point* (NC) *Enterprise*, December 9, 1962.

11. Bob Hoffman, "Exhaust Fumes," *High Point (NC) Enterprise*, November 6, 1963; "USAC & NASCAR Fighting Again," *National Speed Sport News* 31 (November 6, 1963): 3; "NASCAR-ARCA Late Model Races at Charlotte Oct. 17–18," *Illustrated Speedway News* 24 (October 6, 1964): 6; John Marcum, "NASCAR Is Big League," *Stock Car Racing* 8 (September 1973): 38; Edelstein, *Full Throttle*, 207–208; Fielden, *40 Years*, II: 231–232.

12. Fred Lorenzen quoted in Wilkinson, *Dirt Tracks to Glory*, 109; Kim Chapin, "Curtis Lives!," *Sports Illustrated* 28 (February 26, 1968): 48.

13. Hurt, "Dialed In," 127; "NASCAR Drivers to Head North After Firecracker 400 Saturday," *New York Times*, June 28, 1964.

14. Grantham, *South in Modern America*, 194–223.

15. Stephen A. Smith, *Myth, Media, and the Southern Mind* (Fayetteville: University of Arkansas Press, 1985), 46–61; John Shelton Reed, *One South: An Ethnic Approach to Regional Culture* (Baton Rouge: Louisiana State University Press, 1982); Richard N. Current, *Northernizing the South* (Athens: University of Georgia Press, 1983), 110–113; James C. Cobb, *Away Down South: A History of Southern Identity* (Oxford: Oxford University Press, 2005), 212–235.

16. Grace Elizabeth Hale, *Making Whiteness: The Culture of Segregation in the South, 1890–1940* (New York: Pantheon, 1998), 9; Frank M. Blunk, "Auto Racing to Challenge Golf as the King of Augusta Sports," *New York Times*, November 20, 1963; Susan Birrell, "Sport as Ritual: Interpretations from Durkheim to Goffman," *Social Forces* 60 (December 1981): 356; Ray Oldenburg, *The Great Good Place: Cafes, Coffee Shops, Community Centers, Beauty Parlors, General Stores, Bars, Hangouts and How They Get You through the Day*, 2nd ed. (New York: Marlowe, 1997), 14–19. In Oldenburg's schema home was the first place, work the second, and public gathering locations the third.

17. Moore quoted in Otto, *Ed Otto*, 117; Ted Ownby, "Manhood, Memory, and White Men's Sports in the American South," in *The Sporting World of the Modern South*, ed. Patrick B. Miller (Urbana: University of Illinois Press, 2002), 326–342; B.J. Phillips, "Speed Sunday Down South," *Washington Post*, March 20, 1970.

18. "New York Prepares for the Automobile Races," *Chicago Defender*, October 25, 1924; "Leads Stock Car Race for 100 Miles, Then Radiator Goes Hot on Sepia Driver," *Chicago Defender*, January 25, 1941; "Auto Racer," *Chicago Defender*, October 5, 1946; Standalone Photo, *Chicago Defender*, July 30, 1949; "Two Negro Drivers Participate in Stock Car Races," *Chicago Defender*, May 7, 1960; "Ten Mount Union Stock Cars Enter Reedsville Races," *Huntingdon (PA) Daily News*, July 25, 1951. For Wiggins, see Todd Gould, *For Gold and Glory: Charlie Wiggins and the African-American Racing Circuit* (Bloomington: Indiana University Press, 2002).

19. Janet Guthrie quoted in Yost, *200-MPH Billboard*, 143.

20. Brian Donovan, *Hard Driving: The Wendell Scott Story* (Hanover, PA: Steerforth, 2008), 37, 122; Wendell Scott quoted in Wilkinson, *Dirt Tracks to Glory*, 121. Black American Racers' Association chairman Leonard Miller later suggested that the problems for African American drivers were actually compounded by the fact that hostility toward their racing came from both whites and blacks. According to Miller, racing on Sundays was actively discouraged by most black churches, which put prospective drivers in the uncomfortable position of being ostracized both at the track and in their own communities. Len Miller, "Black Power Drive Falters in Racing," *Stock Car Racing* 8 (July 1973): 24–28.

21. "Wendell Scott Breaks Barrier; Lone Negro on Stock Car Circuit," *Chicago Defender*, July 2, 1966; Donovan, *Hard Driving*, 43, 61–62, 75–76.

22. Donovan, *Hard Driving*, 43, 127–128. When Scott received the Curtis Turner Lifetime Achievement Award in 1972, Toy Russell, still the only African American race queen in NASCAR history, was hired to present the trophy and kiss him. He retired from driving the next year. The other black drivers are George Wiltshire (one start in 1971, one in 1975); Randy Bethea (one start in 1975); Willy T. Ribbs (three starts in 1986); and Bill Lester (two starts in 2006).

23. "Stocks 'Little Men' Are Hurting," *National Speed Sport News* 32 (June 10, 1964): 3.

24. Fielden, *40 Years*, II: 141–143; Van Valkenburgh, *Chevrolet*, 78, 174; Levine, *Ford*, I:245–277; Robert Irvin, "Horsepower Race Is On Again," *Washington Post*, June 15, 1962; "Stock Car Group Sets Motor Limit," *New York Times*, June 13, 1962.

25. "Race Official Seeks End of Disasters," *Washington Post*, July 14, 1964; "4 NASCAR Tracks Adopt Safety Tires," *Washington Post*, May 13, 1965; Albert G. Maiorano, "Like That Car in a Stock Race? It's Not in Stock," *New York Times*, April 14, 1963.

26. "Performance from a Police Package," *Washington Post*, January 31, 1965; "Petty Still Without Car at Daytona," *Washington Post*, February 3, 1965; "Chrysler Returns to Stock Racing on Limited Scale," *Washington Post*, June 25, 1965; Frank M. Blunk, "Engine Ruling Expected to Cut Attendance at Stock-Car Races," *New York Times*, January 24, 1965: Chrysler Asks Bill France to Lift Ban on Plymouth Hemi Engine," *Illustrated Speedway News* 24 (November 24, 1964): 9, 15.

27. Van Valkenburg, *Chevrolet*, 174–189; "NASCAR Approves 'Fancy' Engines," *New York Times*, February 13, 1965.

28. "Chrysler to Quit Stock-Car Racing," *New York Times*, July 23, 1966; "Dieringer to Drive Comet for Factory," *Washington Post*, December 18, 1966; Peter Golenbock, *Miracle: Bobby Allison and the Saga of the Alabama Gang* (New York: St. Martin's Griffin, 2006), 59–84.

29. "New Auto Race Division for '68 Listed by NASCAR," *New York Times*, October 22, 1967; "Stock Cars' Influence on Racing Rises," *Washington Post*, October 22, 1967; Phil Holmer, "NASCAR News," *Stock Car Racing* 3 (July

1968): 33. Never one to suffer rivals silently, the combative France dealt another blow to SCCA in 1969 by convincing that organization's executive director John Bishop to defect to the new, France-financed International Motor Sports Association (IMSA), which sanctioned races for foreign sedans and small open-wheelers. "New Group to Spur Small-Car Racing," *New York Times*, July 20, 1969.

30. Fielden, *40 Years*, III: 163–164; "Ford Plan May Boost U.S. Racing," *Washington Post*, July 20, 1967; "Detroit, NASCAR Sign Pact," *New York Times*, October 17, 1968; "Major Jersey Oval Will Open in 1970," *New York Times*, July 27, 1969.

31. "Wallace's Wife Preps for Race Job," *Washington Post*, May 4, 1971; William Greider, "That Season Again," *Washington Post*, August 30, 1971.

32. John S. Radosta, "Stock Drivers Rally and Form Association to Give Them Voice," *Washington Post*, August 24, 1969; Venlo Wolfsohn, "Petty, Top Drivers Provide New Association with 'Clout'," *Washington Post*, August 27, 1969; Howell, *Moonshine*, 37–48.

33. "Alabama Speedway Called Unsafe, Drivers Pull Out," *New York Times*, September 14, 1969; Fielden, *40 Years*, III: 209–217; Joe Menzer, *The Wildest Ride: A History of NASCAR* (New York: Touchstone, 2001), 184–196.

34. "NASCAR Hits Driver Boycott, Demands Pledge of 'Good Faith'," *New York Times*, September 24, 1969; Rae, *American Auto Industry*, 117–129; "Drivers Escape Penalty for Race Boycott," *Washington Post*, September 17, 1969; "Ford Abandons Racing Program Even As 1971 Team Shakes Down," *Washington Post*, November 21, 1970.

35. John S. Radosta, "Auto Racing's Switch Season in Swing," *New York Times*, October 26, 1969; "NASCAR Signs Pact to Televise Races," *New York Times*, December 18, 1969; "Dixie 500 Asked to Post Purse," *Washington Post*, July 29, 1970.

CHAPTER 5

1. Roy Blount, "Million-Dollar Sunday Driver," *Sports Illustrated* 35 (August 9, 1971): 16–17.

2. Elbert Marshall, "Racing Report," *Burlington (NC) Daily Times-News*, August 17, 1971; Bob Myers, "Southern Strategy," *Stock Car Racing* 6 (August 1971): 11, 13, 56

3. Yost, *200-MPH Billboard*, 75–85.

4. "Reynold's Stock Car to Be Displayed Here," *Aiken (SC) Standard*, August 24, 1971.

5. Maury Powell, "France Could Help South Rise Again," *Pasadena Star-News*, July 22, 1970.

6. "Brother Frazier Loyal to Racers," *Hagerstown Daily Mail*, May 20, 1971; Bob Myers, "Brother Bill Frazier: Chaplain of Champions," *Stock Car Racing* 8 (February 1973): 19–23; Perry Allen Wood, *Silent Speedways of the Carolinas: The Grand National Histories of 29 Former Tracks* (Jefferson, NC: McFarland,

2007), 78; Jerry Bledsoe, *The World's Number One, Flat-Out, All-Time Great, Stock Car Racing Book* (Garden City, NJ: Doubleday, 1975), 215–224. Beginning in 1973, Richard Petty sold off one square inch plots of "Petty Country" behind his Level Cross, North Carolina home to help support Frazier's group The Chapel, Incorporated.

7. John S. Radosta, "Mr. NASCAR Calls It a Career," *New York Times*, January 12, 1972.

8. Janet Guthrie, *Janet Guthrie: A Life at Full Throttle* (Toronto: Sport Classic Books, 2005), 267–313.

9. "David Pearson Says No Place for Women in Stock Car Racing," *Galveston Daily News*, January 30, 1977; "Dating Is No Problem Because She Is a Racer," *Galveston Daily News*, March 23, 1977.

10. William Gildea, "Racing Buffs Not Running Out of Gas," *Washington Post*, December 24, 1973; "Energy Crisis Creates Spirit of Cooperation," *National Speed Sport News*, 32 (January 23, 1974): 2; Allen Wolfe, "NASCR Plays 'Energy Game'," *Long Beach Independent*, May 24, 1974; "Auto Racing Outlook," *Florence Morning News*, December 8, 1974; Fielden, *NASCAR Chronicle*, 213.

11. James R. Murray et al., "Evolution of Public Response to the Energy Crisis," *Science* 184 (April 19, 1974): 257–263.

12. Bob Phillips, "Things Are Getting Sticky Out There," *Kingsport News*, March 19, 1974; Benny Phillips, "Talk of 2nd Race Circuit Threatens NASCAR Armor," *High Point (NC) Enterprise*, April 9, 1976; Benny Phillips, "NASCAR Defends Its Position—Nothing Is Settled," Benny Phillips, April 10, 1976; Bob Foley, "NASCAR's 'Plan B' Helping Little Guy," *Kingsport Times*, August 27, 1976.

13. Shav Glick, "Cheating by Drivers Not Really Sinful," *Los Angeles Times*, July 5, 1972; John Frye, "'76 Racing Schedule Established for KARS," *Hagerstown Daily Mail*, February 18, 1976; Benny Phillips, "NASCAR Reinstates '75 Rules," *High Point (NC) Enterprise*, July 4, 1976; "Caught at Talladega," *High Point (NC) Enterprise*, August 7, 1976; "Top Stockers Gather," *Victoria (TX) Advocate*, August 7, 1977. The cheating by top drivers before the 1977 Talladega 500 was only the beginning of a truly unfortunate week for NASCAR. During the race itself, driver David Sisco's mother Irene was killed when she was struck by a pick-up, further cementing the public perception of out-of-control behavior in Talladega's infield.

14. Benny Phillips, "Talks About Racing," *High Point (NC) Enterprise*, March 14, 1971.

15. Yost, *200-MPH Billboard*, 80–82; "Southern Born, Racing Now An American Sport," *Kingsport News*, March 19, 1974; Chapin, *White Lightning*, 199–201.

16. "Granatelli Buys Petty Race Team," *Washington Post*, January 20, 1972; "Millionaire Ranier Pouring Money into Pond's 1976 Racing Campaign," *Petersburg (VA) Progress-Index*, January 3, 1976; Harry March, "The Sports Scene," *Petersburg (VA) Progress-Index*, January 8, 1976.

17. "Waltrip Breezes to Second NASCAR Grand National Win," *Kingsport Times*, October 13, 1975; "Once Hated Waltrip Moving to TV Booth," *Frederick News-Post*, November 16, 2000. In 1974, NASCAR changed the rules so that the Rookie of the Year award was determined solely on the basis of drivers' points.

18. "Waltrip Looks to Future," *High Point (NC) Enterprise*, October 19, 1976; "Waltrip Takes Richmond 400 Despite Surly Race Fans," *Doylestown (PA) Daily Intelligencer*, February 23, 1981.

19. "NASCAR Biggest Spectator Draw in World," *National Speed Sport News* 45 (January 5, 1977): 5; Bob Myers, "Junior Johnson Looks Ahead," *Petersen's Circle Track* 7 (October 1988): 43.

20. Joe Menzer, *The Great American Gamble: How the 1979 Daytona 500 Gave Birth to a NASCAR Nation* (Hoboken, NJ: John Wiley, 2009), 16–22. Tele-PrompTer had offered similar coverage of the Indianapolis 500 since 1964.

21. "NASCAR Events Slated for Showing by CBS," *High Point (NC) Enterprise*, February 8, 1975; "Television Invades NASCAR," *Florence Morning News*, February 15, 1975; Ernie Saxton, "Holbert Gunning for New Title," *Bucks County Courier Times*, November 27, 1977; Jim Spence, *Up Close and Personal: The Inside Story of Network Television Sports* (New York: Atheneum, 1988), 203–204.

22. Fielden, *40 Years*, IV: 251–254; Jerry Garrett, "Yarborough Claims Allison Violated Gentleman's Pact," *Aiken Standard*, February 21, 1979.

23. Menzer, *Great American Gamble*, 22–26; Rocky Entriken, "Good Show, CBS; Boos to NASCAR," *Salina Journal*, February 28, 1978.

24. Al Stilley, "Middle America," *Stock Car Racing*, 7 (December 1972): 14; Chris Economaki, "'They Better Be Careful,' Says Penske of USAC," *National Speed Sport News*, 41 (January 31, 1973): 3.

25. Grantham, *South in Modern America*, 262–280; Jack Temple Kirby, *Media-Made Dixie* (Baton Rouge: Louisiana State University Press, 1978), 133–174; John Edgerton, *The Americanization of Dixie: The Southernization of America* (New York: Harper & Row, 1974), 176.

26. Bruce J. Schulman, *The Seventies: The Great Shift in American Culture, Society, and Politics* (Cambridge, MA: Da Capo, 2002), 102–120; Thomas J. Sugrue and John D. Skrentny, "The White Ethnic Strategy" in *Rightward Bound*, ed. Bruce J. Schulman and Julian E. Zelizer (Cambridge, MA: Harvard University Press, 2008), 174; Richard Pillsbury, "Carolina Thunder: A Geography of Southern Stock Car Racing," *Journal of Geography* 173 (January 1974): 47; Bob Myers, "Humpy Wheeler on the Future of Winston Cup Racing," *Stock Car Racing* 16 (May 1981): 16.

27. Don Cusic, "NASCAR and Country Music," *Studies in Popular Culture* 21 (October 1998): 31–40; Bill Gilbert, "NASCAR Country," *Florence Morning News*, December 31, 1974. The two cultural forms are also connected through RJR. The company's Prince Albert brand of tobacco became the Grand Old Opry's title sponsor in early 1939 and helped get the weekly program on network radio later that year, thereby taking country music national.

28. Marsha G. McGee, "Prime Time Dixie: Television's View of a 'Simple' South," *Journal of American Culture*, 6 (Fall 1983): 100–109; Ted Blake, "The Dukes of Hazzard, Television's Simple South, and Resurrecting the Outlaw Hero," *storySouth*, Issue 4 (Summer 2002): http://www.storysouth.com/summer2002/dukeshazzard.html.

29. "Champagne Hits Spot—Barely," *New York Times*, September 23, 1971; "Revving and Racing into the Promised Land," *New York Times*, September 14, 1978.

CHAPTER 6

1. Ed Hinton, "Attitude for Sale," *Sports Illustrated* 82 (February 6, 1995): 68–76; Karyn Charles Rybacki and Donald Jay Rybacki, "The King, the Young Prince, and the Last Confederate Soldier: NASCAR on the Cusp," in *The Sporting World of the Modern South*, ed. Patrick B. Miller (Urbana: University of Illinois Press, 2002), 294–325.

2. "Earnhardt Favored in Winston 500," *Doylestown (PA) Daily Intelligencer*, May 3, 1987; "Hard feelings Heavy: Driver Rips Waltrip's Track Ethics," *Paris (TX) News*, October 4, 1987; Benny Phillips, ". . . And Still Champion Dale Earnhardt," *Stock Car Racing* 23 (May 1988): 100–107; Jeff Owens, "An American Icon," in *Taking Stock: Life in NASCAR's Fast Lane*, ed. Monte Dutton (Washington, DC: Brassey's, 2002), 37–49.

3. Hurt, "Dialed In," 127; "NASCAR Drivers Will Fight Teamsters Move," *Gastonia Gazette*, October 31, 1977; Carrie Seidman, "Youthful Earnhardt Racing Ahead of the Good Old Boys," *New York Times*, August 4, 1980; "Yankee Bodine Finds Favor with Race Fans at Pocono," *Charlotte Observer*, July 20, 1986; Steve Potter, "Stock-Car Drivers Chasing Earnhardt," *New York Times*, April 19, 1987; Rick Scoppe, "Darlington Man Paints Tribute to Earnhardt," *Aiken Standard*, April 2, 1989; Yost, *200-MPH Billboard*, 134.

4. Mike Rowell, "Basic Training," *Petersen's Circle Track* 2 (March 1983): 60–62.

5. John Hall, "Auto Racing Telecasts Increase," *Syracuse Post-Standard*, April 19, 1982.

6. Fielden, *40 Years*, IV: 319–320; "Rudd, Yarborough Top Race," *Galveston Daily News*, March 14, 1981; Lawrence Hugenberg and Barbara Hugenberg, "NASCAR Fans in Their Own Words: Motivation Expressed in Narratives," in *Sports Mania: Essays on Fandom and the Media in the 21st Century*, ed. Lawrence Hugenberg (Jefferson, NC: McFarland, 2008), 172–186; Glenn Howell, "Last Time Around for the Big Stockers," *Popular Mechanics* 149 (February 1978): 86–88.

7. Levine, *Ford*, II: 91–96.

8. "Changes Make Program a Necessity at Daytona," *Annapolis Capital*, February 14, 1983; John R. Catsis, *Sports Broadcasting* (Chicago: Nelson-Hall, 1996), 138.

9. Bob Myers, "NASCAR: Big Changes for 1981," *Stock Car Racing* 15 (December 1980): 90–91.

10. John Hill, "Racing Experts Fear Impact of TV Glut," *Syracuse Post-Standard*, April 5, 1985; Gaylen Duskey, "And Now for a Few Thousand Words from Our Sponsor," *Aiken Standard*, September 3, 1986; Richard Butsch, *The Making of American Audiences: From Stage to Television, 1750–1990* (Cambridge, MA: Cambridge University Press, 2000), 274; Robert G. Hagstrom, *The NASCAR Way: The Business That Drives the Sport* (New York: John Wiley & Sons, 1998), 56–61.

11. "Despite Violations, Petty Beats Waltrip," Chicago *Daily Herald*, October 10, 1983; "Petty Gets 200th Win in Firecracker 400," *Paris (TX) News*, July 5, 1984.

12. Benny Phillips, "On Tim Richmond," *Stock Car Racing* 23 (May 1988): 14.

13. David Poole, *Tim Richmond: The Fast Life and Remarkable Times of NASCAR's Top Gun* (Champaign, IL: Sports Publishing, 2005), 135–140; Benny Phillips, "Racing's Big Three," *Stock Car Racing*, 21 (March 1986): 35–38; Golenbock, *American Zoom*, 314.

14. Bob Myers, "World 600," *Stock Car Racing*, 17 (September 1982): 42–44, 77–81.

15. Golenbock, *Miracle*, 208–216.

16. J. Brian O'Roark and William C. Wood, "Safety at the Racetrack: Results of Restrictor Plates in Superspeedway Competition," *Southern Economic Journal*, 71 (July 2004): 118–119.

17. Fielden, *40 Years*, IV: 627–641.

18. Dick Berggren, "The Grand National Checkbook," *Stock Car Racing*, 18 (May 1983): 62–63, 81; Smokey Yunick, "Track Tech," *Petersen's Circle Track*, 7 (January 1988): 90–94; Benny Phillips, "NASCAR Racing Grew Into Adulthood in the 1980s," *National Speed Sport News*, 57 (December 20, 1989): 6.

19. Bob Myers, "Stock Report," *Petersen's Circle Track*, 3 (January 1984): 14; Ron Green, "Jimmy Finally Acquires Means To Compete On NASCAR Circuit," Charlotte *Observer*, October 9, 1987; Tom Cotter, "Racing On Empty," *Circle Track & Racing Technology*, 11 (February 1992): 140–147.

20. Bob Myers, "Editorial," *Stock Car Racing*, 17 (October 1982): 12.

21. "Bonnett To Drive For Johnson," Aiken *Standard*, January 26, 1983; Shav Glick, "Vast Stock Car Racing Empire of Hodgdon Ends in Bankruptcy," *Los Angeles Times*, January 24, 1985; Jeff Hammond and Geoffrey Norman, *Real Men Work in the Pits: A Life in NASCAR Racing* (Emmaus, PA: Rodale, 2004), 137, 144; Fielden, *Forty Years*, IV: 432–433.

22. Bob Myers, "Keeping Up With Darrell and Junior," *Stock Car Racing*, 18 (March 1983): 100–101, 114, 118, 124.

23. "Waltrip Starts New NASCAR Team," Aiken *Standard*, June 29, 1986; "Hendrick Looks Back at Two Decades of Racing," Chicago *Daily Herald*, April 30, 2004.

24. "Darlington Track No Easy Cruise," Aiken *Standard*, June 27, 1990; Jeffrey Ressner, "Driving Ambition," Syracuse *Herald-Journal*, June 28, 1990; Lesley Hazleton, "Race Cars as Actors Fuel the Eye in 'Thunder'," *New York Times*,

July 8, 1990; "Races Enjoy Thunderous Experience of Big-screen Movie Making," Chicago *Daily Herald*, July 28, 1990.

25. "NASCAR Founder 'Big Bill' France dies at 82," Chicago *Daily Herald*, June 8, 1992.
26. Allison's brother Clifford died in a stock car accident the same year.

CHAPTER 7

1. Hurt, "Dialed In," 127.
2. Oliver Ryan, "What Fuels the Racing Business," *Fortune* 152 (September 5, 2005): 54–55.
3. Kevin Sack, "He's Good, He's Golden, and Fans Can't Stand It," *New York Times*, October 16, 1997.
4. Bob Myers, "Stock Report," *Circle Track & Racing Technology* 11 (September 1992): 8, 120.
5. Tarik El-Bashir, "For Stock Car World's Reigning Hero, the Villain Treatment," *New York Times*, June 21, 1998; M. Graham Spann, "NASCAR Racing Fans: Cranking Up an Empirical Approach," *Journal of Popular Culture* 36 (Fall 2002): 356.
6. Joseph Siano, "Gordon Eats at a Place Without Slim Jims," *New York Times*, February 19, 1997; Robert Lipsyte, "One Year Later, NASCAR's Discovery Rolls On," *New York Times*, February 12, 2002.
7. Viv Bernstein, "Pop-Tops to Popping Corks," *New York Times*, May 25, 2005.
8. Lars Anderson, "A Six-Pack to Go," *Sports Illustrated* 100 (February 16, 2004): 66–70; Viv Bernstein, "Good Looks and Good Drivers Join to Complete a NASCAR Package," *New York Times*, April 15, 2005; Laura Petrecca, "Marketers Create Their Own Shows," *USA Today*, April 10, 2007.
9. Susanna Rodell, "How Stock Cars Became Icons of Americana," *New York Times*, May 21, 2000; Golenbock, *American Zoom*, 46–47.
10. Viv Bernstein, "Eau de NASCAR: Licensing and the Smell of Money," *New York Times*, March 12, 2006.
11. Yost, *200-MPH Billboard*, 303–304.
12. "Nine Drivers Give Indy Taste of NASCAR," *Logansport (IN) Pharos-Tribune*, June 24, 1992; Art Weinstein, "The Greatest Season?," *NASCAR Scene* 28 (August 5, 2004): 30–35.
13. Joseph Siano, "At the Wave of a Flag, Winston Cup Packs Up," *New York Times*, September 30, 1996.
14. Derek H. Alderman et al., "Carolina Thunder Revisited: Toward a Transcultural View of Winston Cup Racing," *Professional Geographer* 55 (May 2003): 238–249.
15. Rybacki, "The King, The Young Prince," 295; Robert Lipsyte, "The Crossing of Faith and Big-Time Sport," *New York Times*, March 4, 2001. Earnhardt's importance to the sport was reflected in a post-crash study that found the majority of non-Earnhardt fans claimed his crash caused them to suffer some sort of painful reaction. See, Daniel L. Wann and Paula J. Waddill,

"Examining Reactions to the Dale Earnhardt Crash: The Importance of Identification with NASCAR Drivers," *Journal of Sport Behavior* 30 (March 2007): 94–109.

16. "Further Probation for Irate Stewart," *New York Times*, July 12, 2001; David Bukovich, "Hot on the Track, Not under the Collar," *Sporting News* 226 (February 11, 2002): 53; Chris Jenkins, "Junior Feels Like His Dad," *USA Today*, May 17, 2004.

17. Lee Spencer, "Junior: Rock Star and Rock Solid," *Sporting News* 228 (September 20, 2004): 44.

18. Chris Jenkins, "NASCAR Makes Points By Taking Them Away," *USA Today*, July 12, 2002; Viv Bernstein, "Johnson Is NASCAR Star of Stars, and He's Also $1 Million Richer," *New York Times*, May 18, 2003; Dave Caldwell, "3 of Top Nextel Teams Penalized for Cheating," *New York Times*, March 16, 2005; Bill Center, "Shifting into the Season," *San Diego Union-Tribune*, January 11, 2007.

19. Hale, *Making Whiteness*, 9; David Jones, "Confederate Flag-Wavers Tarnish NASCAR Scene," *USA Today*, July 2, 2000; Ina Hughs, "Color Is Alarmingly All White," *Knoxville News-Sentinel*, March 31, 2002; Peter St. Onge, "NASCAR Faithful Feeling the Burn," *Charlotte Observer*, February 16, 2006; "NASCAR Still Proud of Its Heritage," *Raleigh News & Observer*, February 17, 2006; Sammy Fretwell, "Banned Sign Riles Heritage Group," *Columbia State*, July 16, 2006; "NAACP Wants Ban on Confederate Flag," *Columbia State*, May 29, 2009; Tania Valdemoro, "Confederate Group to March in Parade," *Miami Herald*, June 4, 2009.

20. "Why Are Black Colleges Toadying to This Profoundly Racist Organization?," *Journal of Blacks in Higher Education* 26 (Winter 1999–2000): 54–55; "Mauricia Grant, NASCAR," *Chicago Tribune*, June 10, 2008; "Sports Log," *Boston Globe*, December 18, 2008; Rick Bonnell, "Daugherty Talks Passion, A Lifelong Love of Racing," *Charlotte Observer*, August 21, 2009; "NASCAR's Drive for Diversity Program Revamped," *Knoxville News Sentinel*, September 17, 2009

21. Ruy Teixeira and Joel Rogers, *America's Forgotten Majority: Why the White Working Class Still Matters* (New York: Basic Books, 2000); Kemba Johnson, "Forget Football," *American Demographics* 23 (February 2001): 34–36; William Schneider, "Say Hello to NASCAR Dads," *National Journal* 34 (July 13, 2002): 21–22; Mary Douglas Vavrus, "The Politics of NASCAR Dads: Branded Media Paternity," *Critical Studies in Media Communication*, 24 (August 2007): 252. One scholar has suggested that NASCAR's popularity in recent years actually stems from its "whiteness" and conservative values, which correspond to a blossoming of post-9/11 white cultural nationalism. See, Kyle W. Kusz, "From NASCAR Nation to Pat Tillman: Notes on Sport and the Politics of White Cultural Nationalism in Post-9/11 America," *Journal of Sport & Social Issues* 31 (February 2007): 77–88.

22. Matt Bai, "Huntin' for Nascar-Lovin', Moon-Pie-Eatin', Bluegrass-Listenin', Shotgun-Totin' Democrats," *New York Times*, September 15, 2002; John O'Keefe, ""Under Review," *Sports Illustrated* 99 (October 20, 2003): 28.

23. "Ten Hut! Racing into the Military," *USA Today*, May 24, 2002; Viv Bernstein, "In Bid for Recruits, Military Has Allies in NASCAR and Fans," *New York Times*, July 2, 2005; David Wood, "Army Still 'an Opportunity' for Many," *Grand Rapids Press*, December 18, 2005; Yost *200-MPH Billboard*, 227–38.

24. Joshua I. Newman and Michael D. Giardina, "Onward Christian Drivers: Theocratic Nationalism and the Cultural Politics of 'NASCAR Nation'," in *Christotainment: Selling Jesus Through Popular Culture*, ed. Shirley R. Steinberg and Joe L. Kincheloe (Boulder, CO: Westview Press, 2009), 51–82. NASCAR's prerace prayers have also been attacked for their inherent inconsistency and contradictory nature. Shirl J. Hoffman notes that the prayers request utilitarian assistance from God by "ignoring the fact that the contests involved place the fragile human body in unnecessary danger." See, Hoffman, "Recovering a Sense of the Sacred in Sport," in *Sport and Religion*, ed. Hoffman (Champaign, IL: Human Kinetics, 1992), 153–159.

25. Yost, *200-MPH Billboard*, 130–137; Michael Freeman, "NASCAR Seeking One Vision," *MediaWeek* 9 (March 8, 1999): 14; Wayne Friedman, "NASCAR Wants More TV Bucks," *Electronic Media* 18 (November 8, 1999): 1; John Sonderregger, "Pit Stops," *St. Louis Post-Dispatch*, December 31, 2005.

26. Lee Spencer, "Rusty Wallace Astounded by Growth in Race Coverage," *Charlotte Observer*, December 29, 2002; Jim Pedley, "Back in Driver's Seat," *Kansas City Star*, December 18, 2005.

27. Viv Bernstein, "A Cup Without Winston," *New York Times*, February 8, 2003; "NASCAR: Liquored Up," *Multinational Monitor* 25 (November 2004): 4.

28. Tania Ganguli, "NFL Delivers Ratings Hit," *Chicago Tribune*, September 25, 2009.

29. Yost, *200-MPH Billboard*, 279–300; Martin, *American Auto Racing*, 204–206; Tom Sorensen, "This Is Not Your Father's Stock Car," *Charlotte Observer*, January 11, 2007.

30. Tim Haddock, "Stewart Reluctantly in Spotlight," *Los Angeles Daily News*, February 1, 2007.

31. Chris Jenkins, "NASCAR Teams Feeling Detroit's Pain—Automakers' Woes Felt on Track, Too," *Cincinnati Post*, January 26, 2007; Don Coble, "Return of the Fans," *Florida Times-Union*, September 25, 2009.

32. Juliet Macur, "As Growth Hits a Wall, NASCAR Faces a Less Certain Future," *New York Times*, April 15, 2007.

BIBLIOGRAPHY

Alderman, Derek H., et al. "Carolina Thunder Revisited: Toward a Transcultural View of Winston Cup Racing." *Professional Geographer* 55 (May 2003): 238–249.

Amerson, Ann. *The Best of "I Remember Dahlonega": Memories of Lumpkin County, Georgia.* Charleston, SC: History Press, 2006.

Barker, Theo, ed. *The Economic and Social Effects of the Spread of Motor Vehicles.* London: MacMillan, 1987.

Bentley, John. "Souped-Up and Hot." *Sports Illustrated* 1 (November 1, 1954): 16–21.

Berger, Michael L. *The Devil Wagon in God's Country: The Automobile and Social Change in Rural America, 1893–1929.* Hamden, CT: Archon, 1979.

Betts, John Rickards. *America's Sporting Heritage.* Reading, PA: Addison-Wesley, 1974.

Birrell, Susan. "Sport as Ritual: Interpretations from Durkheim to Goffman." *Social Forces* 60 (December 1981): 354–376.

Borgeson, Griffith. *The Golden Age of the American Racing Car,* 2nd ed. Warrendale, PA: SAE International, 1998.

Breen, T.H. "Horses and Gentlemen: The Cultural Significance of Gambling among the Gentry of Virginia." *William & Mary Quarterly* 34 (April 1977): 239–257.

Brown, Allan E. *The History of the American Speedway.* Marne, MI: Slideways, 1984.

Burns, John M. *Thunder at Sunrise: A History of the Vanderbilt Cup, the Grand Prize and the Indianapolis 500, 1904–1916.* Jefferson, NC: McFarland, 2006.

Butsch, Richard. *The Making of American Audiences: From Stage to Television, 1750–1990.* Cambridge, UK: Cambridge University Press, 2000.

Casey, Robert. "The Vanderbilt Cup, 1908." *Technology and Culture* 40 (April 1999): 358–362.

Cash, W.J. *The Mind of the South.* New York: Alfred A. Knopf, 1941.

Catlin, Russ. "Open Wheeling." *Speed Age* 8 (December 1954): 9.

Catsis, John R. *Sports Broadcasting.* Chicago: Neslon-Hall, 1996.

Chapin, Kim. "Curtis Lives!" *Sports Illustrated* 28 (February 26, 1968): 48–60.

———. *Fast as White Lightning: The Story of Stock Car Racing*. New York: Dial, 1981.

Cobb, James J., *Away Down South: A History of Southern Identity*. New York: Oxford University Press, 2005.

Coker, Joe L. *Liquor in the Land of the Lost Cause: Southern White Evangelicals and the Prohibition Movement*. Lexington: University of Kentucky Press, 2007.

Current, Richard N. *Northernizing the South*. Athens: University of Georgia Press, 1983.

Daniel, Pete. *Lost Revolutions: The South in the 1950s*. Chapel Hill: University of North Carolina Press, 2000.

Donovan, Brian. *Hard Driving: The Wendell Scott Story*. Hanover, NH: Steerforth, 2008.

Dutton, Monte, ed. *Taking Stock: Life in NASCAR's Fast Lane*. Washington, DC: Brassey's, 2002.

Edelstein, Robert. *Full Throttle: The Life and Fast Times of NASCAR Legend Curtis Turner*. Woodstock, NY: Overlook Press, 2005.

Fielden, Greg. *Forty Years of Stock Car Racing*. 4 Vols. Surfside Beach, SC: Galfield Press, 1995.

———. *NASCAR Chronicle*. Lincolnwood, IL: Publications International, 2003.

———. *Rumblin' Ragtops: The History of NASCAR's Fabulous Convertible Division*. Surfside Beach, SC: Galfield Press, 1990.

Flink, James J. *The Automobile Age*. Cambridge, MA: MIT Press, 1988.

Gabbard, Alex. *Return to Thunder Road: The Story Behind the Legend*, 2nd ed. Lenoir City, TN: GP Press, 2000.

Golenbock, Peter. *American Zoom: Stock Car Racing—From the Dirt Tracks to Daytona*. New York: MacMillan, 1993.

———. *Miracle: Bobby Allison and the Saga of the Alabama Gang*. New York: St. Martin's Griffin, 2006.

———. *NASCAR Confidential*. Osceola, WI: Motorbooks International, 2004.

———. *The Last Lap: The Life and Times of NASCAR's Legendary Heroes*. New York: MacMillan, 1998.

Gould, Todd. *For Gold and Glory: Charlie Wiggins and the African-American Racing Circuit*. Bloomington: Indiana University Press, 2002.

Grady, Sandy, "Stock Cars." *Speed Age* 10 (February 1957): 57–58.

Grantham, Dewey W. *The South in Modern America: A Region at Odds*. New York: HarperCollins, 1994.

Guttmann, Allen, *From Ritual to Record: The Nature of Modern Sports*. New York: Columbia University Press, 1978.

Hagstrom, Robert, *The NASCAR Way: The Business That Drives the Sport*. New York: John Wiley & Sons, 1998.

Hale, Grace Elizabeth. *Making Whiteness: The Culture of Segregation in the South, 1890–1940*. New York: Pantheon, 1998.

Hall, Randal, "Before NASCAR: The Corporate and Civic Promotion of Automobile Racing in the American South, 1903–1927." *Journal of Southern History*, 63 (November 1997): 629–688.

Hamm, Richard F. *Murder, Honor, and the Law: Four Virginia Homicides from Reconstruction to the Great Depression*. Charlottesville: University of Virginia Press, 2003.

Hammond, Jeff, and Geoffrey Norman. *Real Men Work in the Pits: A Life in NASCAR Racing*. Emmaus, PA: Rodale, 2004.

Harvey, Frank L. "Thunderbolts with Fenders." *Saturday Evening Post* 221 (August 7, 1948): 20–21, 79.

Hinton, Ed. "Attitude for Sale." *Sports Illustrated* 82 (February 6, 1995): 68–76.

———. *Daytona: From the Birth of Speed to the Death of the Man in Black*. New York: Warner Books, 2001.

Hiss, Hanson. "The Knights of the Lance in the South" *Outing* 31 (January 1898): 338–344.

Hoffman, Shirl J., ed. *Sport and Religion*. Champaign, IL: Human Kinetics, 1992.

Howell, Mark D. *From Moonshine to Madison Avenue: A Cultural History of the NASCAR Winston Cup Series*. Bowling Green, OH: Bowling Green State University Popular Press, 1997.

Hugenberg, Lawrence et al., eds. *Sports Mania: Essays on Fandom and the Media in the 21st Century*. Jefferson, NC: McFarland, 2008.

Hurt, Douglas A. "Dialed In? Geographic Expansion and Regional Identity in NASCAR's Nextel Cup Series." *Southeastern Geographer* 45 (May 2005): 120–137.

Hyde, Charles K. *Riding the Roller Coaster: A History of the Chrysler Corporation*. Detroit, MI: Wayne State University Press, 2003.

Ireland, Robert E. *Entering the Auto Age: The Early Automobile in North Carolina, 1900–1930*. Raleigh: North Carolina Division of Archives and History, 1990.

Jensen, Tom, *Cheating: An Inside Look at the Bad Things Good NASCAR Nextel Cup Teams Do in Pursuit of Speed*. Phoenix, AZ: David Bull, 2002.

Johnson, Kemba. "Forget Football." *American Demographics* 23 (February 2001): 34–36.

Jones, Anne B., and Rex White. *All Around the Track: Oral Histories of Drivers, Mechanics, Officials, Owners, Journalists and Others in Motorsports Past and Present*. Jefferson, NC: McFarland, 2007.

Kelly, Godwin. *Fireball: Legends Don't Fall from the Sky*. Daytona Beach, FL: Carbon Press, 2005.

Kirkland, Tom, and David Thompson. *Darlington International Raceway, 1950–1967*. Osceola, WI: MotorBooks International, 1999.

Kline, Ronald, and Trevor Pinch. "Users as Agents of Technological Change: The Social Construction of the Automobile in the Rural United States." *Technology and Culture* 37 (October 1996): 763–795.

Kusz, Kyle, W. "From NASCAR Nation to Pat Tillman: Notes on Sport and the Politics of White Cultural Nationalism in Post-9/11 America." *Journal of Sport & Social Issues* 31 (February 2007): 77–88.

Levine, Leo. *Ford, The Dust and the Glory: A Racing History*. 2 Vols. Reprint, Warrendale, PA: SAE International, 2000.

"Louise Smith." *Sports Illustrated* 104 (April 24, 2006): 29.

MacGregor, Jeff. *Sunday Money: A Hot Lap Around America with NASCAR*. New York: HarperPerrenial, 2005.

Menzer, Joe. *The Wildest Ride: A History of NASCAR*. New York: Touchstone, 2001.

Miller, Patrick B., ed. *The Sporting World of the Modern South*. Urbana: University of Illinois Press, 2002.

Newman, Joshua I. "A Detour Through 'NASCAR Nation': Ethnographic Articulations of a Neoliberal Sporting Spectacle." *International Review for the Sociology of Sport* 42 (September 2007): 289–308.

Oldenburg, Ray. *The Great Good Place: Cafes, Coffee Shops, Community Centers, Beauty Parlors, General Stores, Bars, Hangouts and How They Get You through the Day*, 2nd ed. New York: Marlowe, 1997.

Olds, R. E. "The Farmer and the Automobile." *Colman's Rural World* 66 (March 20, 1913): 13.

O'Reilly, Don. "Inside Auto Racing," *Illustrated Speedway News* 24 (October 27, 1964): 8, 10.

O'Roark, Brian J., and William C. Wood. "Safety at the Racetrack: Results of Restrictor Plates in Superspeedway Competition." *Southern Economic Journal* 71 (July 2004): 118–129.

Otto, Edgar, and Joann Biondi. *Ed Otto: NASCAR's Silent Partner*. Newburyport, MA: Coastal 181, 2008.

Ownby, Ted. *Subduing Satan: Religion, Recreation, and Manhood in the Rural South, 1865–1920*. Chapel Hill: University of North Carolina Press, 1990.

Packard, Sam. "Four Days in December." *Winston Cup Illustrated* 17 (February 1998): 74–77.

Pierce, Dan. "The Most Southern Sport on Earth: NASCAR and the Unions." *Southern Cultures* 7 (Summer 2001): 8–33.

Pillsbury, Richard. "Carolina Thunder: A Geography of Southern Stock Car Racing." *Journal of Geography* 173 (January 1974): 39–47.

Poole, David. *Tim Richmond: The Fast Life and Remarkable Times of NASCAR's Top Gun*. Champaign, IL: Sports Publishing, 2005.

Preston, Howard Lawrence. *Automobile Age Atlanta: The Making of a Southern Metropolis, 1900–1935*. Athens: University of Georgia Press, 1979.

———. *Dirt Roads to Dixie: Accessibility and Modernization in the South, 1885–1935*. Knoxville: University of Tennessee Press, 1991.

Punnett, Dick, *Beach Racers: Daytona before NASCAR*. Gainesville: University Press of Florida, 2008.

Quattlebaum, Julian K. *The Great Savannah Races*. Athens: University of Georgia Press, 1983.

Radbruch, Don. *Dirt Track Auto Racing, 1919–1941*. Jefferson, NC: McFarland, 2004.

Rae, John B. *The American Automobile Industry*. Boston: Twayne, 1984.

Raitz, Karl B. *The Theater of Sport*. Baltimore, MD: Johns Hopkins University Press, 1995.

Rao, Hayagreeva. "The Social Construction of Reputation: Certification Contests, Legitimation, and the Survival of Organizations in the American Automobile Industry: 1895–1912." *Strategic Management Journal* 15 (Winter 1994): 29–44.

Raper, Arthur. *Preface to Peasantry: A Tale of Two Black Belt Communities*. Chapel Hill: University of North Carolina Press, 1936.

Reed, John Shelton. *One South: An Ethnic Approach to Regional Culture*. Baton Rouge: Louisiana State University Press, 1982.

Rubin, Louis D. Jr., ed. *The American South: Portrait of a Culture*. Baton Rouge: Louisiana State University Press, 1980.

Rudeen, Kenneth. "They Laughed When NASCAR's Stock Cars Took to the Road at Elkhart Lake." *Sports Illustrated* 5 (August 20, 1956): 81–82.

Schneider, William. "Say Hello to NASCAR Dads." *National Journal* 34 (July 13, 2002): 21–22.

Smith, Stephen A. *Myth, Media, and the Southern Mind*. Fayetteville: University of Arkansas Press, 1985.

Sobel, Robert. *Car Wars: The Untold Story*. New York: E. P. Dutton, 1984.

Spann, Graham M. "NASCAR Racing Fans: Cranking Up an Empirical Approach." *Journal of Popular Culture* 36 (Fall 2002): 352–360.

Steinberg, Shirley R., and Joe L. Kincheloe, eds. *Christotainment: Selling Jesus Through Popular Culture*. Boulder, CO: Westview Press, 2009.

Struna, Nancy L. *People of Prowess: Sport, Leisure, and Labor in Early Anglo-America*. Urbana: University of Illinois Press, 1996.

Thompson, Neal. *Driving with the Devil: Southern Moonshine, Detroit Wheels, and the Birth of NASCAR*. New York: Random House, 2006.

Tindall, George B. *The Emergence of the New South, 1877–1945*. Baton Rouge: Louisiana State University Press, 1967.

Twelve Southerners. *I'll Take My Stand: The South and the Agrarian Tradition*. Reprint, Baton Rouge: Louisiana State University Press, 2006.

Vandiver, Frank E., ed. *The Idea of the South: Pursuit of a Central Theme*. Chicago: University of Chicago Press, 1964.

Van Valkenburgh, Paul. *Chevrolet—Racing? Fourteen Years of Raucous Silence! 1957–1970*. Warrendale, PA: SAE International, 2000.

Vavrus, Mary Douglas. "The Politics of NASCAR Dads: Branded Media Paternity." *Critical Studies in Media Communication* 24 (August 2007): 245–261.

Vlasich, James A., ed. *Horsehide, Pigskin, Oval Tracks and Apple Pie: Essays on Sports and American Culture*. Jefferson, NC: McFarland, 2006.

Wann, Daniel L., and Paula J. Waddill. "Examining Reactions to the Dale Earnhardt Crash: The Importance of Identification with NASCAR Drivers." *Journal of Sport Behavior* 30 (March 2007): 94–109.

White, Rex. *Gold Thunder: Autobiography of a NASCAR Champion*. Jefferson, NC: McFarland, 2005.

Whitener, Daniel Jay. *Prohibition in North Carolina, 1715–1945*. Chapel Hill: University of North Carolina Press, 1945.

Whitlock, Joe. "Behind the Legend of the Smoke-Filled Room." *Grand National Illustrated* 6 (March 1987): 50–57.

"Why Are Black Colleges Toadying to This Profoundly Racist Organization?" *Journal of Blacks in Higher Education* 26 (Winter 1999–2000): 54–55.

Wik, Reynold M. *Henry Ford and Grass-Roots America*. Ann Arbor: University of Michigan Press, 1972.

Wilkinson, Sylvia. *Dirt Tracks to Glory: The Early Days of Stock Car Racing as Told by the Participants*. Chapel Hill, NC: Algonquin, 1983.

Wolfe, Tom. *The Kandy-Kolored Tangerine-Flake Streamline Baby*. New York: Farrar, Strauss, and Giroux, 1965.

Wyatt-Brown, Bertram. *Southern Honor: Ethics and Behavior in the Old South*. New York: Oxford University Press, 1982.

Yost, Mark. *The 200-MPH Billboard: The Inside Story of How Big Money Changed NASCAR*. St. Paul, MN: Motorbooks, 2007.

INDEX

About the Author

SCOTT BEEKMAN is an assistant professor of history at the University of Rio Grande. He is the author of *William Dudley Pelley: A Life in Right-Wing Extremism and the Occult* and *Ringside: A History of Professional Wrestling in America*.